Organizational Design

In today's volatile business environment, it is more important than ever that managers, whether of a global multinational or a small team, should understand the fundamentals of organizational design. Written specifically for executives and executive MBA students, the new edition of this successful book provides a step-by-step "how to" guide for designing an organization. It features comprehensive coverage of the key aspects of organizational design, including goals, strategy, process, people, coordination, control, and incentives. These aspects are explained through the use of a unique series of 2×2 graphs that provide an integrated, spatial way to assess and plan organizational design. The new edition features a number of important improvements, including a new framework for understanding leadership and organizational climate, the introduction of the concept of manoeuvrability, and a completely new chapter examining joint ventures, mergers, partnerships, and strategic alliances.

Richard M. Burton is Professor of Strategy and Organization at the Fuqua School of Business, Duke University.

Børge Obel is Professor of Organization and Director of the Interdisciplinary Center for Organizational Architecture, Aarhus University.

Gerardine DeSanctis was Thomas F. Keller Professor of Business Administration at the Fuqua School of Business, Duke University.

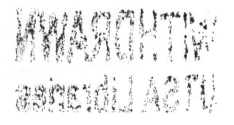

Organizational Design

A STEP-BY-STEP APPROACH

Second Edition

Richard M. Burton
Børge Obel
Gerardine DeSanctis

CAMBRIDGE
UNIVERSITY PRESS

CAMBRIDGE UNIVERSITY PRESS
Cambridge, New York, Melbourne, Madrid, Cape Town,
Singapore, São Paulo, Delhi, Tokyo, Mexico City

Cambridge University Press
The Edinburgh Building, Cambridge CB2 8RU, UK

Published in the United States of America by Cambridge University Press, New York

www.cambridge.org
Information on this title: www.cambridge.org/9780521180238

First edition published 2006
Second edition published 2011

Printed in the United Kingdom at the University Press, Cambridge

A catalogue record for this publication is available from the British Library

Library of Congress Cataloguing in Publication data

Burton, Richard M.
Organizational design : a step-by-step approach / Richard M. Burton,
Børge Obel, Gerardine DeSanctis. – 2nd ed.
          p.   cm.
Includes bibliographical references and index.
ISBN 978-1-107-00448-1 – ISBN 978-0-521-18023-8 (pbk.)
1. Organization.   2. Corporate culture.   3. Psychology, Industrial.
I. Obel, Børge.   II. DeSanctis, Gerardine.   III. Title.
HD31.B8523 2011
302.3′5–dc22   2010053595

ISBN 978-1-107-00448-1 Hardback
ISBN 978-0-521-18023-8 Paperback

Contents

Step 1
GETTING STARTED   1

Step 2
STRATEGY   21

Step 3

STRUCTURE   57

Step 4

PROCESS AND PEOPLE   109

Step 5

COORDINATION AND CONTROL   163

Figures

Tables

Preface to first edition

In writing this book, we had specific readers in mind. We dedicate this book to our executive students at The Fuqua School of Business and at the Aarhus School of Business, Denmark. Executive students are very special professionals who come from around the world and bring their varied experience. They have a goal to acquire new knowledge to act and take decisions that will make a difference in their world. In particular, they want to improve the performance of their firm, unit, or organization. From our first detailed outline to the final editing from Cary, Durham, and Aarhus – whether in person, video conference or elaborate email – they were ever with us.

Experience and science are two great teachers. Most of us spend most of our time in organizations at work, home, worship and leisure. Over time, we amass a wealth of experience through observation and action to apply in the design of organizations; simply, we use our experience to design. But this experience is limited and we can enhance it by blending it with the science of organization design. The science of organization design is an accumulation of knowledge by many individuals who, over many years, have conducted research on the performance of organizations under many conditions. It informs us about how to take action to design an organization. The scientific foundation of this book comes from almost a century of research we call the multi-contingency approach of Organizational Design.

The executive wants to understand, to diagnose, and take action. Experience and science are complementary and mutually supportive. In our classes we try to build upon our executive students' varied experiences with the science of organization design to enhance their ability as executives to take informed decisions and actions. As leaders in their firms they want to know what is wrong, why it is wrong, and what can be done. In this book we approach their questions systematically. We begin with the goals of the organization; then we develop an understanding of the environment; examine the strategies; tease out the structure and the IT infrastructure; examine the leadership style; observe the climate; and scrutinize the incentives. Using our experience and the science of good design, we analyze what works well and what does not work well, or not at all. Good design fits together; poor design has misfits and the organizational performance suffers. Design is the diagnosis of misfits and the action to fix them.

What is a good way to read and use this book? The book begins with organizational goals and builds up a comprehensive integrated model for a good organizational design. Skip around, examine the figures and tables; answer the diagnostic questions to get started. For whatever approach you find comfortable, you should pick an organization such as your own firm to use for analysis of, and reflection on, the concepts. Along the way, you should diagnose the organization and think about the actions you want to take to make your organization perform better.

Many have helped in a number of ways. There are our executive students who provided the motivation. Over the last two years, Dr Katy Plowright, our editor at Cambridge, has been the patient yet demanding task master; she has been our anchor and our guide. Further, we have had the support of a number of editors at Cambridge; they have been most helpful. Dorthe Døjbak Håkonsson of the University of Southern Denmark and Min Li of the Fuqua School read the penultimate draft and made many improvements. Karin Søby of the Aarhus School of Business read and corrected the manuscript. Finally, we want to thank our friends and families, who have been there when we needed them most – all the moments between the blank screen and a book.

RICHARD M. BURTON
GERARDINE DESANCTIS
BØRGE OBEL
August 12, 2005

On August 16, 2005, Gerry DeSanctis passed away. Gerry was charming, patient, supportive and kind as well as disciplined, determined and strong willed. She had passion for her students and was a complete teacher. We were privileged to work with her in writing this book. She made us better, both in our work and our spirit. It was a wonderful opportunity and an experience that bonded our friendship.

Gerry had deep courage. She is our incredible colleague and beloved friend. In her parting words, "I'll always be with you."

RICHARD M. BURTON
BØRGE OBEL
September 10, 2005

Preface to second edition

Since the first edition in 2006, many things have changed. The world economic crisis, which is most evident in the financial sector, has changed our world from expected growth to more restrictions and more nuanced changes. Yet, the fundamentals of organizational design remain relevant – perhaps even more so. The step-by-step approach which focuses on the identification and fixing of misfits addresses today's challenges; an information-processing view of organization captures the basic processes of organization; and a design is essential to good performance for the organization. In short, the basic ideas for a good design remain, even if some of the parameter values are modified.

Yet, we have made some significant changes in this second edition. We have: added a number of examples to illustrate the fundamentals and provide a timely context for the reader; introduced emotions as an underlying frame for leadership and climate; expanded the dynamic fit ideas and included time more explicitly; and deepened the examination of joint ventures, mergers, partnerships, and strategic alliances.

Paula Parish of Cambridge University Press has been a very supportive editor. Dorthe Døjbak Håkonsson of the Aarhus School of Business, Aarhus University has shared our joint research which is central to the changes in this edition.

And finally, thanks to the many individuals who used the first edition and inspired us to undertake this revision.

RICHARD M. BURTON
BØRGE OBEL
September 3, 2010

An outline of the step-by-step approach

STEP 1 GETTING STARTED
    1. Goals

STEP 2 STRATEGY
    2. Strategy
    3. Environment

STEP 3 STRUCTURE
    4. Configuration and complexity
    5. Geographic distribution and knowledge exchange

STEP 4 PROCESS AND PEOPLE
    6. Task design
    7. People
    8. Leadership and organizational climate

STEP 5 COORDINATION AND CONTROL
    9. Coordination, control, and information systems
    10. Incentives

STEP 1
Getting started

1

Define the scope of the organization and assess its goals

Introduction: The executive challenge of designing the organization

In today's volatile world, organizational design is an everyday, ongoing activity and challenge for every executive, whether managing a global enterprise or a small work team. Globalization, worldwide competition, deregulation, and ever-new technologies drive the ongoing reassessment of the organization. The executive response has been many new forms of *organizational design*: virtual, learning, modular, cellular, network, alliance, or spaghetti – to name a few. New organizational forms challenge old ways of organizing for efficiency and effectiveness. Yet fundamental design principles underlie any well-functioning organization. Organizations still require a formal design. The fundamentals are: what are our goals? What are the basic tasks? Who makes which decisions? What is the structure of communication, and what is the incentive structure? Fenton and Pettigrew (2000, p. 6) state that "a closer inspection of the literature reveals that many of the new forms are not entirely new but reminiscent of earlier typologies, such as Burns and Stalker's (1961) organic and mechanistic forms and Galbraith's preoccupation with lateral relations." Thus fundamental concepts and principles of organizational design remain very important for the modern organization of today and tomorrow.

IBM has been through five major organizational design changes recently. It has moved from country organizations to global business units, toward a more multi-dimensional matrix, and increased collaboration both within IBM and between IBM and other organizations. Many organizations overlook the importance of redesigning their organization. IBM has been very aware of the importance of continuing redesigning the organization for many years. However, top executives frequently neglect the need for a new design because of organizational inertia. This neglect to get the design right is very costly for the firm. In this book we provide a way to diagnose the need for a new design, as well as an approach to choose the most appropriate design.

To address the challenge of designing the organization we adopt a multi-contingency information processing view (Burton and Obel, 2004). Based on a large body of research, this view says that an organization's design should be chosen based on the particular context, and further that the description of the context should be multi-dimensional, including both structural and human components. Structural components of organizational design include goals, strategy, and structure. Human components include work processes, people, coordination and control, and incentive mechanisms. Together, these components provide a holistic approach to the organizational design challenge.

Organizational design starts with the organization's goals, and from there we work from the top to the bottom, considering strategy, structure, process, people, coordination, and control. This is a top-down approach to design. We could start the design process using the reverse approach, that is, by specifying how we want to coordinate and control work tasks and then designing the organization from the bottom to the top, designing tasks ahead of strategy; but such an approach would eliminate some possible good designs because the tasks of the organization can be affected by its goals and strategy. So we recommend a top-down approach that is complemented by iterative incorporation of lower-level issues on the top-level design. Political and implementation issues may suggest that the organization be designed bottom-up. Here again the top-down approach may have to be done in an iterative fashion, and further caution has to be exercised to ensure that lower-level design and choice of tasks do not eliminate some good alternative designs.

Overview of this book

In this book, we keep to the basics of organizational design. Organizational design involves two complementary problems: (1) how to partition a big task of the whole organization into smaller tasks of the subunits; and (2) how to coordinate these smaller subunit tasks so that they fit together to efficiently realize the bigger task or organizational goals. By complementary, we mean that the smaller tasks must be defined and arranged in a way that allows effective coordination. We consider these issues for "older," classic organizational forms as well as "newer," modern organizational forms.

We present a step-by-step approach which is a "how to" method for designing an organization. Each step and its subcomponents provide fundamental building blocks for any organization, and we guide you through the process of assessing each building block as well as planning for change. To simplify and show continuity in our approach, the components of each building block are mapped onto a series of two-dimensional graphs that clearly illustrate managerial options. The graphs are interlocking, such that a specific quadrant in any one graph corresponds to the same quadrant in all other graphs. In this way, you can visualize the relationships among the organizational design components and readily identify where there are *misfits* in your organization's design. Misfits are misalignments within the organizational design components that can lead to deterioration in the firm's efficiency and effectiveness.

Misfits lead to a decrease in organizational performance, either today or in the future. Misfits thus are the starting point for the implementation of change. As such, misfits are the engine of the organizational design process. If your organization changes in response to design misfits, rather than waiting for financial or other performance problems to arise, goal attainment is more likely to be achieved.

The graphs that we will provide for each design component will allow you to visualize and plot the current location of an organization and then identify the desired point to which you would like the organization to move. In this way, you can see where you are and where you want the organization to be in the organizational design space. While diagnostic questions and the two-dimensional graphs give you an easy way to get an overview, the ideas of the book have also been included in the OrgCon® software.[1] This software presents a more elaborate version of the approach presented in this book and provides a set of analytic and graphical tools that will ease the process of design. Meanwhile, you can use this book on its own, and the software is not required to complete the step-by-step approach and design your organization.

Organizational design is an ongoing executive process that includes both short-term, routine changes, as well as intermittent, larger-scale changes. We will address the dynamics of design, including misfit management, for both routine and larger-scale changes in the context of organizational design throughout this book.

---

[1] OrgCon can be obtained from www.ecomerc.com.

Our step-by-step approach is based on an information-processing view of the firm. This provides you with a framework and a toolkit for understanding a wide range of organizations in product and service industries across global boundaries. The approach helps you to interpret the history of organizations, assess and redesign complex organizations of today, and plan for the more information-rich organizations of tomorrow. We next describe the information-processing view and then move on to defining the scope of the organization and assessing its goals.

The information-processing view

The information-processing view uses the following logic. An organization uses information in order to coordinate and control its activities in the face of *uncertainty* where uncertainty is an incomplete description of the world (Arrow, 1974, p. 34). By processing information, the organization observes what is happening, analyzes problems, and makes choices about what to do, and communicates to others. Information processing is a way to view an organization and its design. Information channels "can be created or abandoned and their capacities and the types of signals to be transmitted over them are subject to choice, a choice based on a comparison of benefits and costs" (Arrow, 1974, p. 37). Both information systems and people possess a capacity to process information, but "this capacity is not, however, unlimited and the scarcity of information-handling ability is an essential feature for the understanding of both individual and organizational behavior" (ibid.). Work involves information processing; individuals conduct information- and knowledge-based activities. They talk, read, write, enter information in databases, calculate, and analyze. Various media are available to facilitate information processing – from pens and face-to-face conversation, to computers, networks and video meetings. Innovations in information technology affect both the organization's demand for information processing and its capacity for processing information.

The step-by-step approach presented in this book is based on the fundamental assumption that the work of an organization can be seen as information processing: observing, transmitting, analyzing, understanding, deciding, storing, and taking action for implementation. These issues may be labeled with other words like learning, tacit versus explicit knowledge, knowledge management, and data mining, but the basic idea is the same. Organizations are information-processing entities. Therefore, we want to design organizations so that they process information effectively and efficiently.

The basic design problem is to create an organizational design that matches your organization's demand for information processing with its information-processing capacity. Galbraith (1973, 1974), in his seminal work, put it this way: "the greater the uncertainty of the task, the greater the amount of information that has to be processed between decision makers" (Galbraith, 1974, p. 10). Task (or work) uncertainty can arise from a firm's technology and the business environment in which the firm operates (Thompson, 1967) as well as other sources. If the information-processing demand comes from many routine and predictable tasks with an efficiency focus, then formalization in the form of rules and programs can increase the number of tasks that can be handled. As an example, an online retail store in which the shopping and purchase process is rather routine can use rules and programs to increase the number of customers it processes per day. Task uncertainty is low, so the rules and programs are used to manage exceptions. When there are uncertainties associated with the tasks, then information processing is referred up the hierarchy to a level where an overall perspective exists. This is the traditional use of exception-based hierarchical decision-making. Unfortunately, such hierarchical decision-making can handle only a limited amount of uncertainty. If the uncertainty demands exceed the capacity of the hierarchy, then targets or goals have to be set for the various tasks, making the tasks somewhat independent. Coordination of work has moved from an efficiency orientation to an effectiveness orientation. Organizations thus face a tradeoff: they can either reduce their need for information processing or increase their capacity to process information (Galbraith, 1974). These are the two managerial options.

The first option is to reduce the organization's need for information processing by increasing slack resources. For example, if the organization uses a just-in-time (JIT) inventory approach, which requires precise coordination, then the organization might shift to having buffer inventory. Buffer inventory replaces the need to process the information required for JIT. As another example, information-processing needs can be reduced by creating self-contained tasks that do not require coordination among them in order to deliver the firm's product or service. For example, a two-product firm can create two self-contained single-product divisions that need not communicate in order to meet their customers' needs. Of course, this strategy of reducing the need for information processing may incur high opportunity costs from loss of coordination of interdependencies. Single-product divisions may ignore interdependencies in production or marketing, which may be costly in terms of lost opportunities. Thus, reducing information needs must be balanced with the returns from coordinated activities.

A second option is to increase the organization's capacity to process information. For example, in a hierarchical organization, the hierarchical processing of information can be increased by investment in a vertical information system. An information system may increase the speed and amount of information that can be exchanged. The introduction of satellites, information computer networks, the Internet and integrated CAD-CAM systems can increase the information-processing capacity of the organization. Upgrading the skills of the workforce, hiring more educated people with broader abilities, using mobile communication devices, or holding face-to-face meetings where people can share information are other ways to increase information capacity. Information-processing capacity can also be increased by creating lateral communications across the organization. Direct contact, liaison roles, task forces and permanent teams are other examples of strategies that will increase the firm's information-processing capacity.

The development of new information technologies, methods for organizational learning and technologies for knowledge management require a revisit of traditional strategies for managing a firm's information-processing capacity. Interactive information networks, multimedia systems, and generally the speed and amount of information that can be processed all have served to increase the information-processing capacity of firms. At the same time, the volume of information that firms must process continues to increase. There are more things we want to know about our customers' buying behavior, more research to be gathered for product development and production, more details in the service we want to provide, and so on. So the challenge of designing the organization in a way that best meets demands for information processing remains.

Without doubt, organizations are information-processing entities, and both the information-processing capacity and demands on firms have surged as the cost of information-processing technology has decreased. Along with this trend, there has been a reduction in slack resources in most companies, a slight increase in the use of self-contained units, a large investment in computer-based technologies, and a large increase in lateral communications. All this has led to "leaner and meaner" organizations, less inventory, less equipment, and fewer employees, particularly middle managers. Those who remain use information much more quickly and efficiently. This introduces the issue of information management by the human resources in the organization. Many organizations have invested in the technical side of knowledge-management and other information systems without getting the benefits, often because the human side was neglected. For this reason, we will emphasize the human side of organizational design in our step-by-step approach.

Select an organization for analysis

Let us get started with our step-by-step approach. For the purpose of analysis you should think about the definition of an organization in theoretical terms. In such terms an *organization* can be defined as "a consciously coordinated social entity, with a relatively identifiable boundary, which functions on a relatively continuous basis to achieve a common goal or a set of goals" (Robbins, 1990, p. 4). Thinking about your organization in these terms will allow you to manage its design and not be overwhelmed by the many, extensive set of activities involved in managing your organization every day. As you will see, this definition corresponds well to the components in our five-step approach.

Now select a specific organization for your use throughout this book. We will walk through the design of that organization in a step-by-step fashion. The organization can be a team, department, division, an entire company, or even a set of companies (such as a holding corporation or a strategic alliance). Your choice of an organization becomes the *unit of analysis* for the entire five-step design process. It is important to stick with the same unit of analysis as we go through this design process. At the end of each chapter we will state a number of diagnostic questions for you to answer that relate to the organization you have chosen. Your answers to the diagnostic questions will be the basis for the organization's design.

Define the scope of the organization

Let us start with a brief explanation of how you should scope your organizational design problem. This is a necessary starting point for analysis. We use the term "organization" or "firm" in the generic sense to refer to the team, business unit, company, or larger enterprise. For most readers the organization

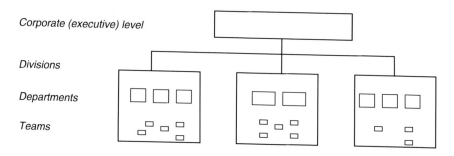

Corporate (executive) level

Divisions

Departments

Teams

Figure 1.1 Levels in the organizational design process.

is a business firm, but the method we present applies to nonprofit firms, partnerships, joint ventures, educational institutions, hospitals, churches, government agencies – any type of organization in practically any kind of setting.

As stated earlier, organizational design involves two complementary problems: (1) how to partition a big task into smaller subunit tasks, and (2) how to coordinate these smaller subunit tasks so that they fit together to efficiently realize the bigger task and organizational goals. The smaller tasks must be defined and arranged in a way that allows effective coordination. For example, the big task of General Motors or IBM is broken down into divisions and departments. For a project team, the project task must be broken into individual tasks. These smaller tasks are then integrated so that the large corporation or project realizes the desired goals. In all organizations, these fundamental, complementary problems of breaking down big tasks and putting smaller ones together are repeated again and again in many forms.

You should think about the design process as a set of cascading organizational design tasks where you go through the step-by-step process for each task (see Figure 1.1). Often the best place for you to start will be at the corporate level: you should design the upper echelons first. Once that part has been designed, move on to the next levels, which could be departments or divisions, as we shall discuss in subsequent chapters. For example, you first design the divisions in a divisional organization and then you determine how the divisions should be coordinated with one another. Each division can be different from the other – one functional, another matrix. In the cascading process, it is important to consider only one "organization" at a time; do not mix the design of the whole organization as a set of divisions with the design of any one division. More formally, keep the unit of analysis consistent. This process may be replicated in an iterative fashion. The idea of equifinality (Doty et al., 1993) is that for a given situation there may be more than one feasible design option from which to choose. Therefore, you may have to go through the design cascade for more than one option.

Assess the organization's goals

You should start by assessing the relative importance to the organization of two fundamental goals, efficiency and effectiveness. *Efficiency* is a primary focus on inputs, use of resources, and costs. *Effectiveness* is a focus more on outputs, products or services, and revenues. These are competing priorities. Some organizations place a higher priority on efficiency, focusing on minimizing the costs of producing goods or services. Other organizations emphasize effectiveness, focusing on generating revenues or seizing leading-edge innovation in the marketplace. All organizations value both efficiency and effectiveness to some degree, but the question is: which is the dominant priority? For example, no-frills airlines such as Southwest Airlines and Jet Blue focus primarily on efficiency. Firms with significant R&D investment, such as 3M Corporation or a biotech firm, focus primarily on effectiveness. Some organizations focus simultaneously on high efficiency and high effectiveness, such as Singapore Airlines and General Electric.

Few organizations state their goal directly in terms of efficiency or effectiveness. Vestas, the leading manufacturer of windmills, states its overall goal to be No. 1 in the world in modern energy. This statement means that the goal must be a comparison with the industry. The term "modern energy" signals a focus on effectiveness and new technologies. To be No. 1, it also requires a focus on efficiency as it must be cost competitive with Chinese firms.

Now, consider a company owned by a private equity fund that has a goal to obtain a specific rate of return on the invested capital within a given number of years. This goal signals a primary focus on cost and efficiency with little focus on longer term innovation. The goal also sets the time frame, which will be important for the choice of the organizational design.

Some business schools have a goal to become a Triple Crown business school obtaining all three of the AACSB, EQUIS and AMBA accreditations. This goal sets the focus on absolute specific ends – almost disregarding the competitors. Other business schools focus on their *Financial Times* business schools ranking. The success of this goal is highly dependent on what other competitive business

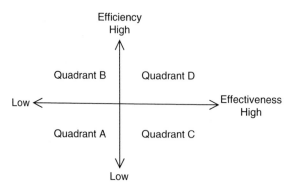

Figure 1.2 The goal space.

schools do. Thus, some goals are relative to the competition while other goals are directed towards absolute measures.

To access the company goals for our model you have to inspect the official goals and analyze them to assess if the goal has a focus on efficiency, effectiveness or a balanced combination. You also have to be aware that sometimes the goals that direct the top management are merely implicitly stated. Under the leadership of Mark Hurd, the focus of HP was primarily on cost cutting with a focus on efficiency. "Mr. Hurd conspicuously arrived at HP without a vision. Instead he slashed cost ...." (*Financial Times*, August 10, 2010) – a goal that was different from the official stated objectives.

As shown in Figure 1.2, efficiency and effectiveness are two dimensions – not ends on a single scale. You should rate your organization on both goal dimensions. In this two-dimensional model four different kinds of goal states are possible. Quadrant A represents the organization with a relatively low emphasis on both efficiency and effectiveness. It has little focus on using resources well and it has few or no specific goals related to higher-level ideas or targets. Such organizations exist and some even with great success. This could be the case of a monopoly, or it could be an early start-up.

A firm in quadrant B has its focus on utilization of the smallest amount of resources necessary to produce its products or services. Firms here continue to do what they have done in the past, refining for continued improvement. Such companies often exist well in stable environments where they can defend their position with a low-cost focus.

Firms in quadrant C are just the opposite. Here the organization has higher focus on effectiveness but a lower focus on efficiency. This means that the organization focuses on its goals, but takes less care to attend to the efficient use of resources. This could be the case in highly volatile environments or in situations where the organization constantly develops new ideas and has a first mover advantage and, as such, treats the costs of resources as a secondary concern.

The final goal position is quadrant D, where there is an emphasis on both efficiency and effectiveness. Firms in this quadrant confront competitive, complex and volatile environments that require both product innovations and low cost in order to compete successfully. Organizations in quadrant D pursue the dual goals of efficiency and effectiveness with equal vigor.

The goal position of the organization affects its information-processing requirements. For example, efficiency can be related to first-order learning, which is "a routine, incremental conservative process that serves to maintain stable relations and sustainable existing rules" (March, 1991). Effectiveness, on the other hand, can be associated with second-order learning, where existing rules are modified and new knowledge in the organization has to be facilitated. Information requirements are much greater if the organization's primary goal is effectiveness rather than efficiency. Efficiency and effectiveness also require different managerial approaches to environmental scanning and incentives and thus demand different organizational designs. From this discussion there seems to be a tension, or competition, between efficiency and effectiveness.

Most executives want to obtain the right balance between efficiency and effectiveness, and almost everyone agrees that modern organizations should focus on both dimensions. But how do you obtain a balance? Some scholars have argued that organizations focus on efficiency and effectiveness sequentially by going through an evolutionary period with a focus on efficiency disrupted by revolutionary periods of change where effectiveness is the focus (e.g., Tushman and Romanelli, 1985). The balance is thus achieved over time rather than simultaneously. Many managers, on the other hand, argue that the efficiency–effectiveness foci are ongoing simultaneously, although the emphasis can vary.

The way the balance is obtained is important. The solution to the balancing could be that one subunit of the organization is efficient and another effective; one subunit runs the current operations while another focuses on innovation. But such an approach may not work. A well-known failure is Xerox's experience of placing its operations in Rochester, NY, and its research at Xerox PARC in Palo Alto, CA. These were separate business units that did not coordinate with one another. As a result, other firms, not Xerox, brought the Windows-based operating system and the Ethernet network protocol to the market.

Although Xerox simultaneously achieved both effectiveness and efficiency, the company failed to obtain the proper balance.

Recently, organizational scientists have argued that pursuit of efficiency and effectiveness must be present everywhere in the organization at all times. In a thorough study of ten multinational firms researchers found that successful business units were able to simultaneously develop capacities related to *both* efficiency and effectiveness (Gibson and Birkinshaw, 2004). Put in terms of our diagram in Figure 1.2, this means that quadrant D is the ideal state. As we shall see, this is the most complex organizational design to develop and maintain, and so not all firms are able to take this approach. Many, many firms find themselves in quadrants B and C for this reason. Nonetheless, if your organization can be both highly effective and highly efficient, then you are in the best position to compete successfully in the marketplace if you are facing a highly volatile environment.

To summarize, the choice of a goal state in relation to efficiency and effectiveness has profound consequences for the information-processing demands and capacity of an organization. The efficiency–effectiveness goal state for your firm significantly affects your choice of the proper organizational design.

Diagnostic questions

To begin the organizational design process, choose the unit of analysis and keep that fixed throughout the step-by-step method: the top management layer of a large firm, a small firm, a division within a large firm, a department or a project. Thus, we advise starting with the whole firm by taking a cascade approach from top to bottom to obtain a complete analysis. Start at the executive level of the organization, go through the five-step design process, and then repeat the process for each major department or business division. You may have to iterate more than once. Of course the task of your design approach may not be the total firm. But our advice is to start at the top of the unit you are considering.

Next, assess where the organization is located on the efficiency/effectiveness diagram of Figure 1.2. Write down the arguments for the location using the vocabulary of your organization. You will need that later when you consider making changes. Answer the questions below.

1. What is the unit of analysis for the step-by-step approach?

2. What does the organization do? What is its major work activity?

3. How does the organization score on efficiency?

1	2	3	4	5
very low		moderate		very high

4. How does the organization score on effectiveness?

1	2	3	4	5
very low		moderate		very high

5. Plot the organization in the efficiency/effectiveness graph of Figure 1.2.

6. Where would the organization like to be in the efficiency/effectiveness graph of Figure 1.2?

Misfits and balancing competing design dimensions

As the last two diagnostic questions indicate, the organization design process consists of two important questions: Where are you, and where do you want to be? With regard to organizational goals, there are two things for you to consider about your unit analysis. First, where is the firm in Figure 1.2? Second, where would the organization like to be in this design space?

Let us use Figure 1.3 to think through these questions. Suppose that the organization is currently at point C in the diagram. Your focus is on effectiveness. Suppose that the competitive environment has changed such that the firm now must compete more on efficiency. Thus you might desire to move the organization to the quadrant of point D. However, before making this change, a more comprehensive review of the organization's design is needed. You need to diagnose the consequences of such a change. This means working through the five steps in our organizational design approach and determining where each major design dimension is located in the two-dimensional organizational design space. For example, it may be that the

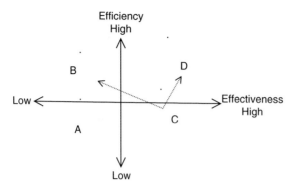

Figure 1.3 Making changes in the efficiency/effectiveness space.

organization's structure and work processes, for the most part, lie in the quadrant of point C (thus explaining your firm's success in achieving effectiveness). Suppose the competitive environment and business strategy (which we will consider in Chapters 2 and 3), on the other hand, lie in the quadrant of point B. As a result, there are misfits in the organizational design. That is, the design components do not all lie within the same quadrant. To address the misfit problem, you have a choice: either move the structure and work processes toward the quadrant of point B (thus aligning the organizational dimensions together in the same area of the design space), or change all of the design dimensions such that they move toward point D. The latter is a much more significant management change than the former, and you should carefully evaluate the implications of this design option before deciding on a plan. Our step-by-step approach will allow you to assess the consequences of various change strategies and their effects on goals, strategy, structure, process and people, and coordination and control.

As noted earlier, the quadrant associated with point D is an ideal location in the organizational design space. Indeed, much of the managerial hype of the day suggests to managers that all firms should be located in this place. But the organizational design space of point D is more costly than a singular focus of either efficiency or effectiveness and so may not be appropriate for all firms. Balance is a key theme of this book; organizational design entails developing design dimensions that are in alignment, thus avoiding misfits that lead to performance decrement.

Several studies (Burton et al., 2004; Burton and Obel, 2004) have shown that proper alignments of an organization's design indeed result in superior performance. In many instances, this means operating within the quadrants associated with points B and C and developing organizational design components that support an acceptable tradeoff between the dual goals of efficiency and effectiveness. Though the quadrant associated with point D may be ideal, it is not always the most suitable goal for management due to design constraints. Organizations that operate within the quadrants associated with points B and C can be extremely successful. Only quadrant A is to be avoided in the long run unless the firm operates in a highly protected environment, is a very small organization, or is living through the early period of a start-up venture. Organizations that find themselves in quadrant A of the design space usually should plan for change, and our five-step approach, as we shall see, can help identify what the needed changes are and how to proceed.

Again, many executives may wish their organization to be high in both efficiency and effectiveness. This is possible and may be desirable, but this design space is difficult to develop and maintain, especially if the organization's design components currently lie outside of this quadrant. An organization can more likely move itself toward point D if it has other design factors that fall into this same quadrant.

It is important for you to work through all of the steps of our design process and their subcomponents to determine a good fit among the many components of your organization's design. A partial approach, completing only some steps but not others, will be suboptimal. For example, if you assess the organization's strategy but not its processes or coordination, you cannot see what is necessary for the strategy to be effectively realized. Only when the picture of the organizational design is complete does it become meaningful.

Summary

This chapter introduced our step-by-step approach for organizational design based on the multi-contingency approach (Burton and Obel, 2004). We discussed the scope of the design process, which includes the choice of the unit of analysis and deciding where your organization is and/or would like to be located on the efficiency/effectiveness diagram. The basic idea of viewing the organization from an information-processing perspective was presented. Further, a series of questions that you should answer for the organization (unit of analysis) have been provided as the starting point for the organization's design.

Glossary

Effectiveness: an organization's goal priority that contrasts with efficiency; a focus on outputs, products or services, generating revenues, or seizing leading-edge innovation in the marketplace.

Efficiency: an organization's goal priority that contrasts with effectiveness; a focus on inputs, use of resources, and costs, especially minimizing the costs of producing goods or services.

Fit: organizational design components that all lie within the same quadrant, thus balancing the firm's efficiency and effectiveness. Further, the information-processing capacity of the firm is balanced with the demand to enhance performance.

Misfits: organizational design components that do not all lie within the same quadrant, thus threatening the firm's efficiency and effectiveness.

Organizational design: the complete specification of strategy, structure, processes, people, coordination and control, and incentive components of the firm.

Uncertainty: an incomplete description of the world.

Unit of analysis: the organization that is being designed, whether a team, business unit, department, division, firm, or larger enterprise; the unit of analysis must be held constant throughout the step-by-step design process.

Where are you in the step-by-step approach?

▷ STEP 1   GETTING STARTED

(1) Goals

So far, you have specified the scope of the organization (your unit of analysis) and the goals in terms of efficiency and effectiveness. Before continuing, review your firm's current position in Figure 1.3 very carefully as this position will be the anchor point as you proceed through the next steps. Does the position correspond well to the vision and mission statements of your organization? Is there general agreement in the organization about this position? Are you located in Figure 1.3 where you want to be, or are you in a position that you would like to change? That is, do you want to change the goals of the organization so that it is located in a different place in Figure 1.3? Please keep in mind the two situations: where the organization is and where you want the organization to be. As we proceed through the upcoming steps, you will see whether your organization's design fits where you are, or not, and whether it fits where you would like the organization to be, or not. Before you proceed to step 2, make sure that you have decided whether your analysis is for the current or a future situation and be consistent in your analysis throughout the book. You may do the analysis for both situations and make comparisons.

Once you have reviewed your organization's scope and goals, then you are ready to go on to step 2.

STEP 2   STRATEGY

Next, you will examine your firm's strategy and the firm's environment.

(2) Strategy
(3) Environment

STEP 3   STRUCTURE

STEP 4   PROCESS AND PEOPLE

STEP 5   COORDINATION AND CONTROL

STEP 2
Strategy

2   Strategy

Introduction

In the previous chapter you described an organizational unit of analysis and its goals. The next step in our step-by-step approach is to describe the strategy of the organization and the environment in which it operates. In this chapter we focus on strategy. A firm's strategy[1] helps determine its organizational design. Our focus here is on describing your firm's strategy – not how or why the choice of a strategy is made. Chandler (1962) stated the fundamental relation in his now famous dictum, "structure follows strategy." That is, given a strategy, there are some organizational structures which can implement that strategy better than others. Strategy is the end; structure is the means. *Strategy* is the operationalization of the firm's goals of efficiency and/or effectiveness; and the structure is the means to achieve them. In this chapter we will discuss which strategy should be pursued to obtain the goals decided in Chapter 1. This has to be done taking into account the environment in which the firm operates. Thus, "achieving high performance in a business results from establishing and maintaining a fit among three elements: the strategy of the firm, its organizational design, and the environment in which it operates" (Roberts, 2004, p. 12).

A firm's strategy reflects management's assessment of the firm's situation and its choice of how to pursue the firm's goals. Strategy can be described in a number of ways. For example, strategy can be described in terms of five forces of the firm's economic situation (Porter, 1985): suppliers, buyers, substitutes,

---

[1] We use firm in this chapter as a matter of convenience, but the analysis applies to any unit of analysis, be it a department or a team.

potential entrants, and the rivalry among existing competitors. These five forces yield three possible strategies: cost leader, product differentiator, or niche player. In marketing, strategy can be described as the choice of the four Ps: product, price, promotion, and place: that is, which product the firm should produce; what its price is; how it should be promoted and advertised; and how it should be distributed (Kottler, 2000). On the input side of the firm, operations strategy is the choice of the firm's supply chain including the chain management and outsourcing. This involves the choice and management of the resources and capabilities (Makadok, 2001). Your choice of a strategy for your firm is always a question of what the firm should do in its situation to meet its goals of efficiency and effectiveness.

A simple and powerful way to describe a firm's strategy is in terms of the following typology (Miles and Snow, 1978): (1) reactor, (2) defender, (3) prospector, and (4) analyzer without or with innovation. This typology has proved to be very robust and is frequently used today (Hambrick, 2003). The dominant strategic approach is reflected in such actions as capital investment, concern for quality, price level compared to competitors, preference for product innovation, and preference for process innovation. Many factors make up a firm's strategy, but the most important thing is its approach to innovation: whether it exploits its current situation and whether it adopts the strategy of exploring new innovations (March, 1991).

Exploration includes search, variation, risk-taking, and innovation. Exploration is the process of seeking new technologies or new ways of doing things. *Exploitation* includes refinement, efficiency, selection, and implementation (March, 1991). Exploitation is taking advantage of current or known technologies to do things in a new or novel way. Originally, exploration and exploitation were developed to analyze organizational learning and the nature of knowledge, both of which are related to firm strategy. Strategy is the application of knowledge, and learning is a change in the knowledge base to develop new strategies. Fundamentally, strategy choice, knowledge usage and learning are all concerned with how the firm chooses which actions to take based upon limited information.

Exploration and exploitation are dimensions of strategy that can be used to form the basis for categorization of a firm's strategy into one of four types (Håkonsson et al., 2005). If your firm is a *reactor* it is low on both exploration and exploitation; it lacks an intentional strategy toward innovation. It makes adjustments when forced or when there is an urgent need or problem. If your firm is a *defender* it is high on exploitation and low on exploration; it is

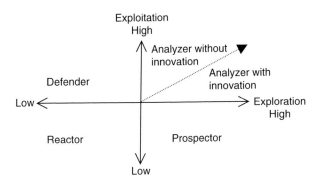

Figure 2.1 The strategy space.

innovative only in narrow, limited areas. Its innovation is confined and highly focused. If your firm is a *prospector* it is high on exploration and low on exploitation; it takes an aggressive approach to innovation, systematically searching for new opportunities. It experiments regularly with change. *Analyzers* take a mixed mode approach to innovation. If your firm is an *analyzer without innovation* your strategy is similar to a defender but with more emphasis on exploration. If your firm is an *analyzer with innovation* your strategy is similar to a prospector but with more emphasis on exploitation. Figure 2.1 displays the strategic space of exploration and exploitation along with the four basic types of strategy that relate to these dimensions.

Now let's consider these strategic types in more detail. In Figure 2.1, begin in the lower left corner, move to the upper left, then to the lower right and finally to the upper right corner. This is a convenient way to compare and contrast the strategies. Although the descriptions and examples given here are provided for the firm as a whole, we emphasize that strategies can be used to describe a business unit, division, department, or team – that is, for smaller units of analysis. In the case of smaller units, exploration and exploitation must be considered relative to other, equivalent units of analysis (e.g., other departments or teams, whether inside or outside the firm) that compete with your unit for success in the "marketplace."

Reactor

The reactor is neither an explorer nor an exploiter of the firm's opportunities. Generally, the reactor strategy is neither efficient nor effective in terms of achieving the firm's goals. The reactor acts without a focus on exploration or exploitation; instead, the reactor tries to adjust to the situation after it is possible to capture any opportunities that may have been present but are now lost. There is no innovation. The executive does not systematically anticipate, plan, or project into the future. The organization does not take a deliberate position to become efficient or effective. At the other extreme, the reactor may be a dreamer that pursues innovation without any focus; the dreamer is neither efficient nor effective. Information processing demands are likely to be low on detail and focus, and at the same time be rather inwards-focused.

If your firm is a reactor, you make decisions based largely upon bad news as it becomes known to you, whether this is poor performance such as decreased profits or earnings, events such as a loss of a major customer, or internal problems such as conflicts or inappropriate utilization of resources. Problems emerge as surprises and are dealt with as they occur. A reactor strategy is often observed in organizations that are in transition. A good example is a firm after a merger, where the focus is on the internal reorganization and management power struggles; the interest in both exploitation and exploration can be lost.

If the reactor strategy is followed for the long term, your firm ultimately will be caught with more bad news, most likely in the form of poor performance in the marketplace or internal processes that cannot be managed in the available time. The organization will go out of existence as it will eventually not be able to obtain sales or capital and perhaps human resources. Thus, it is difficult to give examples of existing companies that can be categorized as following the reactor strategy. They often die if they have a reactor strategy for too long. Inefficient and ineffective government organizations and firms in the midst of bankruptcy are known for following reactor strategies. The one-time computer giant Digital Corporation could in its later years be categorized as a reactor. It basically did not develop new technology after its famous VAX computer, and it completely missed the entrance of the PC into the market. It reacted too late with a too high cost structure. The pieces of Digital that are left are now part of Hewlett-Packard.

Defender

Now move to the upper left corner of Figure 2.1. If your firm has a greater focus on exploitation than on exploration, then your strategy is a defender. The defender is high on exploiting its resources and situation, but low on exploring anything new or being innovative. The executives inside a defender firm are focused on keeping the organization's position in the market. There is less emphasis on developing new ideas, products or services. Instead, there is an emphasis on maintaining a competitive position, which may be measured in terms of market share or profitability. Sales forecasting, as an extrapolation of the past, is a frequent tool used to support the defender strategy; that is, the past is projected as the future. Plans are developed to keep the position and fend off competitors, or at least keep them from encroaching into the well-defined territory of the defender. The defender usually has very competitive prices or a product niche that it works hard to keep others from penetrating. To remain competitive, a defender strategy requires detailed and focused information to enable continuous refinement (rather than innovation) of current products and production methods.

The defender maintains its position by being efficient in the utilization of resources. This strategy keeps the defender invulnerable to less efficient competitors. The defender can make changes in existing processes for existing products and services, but the goal is to be efficient and maintain its position. Thus the defender firm focuses on process innovation and has efficiency as the primary goal, as discussed in Chapter 1. On the other hand, effectiveness is low (relatively speaking) in a defender firm.

If your firm is a defender you will find that you cannot change much or change quickly. A high capital requirement is often a barrier to entry in the defender's industry. Thus there is a steady strategy of repeatedly doing the same thing efficiently. The emphasis on quality may be high as a means to prevent new entrants from coming into the market or to prevent existing competitors from taking over the firm's market share.

The defender can do well for a long time. Its vulnerability comes when its products or services are no longer desired in the market. Another threat is if new technology reduces high capital requirements, thus allowing competition from new entrants. Similar threats may come from new regulation or deregulation, as we have seen in industries such as transportation and telecommunications.

A defender is slow to make significant change. When buyers stop purchasing its products, the defender is not in a good position to develop new products or new markets. Slowness to change, combined with a high focus on efficiency makes the defender vulnerable in the long run.

One good example is LEGO, the Danish plastic brick children's toy company. It has kept its focus on toy bricks for decades. Prior to 2000 LEGO was making a handsome profit and was a growth company for many years. It protected its position with aggressive marketing, defending patents, copyrights and trademarks, and with an ongoing process of automating the production as much as possible. During the period 2000–4 LEGO struggled to make changes to meet new demands for more electronically based toys; it was not well situated to move from adopting a defender strategy to a more innovative strategy. LEGO had gone for a number of years with an inconsistent and continuously shifting strategic focus, with consequent severe financial losses. In 2004 Jørgen Vig Knudstorp became the new CEO. He realized LEGO had to return to the defender strategy with a renewed focus on LEGO's core product: the interchangeable plastic brick. He stated in an interview: "By 2004, when I became CEO, things had gone awfully wrong at the LEGO Group. To survive, the company needed to halt a sales decline, reduce debt, and focus on cash flow. It was a classic turnaround, and it required tight fiscal control and top-down management." Today LEGO is again very successful; in 2009 it recorded its highest profit ever.

Another defender strategy example is Coca-Cola, Inc., which has been defending its Coke brand fiercely, investing more resources in defensive moves than in new product development.

Prospector

The prospector is located in the lower right corner of Figure 2.1. The prospector is high on exploration of its opportunities but low on exploiting its current situation. Thus if you have a very high focus on exploration but a very low focus on exploitation, then your firm's strategy is a prospector. The prospector focuses on innovation of new things to the detriment of being efficient and exploitative of existing opportunities. It searches continually for new market opportunities and experiments regularly with new ideas, new technology, and new processes. The prospector firm is the creator of change, and so other firms must adjust to its actions. But the prospector is not much concerned with exploiting its situation or developing efficiencies in its use of resources. Prospector strategies require continuous scanning of the external environment and dealing with a lot of new, varied information.

The prospector maintains its competitive position by being new and making changes to the competitive situation that others must adjust to. The prospector constantly questions the status quo, and this puts it in its own niche and allows it to enjoy first-mover advantages. The prospector can make large changes in products and services much more readily than the defender. It is driven by the effectiveness goal as discussed in Chapter 1. The prospector's efficiency is low, but due to the competitive situation it may survive with a higher cost structure by demanding high prices.

The prospector firm is change-oriented, preferring the new over the status quo. Quality is not the primary concern, nor is being price competitive. Instead, these issues are subsumed by the novelty of new products or services. Of course, quality and price will become important to the customer, especially when other firms enter to match the prospector's latest innovation. The prospector's reaction is to seek a new product or service, thus leading the market in innovation. A new product or service is continually required for the prospector to prosper.

This strategy is risky. On the upside, a new product or service may have enormous payoffs. On the downside, the prospector firm can quickly exhaust its resources since usually it operates within a limited time frame for success; in other words, new product (or service) development life cycles must be relatively short. The prospector can do well for a long time. Its vulnerability comes when it fails to innovate and provide new products and services to the market within life cycle demands.

Many start-up ventures, for example, in the biotechnology industry today can be categorized as prospectors. 3M is often cited as having a prospector strategy with its constant development of new and innovative products. Google is taking a similar tack with its continual innovation of new Internet-based information services. Most firms in biotech are prospectors focusing on innovation.

Analyzer without innovation

If you have a strong focus on exploitation and weak focus on exploration, then your strategy is an analyzer without innovation. The analyzer without innovation is very similar to the defender except that it does have a passive innovation strategy or a copy strategy. The analyzer without innovation looks to what other firms are doing that is successful and then imitates with similar products or services to meet customer needs. The analyzer without innovation is high on exploitation of its resources and situation but very moderate on exploration while copying innovations of others. It is the upper middle of Figure 2.1.

Similar to the defender, the analyzer without innovation is focused on keeping the organization's position in the market; meanwhile, it is attentive to what others are doing. Some firms are quite good at being quick followers by observing what others do successfully and then moving quickly to do the same, or very similar. This strategy can be in part defender as the follower moves quickly to keep its position; or it can be more projective where the firm actually goes beyond what the originator did. In either case, it is an imitation or copying strategy where it is important to recognize what others are doing successfully and then follow.

The analyzer without innovation maintains its position by being efficient in the utilization of resources and following others; this maintains a degree of invulnerability to the moves of competitors. The analyzer without innovation can make small changes in existing processes for existing products and services, but the purpose is to be efficient and maintain its position. It can innovate in its defense of market position by following others if necessary. The analyzer without innovation primarily pursues the efficiency goal as discussed in Chapter 1. Its effectiveness goal is moderate.

Usually the analyzer without innovation does not change much, but the point is that it can change by following others. The analyzer without innovation is adept at doing much the same thing efficiently, but with a few changes from time to time.

The analyzer without innovation can do well for a long time, particularly by following what others do with aggressive intent. The challenge for the analyzer without innovation is to select well what to follow. Its vulnerability comes when it follows the wrong trend or fails to imitate quickly enough, so that its products or services are no longer desired in the market. If customers stop purchasing its products or services, the firm that pursues this strategy is not in a good position to develop its own new products or new markets. Because it is not easy to follow quickly, the firm that selects the analyzer without innovation strategy must be organized to detect and imitate quickly. The external information demands are to observe obvious success in sufficient depth to imitate.

In the fashion industry you see numerous analyzers without innovation. They go to Paris to spot the trend of the year and then copy the Haute Couture in a mass-market fashion. Magazine and television productions often do the same thing. They succeed by aggressively and adeptly imitating the latest approaches to finding customers that have been established by the market leaders. The PC market has a number of low-cost imitators who sell inexpensive computers.

Analyzer with innovation

If your firm has a focus on both exploration and exploitation, then your strategy is an analyzer with innovation. The analyzer with innovation is a dual strategy combining aspects of both a defender and a prospector. It exploits its current position of resource utilization and market position, and at the same time it adopts an active innovation strategy of developing new products, services, and their delivery processes. The analyzer with innovation is both efficient and effective. It is the upper right of Figure 2.1.

The analyzer with innovation is active in exploration as it purposefully innovates and searches for new products and services. It goes beyond just looking at what others do and instead surveys more widely in technology and markets to look for opportunities that it can develop into new products and services. Some firms have a market-driven approach to innovation as they look at market or customer needs and then try to innovate to meet those needs. They may limit themselves to markets they know well, or they may look for new markets as well. Other firms take a more technology-driven strategy in which they invest in more basic technology and try to capitalize on the results of the technological developments.

If you pursue the strategy of analyzer with innovation, you must have a dual focus on defending your firm's position in its markets while at the same time innovating with new products and services. This is a difficult balance requiring great skill and managerial expertise. The firm must emphasize developing new ideas, products, and processes. Success means producing new products and services on a regular basis. At the same time there is an emphasis on keeping the firm's position in terms of market share or profitability. Plans are developed to defend the firm's position and fend off competitors while at the same time exploring new frontiers. The analyzer with innovation requires the best, most complex of organizational designs.

There is a downside to this strategy. The analyzer with innovation is vulnerable in that it can fail to maintain the combination of exploration and exploitation needed to keep its existing markets for short-term economic performance and innovation in new products to meet future opportunities. The dual goals of efficiency and effectiveness create conflict that must be cleverly reconciled within a flexible and robust organizational design.

Xerox might be categorized as one of the less successful analyzers with innovation. It had both exploitation and exploration in its strategy, but these strategies are pursued separately, by different divisions located very far apart with different management structures. Despite the fact that Xerox has developed very novel and innovative products over the years, the firm has rarely managed to successfully transfer new ideas from development to production to sales. A successful analyzer with innovation strategy requires both exploitation and exploration embedded in the whole organization as part of the design (Gibson and Birkinshaw, 2004).

IBM seems to be a more successful example. The firm invests in new product development and new forms of service offerings but constantly looks at what is going on in the market. One example of this is the use of the Linux operating system in many of their new products and systems, as well as their recent acquisition of a major consulting firm. These moves are undertaken with great care, following careful analysis of market trends, but they are aggressive, risk-taking moves that bring innovation into the company.

You can obtain the right balance of exploitation and exploration by having some parts of the organization focus on exploitation, i.e., defender, and other parts focus on exploration, i.e., prospector. This separation requires a mechanism for selecting the new exploratory ideas, services or products that can later be exploited, and further how and when the transfer should be done. As mentioned above, the Xerox case is a very good example which shows that such an approach is difficult and may fail even if both the explorative part as well as the exploitative part of the organization are doing very well. An alternative approach is the ambidextrous strategy, where both exploration and exploitation take place concurrently in every part of the organization. For the ambidextrous strategy, the focus is on incremental and radical innovation as well as product and process innovation. A complex ambidextrous strategy requires special attention to leadership style and organizational setup (Raisch and Birkinshaw, 2008). We will look at these issues in subsequent chapters.

Diagnostic questions

Now continue with the analysis of your chosen organization. Recall that in Chapter 1 you chose a unit of analysis and assessed its goals on the dimensions of efficiency and effectiveness. Locate this same organization (the same unit of analysis) on the exploration–exploitation dimensions of Figure 2.1. Then you can categorize the firm's strategy as a reactor, defender, analyzer without innovation, analyzer with innovation, or prospector. Answer the diagnostic questions below. By working through these diagnostic questions, you can locate where the firm is in the strategy space.

1. What is the unit of analysis that you chose in Chapter 1? Use this unit of analysis as the organization when answering the questions below.

   The questions below will help you locate your organization on the exploration and the exploitation dimensions. For each item within question 2 and question 3, use a 1 to 5 rating scale to score your chosen organization as follows:

1	2	3	4	5
very low		moderate		very high

2. Exploration:
   a. How innovative are the organization's products, (1)–(5)? ___
   b. What is the price compared to the value of the product, (1)–(5)? ___
   c. What is the price level compared to the quality level, (1)–(5)? ___
   d. How frequently does the firm develop new products (1)–(5)? ___
   e. How difficult is it for other firms to develop related products (1)–(5)? ___

   Now mark the organization's location on the exploration axis in Figure 2.2.[2] If the score you gave is greater than 3, then the organization is high on exploration. If the score you gave is less than 3, then it is low on exploration.

---

[2] The detailed questions that we include throughout this book come from either research instruments used to measure the particular concept or a dissection of the definition of the concept. The detailed questions will help you focus on how to score exploration and exploitation. We suggest that you use an averaging or weighted averaging procedure of the detailed scores to get to the overall score. If you do not agree with the average, then you may use your own judgment to adjust it. You may use other detailed questions to get the score if that fits your chosen firm or industry better. For example, in some industries the number of patents is used to compare the degree of innovation across firms, so if that is appropriate for your firm, that question could augment or replace a question listed here.

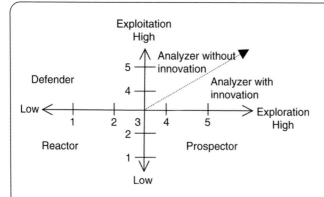

Figure 2.2 Locate your organization in the strategy space by rating the levels of exploration and exploitation.

3. Exploitation:

   a. What is the organization's degree of process innovation, (1)–(5)?____

   b. What are its prices compared to the competition (1)–(5)?____

   c. What is its quality in terms of its standardization and reliability (1)–(5)?____

   d. What is the number of products the organization has compared to its competitors (1)–(5)?____

   e. What are the barriers to entry in its industry (1)–(5)?____

   Now mark the organization's location on the exploitation axis in Figure 2.2. If the score you gave is greater than 3, then the organization is high on exploitation. If the score you gave is less than 3, then it is low on exploitation.

4. Now with these values of exploration and exploitation, locate the organization on the graph. What is its strategy?

   Next we want you to examine how your organization's strategy fits with the goals that you chose in Chapter 1.

Fit and misfits

What goals fit well with your strategy?[3] If the organization's strategy does not align with its goals, then there are misfits that need to be addressed. What are the misfits and what can you do about them? As an example, suppose your chosen organization has a defender strategy which has a focus on exploitation. This strategy is a fit with the efficiency goal. Now go back to Chapter 1 to verify that your goals were primarily efficiency. If so, your organizational strategy and goals fit. There is no misfit. On the other hand, if your goals do not fit the defender strategy, then you have a misfit, which calls for some change to bring your organization into alignment. Suppose your goals are to be both efficient and effective. Then a better strategy would be an analyzer, either with innovation or without innovation. Now you have a choice either to change your organization's goals to fit the defender strategy, or to change the strategy to an analyzer to fit your goals.

Table 2.1 shows the mapping of strategy types and organizational goals. These correspond to the four quadrants of our organizational design space. Each of the four columns in the table marked A, B, C, and D shows situations of fit among the strategy and goal components of the organizational design space. In other words, for an organization to have good fit, your strategy and goals should fall within the same column in this table.

First, take the strategy you identified in this chapter as given and see which matching goal is acceptable. If your goal matches your strategy, then the organization has no misfits; however, if strategy and goals are not in the same column of the table, then there is a misfit between the organization's strategy and goals, and one or the other should change in order to bring the organization into alignment. What would be required by your organization to adopt a revised goal?

Second, try the reverse approach. Take the goal you identified in Chapter 1 as given and see what matching strategy is acceptable, given the information in Table 2.1. If there is a misfit, what would be required by your organization to adopt this revised strategy? For example, is a greater emphasis on exploration feasible or a switch from exploitation to exploration? Think through the possibilities in light of your firm's particular situation.

---

[3] The balancing of the information-processing demand with capacity has been discussed in the research literature in terms of fit and misfit (Venkatraman, 1989; Burton et al., 2002).

Table 2.1 Fit between strategy and organizational goals

Corresponding quadrant in organizational design space	A	B	C	D	
Strategy types	Reactor	Defender	Prospector	Analyzer with innovation	Analyzer without innovation
Organizational goals	Neither	Efficiency	Effectiveness	Efficiency and effectiveness	

Finally, think about whether it would be preferable for your organization to change the strategy or change the goal. How would you implement such changes? As you move ahead in the book, we will develop a more complete picture of your organization and examine alternatives for managing and changing your organization as needed.

In later chapters, we will add organizational design alternatives which will expand the table presented here. The organizational design space will become more complex, but you will be able to develop more complete and better alternatives for achieving an organization's goals. In the next chapter, we will complete Step 2 by examining the environment of the organization.

Summary

This chapter has continued our step-by-step approach by examining the strategy of an organization. You first described the strategy of an organization in terms of degree of exploration and exploitation, categorized as: reactor, defender, analyzer without innovation, analyzer with innovation, or prospector. You then examined the fit of the strategy with your goals as assessed in Chapter 1. If there are misfits between the organization's strategy and goals, you should think about actions you might take to either adjust the strategy or adjust the goals so that these can be aligned.

In the next chapter, we will examine the organizational environment.

Glossary

Ambidexterity: a dual simultaneous focus on exploitation and exploration.

Analyzer with innovation: a strategy that is similar to a prospector but with more emphasis on exploitation.

Analyzer without innovation: a strategy that is similar to a defender but with more emphasis on exploration.

Defender: a strategy that focuses on exploitation and innovation only in narrow, limited areas.

Environment: the marketplace, the regulatory and legal situation, the opportunities and other aspects of the context in which the firm operates.

Exploitation: refinement, efficiency, selection, and implementation by the firm.

Exploration: search, variation, risk taking, and innovation by the firm.

Organization: a collection of people identified socially as a firm or one of its subunits; deliberately formed, goal-directed, bounded, and functions on a relatively continuous basis.

Prospector: a strategy that takes an aggressive approach to innovation, systematically searching for new opportunities. It experiments regularly with change.

Reactor: a strategy that lacks an intentional strategy toward innovation. It makes adjustments when forced or when there is an urgent need or problem.

Strategy: the firm's position on exploration and exploitation.

Structure: the partition of tasks by work roles and the reporting relationships among the work roles.

3 Environment

Introduction

In our step-by-step approach, you have described the goals and strategy for your unit of analysis. In this chapter, we focus on the environment that surrounds an organization. The *environment* is everything outside the boundary of the organizational unit of analysis. When you think about the environment for a firm, think about what could have an effect on the way the organization performs. It could be: its customers, its competitors, its suppliers, the financial market, or the political system. If your unit of analysis is a department, then the other departments in the organization are a part of its environment. The environmental imperative states that the organizational design is determined in large part by the environment of an organization. In brief, the environment is for the most part given for a firm, and the firm should then adjust its design to fit the environment. The performance of the firm depends upon how a firm makes the organization fit with the environment. Scott (1998) calls this the rational view of organizing. This also fits with the open systems view of organizational design:

Open systems theory can be defined as a theory of organization that views organizations not as simple "closed" bureaucratic structures separate from their surroundings, but as highly complex entities, facing considerable uncertainties in their operations and constantly interacting with their environment. This system also assumes that organizational components will seek "equilibrium" among the forces pressing on them and their own responses to their forces. (Milakovich and Gordon, 2001, p. 165)

There are a number of ways to describe an organization's environment. Early on, Ashby (1956) described the environmental variety as the number of distinct elements, whereas Lawrence and Lorsch (1967) used uncertainty. Burton and Obel (2004) used a four-dimensional description: complexity, which is the number of factors in the environment and their interdependency; uncertainty, which is the variance among the factors; equivocality, which is the ignorance and confusion about the existence of some factors; and hostility, which is the extent of malicious external threats. These four factors are modifications of earlier descriptions. Lawrence (1981) began with four descriptors: instability, ignorance of data, number of variables, and interdependence of variables. He then reduced these four to two: unpredictability and complexity. Duncan (1972) used environmental change or dynamism, and environmental complexity. Later, Bourgeois and Eisenhardt (1988) defined a high-velocity environment as one where changes are rapid and discontinuous so that information is often unavailable. More recently, Siggelkow and Rivkin (2005) also described the environment in terms of turbulence and complexity.

Among all of these descriptions, there are some common aspects. First, they are general properties of an organization's environment, not a detailed listing of all of the elemental factors themselves. Second, the measures are perceptions made by the management of the firm; they are not necessarily objective. This does not mean they are inaccurate, but that management creates its own understanding of the environment and the implications for design. Third, whatever the particular environmental description used, the environment is a large determinant of the organizational design, i.e., the environmental imperative means that the environment is a major determinant of how an organization should be designed. Contingency theory and the principle that structure follows strategy discussed in Chapter 2 – all follow the common theme that there must be a fit between the environment and the organization.

The environment creates both limits and opportunities for a firm's strategy and, subsequently, its structure. Lawrence and Lorsch (1967), for example, argued that increased environmental uncertainty leads to increased organizational differentiation. They define differentiation to mean that an organization has departments that are different in both tasks and orientation. Lawrence and Lorsch studied three well-defined industries that they categorized as ranging from low to high uncertainty. They found that increased uncertainty in the environment required increased differentiation in the organizational structure in order for the organization to be efficient. Then integration is required to make the different departments work in coordination. Integration devices typically include rules and procedures, configurational plans, the authority of the hierarchy, and decision-making committees.

The way you should define the environment is in terms of what you know affects your organization. If a firm is a monopolist, it does not have any relevant competitors. On the other hand, if a firm is in a very strong competitive market, the most significant dimension in its environment may be its competitors. If a firm sells goods in a seasonal industry, then cycles of consumer demand are an important dimension of its environment. Thus some dimensions describe the environment of one firm whereas other dimensions describe the environment of another firm. Some organizations have many important and somewhat interrelated factors in their environment, whereas others have much simpler environments with few and unrelated factors. Further, some factors have a direct effect on firm performance and some have an indirect effect. A change in exchange rates may directly affect the costs and revenue of particular activities or products. Similarly, a change in government subsidies may directly determine the viability of an industry. For example, sales of windmills in the US are directly dependent on US government subsidies. In the early days of the Bush administration it was unclear whether the administration would continue to support the windmill industry or not. The choice of the government in this case had a direct and significant impact on the companies producing windmills. Recently, the Obama administration has placed an increased emphasis on multiple energy sources, including wind. Other factors have more indirect effects. For example, the deregulation of the aviation industry had the effect that new competitors could enter the market, but it was not clear how they would enter, when they would enter, or what strategies a mature airline could initialize to prevent or postpone particular types of competitors from entering the market. Here the deregulation affected the environment but in a more indirect way, and there was uncertainty about what would happen.

The environment thus refers to the forces surrounding an organization that impact its performance. For the firm as a whole, the environment usually is the competitive marketplace. For a department or business unit, it includes upper management and the other units of the firm that affect the business of the department. For a team, the environment is the department, other organizational units in which the team operates, and possibly other teams that influence the team's workload and its success in carrying out its tasks. It is important to assess an organization in terms of its immediate environment and to do so as part of the ongoing process of organizational design. If a firm switches industries, its environment will change (as it moves into a new marketplace). If a firm undergoes internal reorganization, the environment for a given department, business unit, or team may change. Likewise, if one business unit operates in country A while another operates in country B, there are likely to be different environments due to differences in customs, regulations, and so forth, across the two countries. Again, the environment of an organization should be assessed in terms of the forces affecting the organization, whether these forces lie within the larger organization in which the focal organization operates, or whether these are forces that lie outside in the external marketplace.

When you think about the forces that describe a firm's environment, can you predict how they will affect the firm? Do you know what competitors will do? Can you predict what new regulations the political system will initiate in the future? Sometimes you can and sometimes you cannot. If the European Parliament has agreed upon a new framework, you can estimate to a certain extent how local regulations will change. But you may not know *when* the local governments will pass the new laws. If you are a vertically integrated company you may be able to control the value chain to some degree, but in other situations you may be very dependent on your suppliers and you may not know their reaction. When the financial crisis hit the banking industry in 2008, it was not clear what the implications would be. Would the crisis be short- or long-term? Would the financial crisis be followed by an economic crisis? Would there be governmental interventions, and what might they be? Thus the environment has some degree of uncertainty. Obviously, good information can be very valuable, but such information did not exist.

It may be rather straightforward to state which factors in the environment are likely to affect the actions and performance of a firm, but it may be much more difficult to estimate the degree of uncertainty associated with those factors. Some of the uncertainty may be stated in probabilistic terms, whereas other parts of the uncertainty may be much more difficult to estimate probabilistically. For example, there may be new aspects of the environment that your chosen organization has never before experienced. This could be a new technology or a new type of regulation.

The characterization of an organization's environment in terms of complexity and uncertainty is important and relevant because an increase in both the complexity of the environment and the uncertainty of the environment increases the demand for information processing in the organization. If there is a high degree of complexity, more elements have to be monitored and the effect of change has to be estimated. If there is a high degree of uncertainty, more plans may have to be established and a higher degree of flexibility may be needed.

Should the description of an organization's environment be objective or subjective? This issue was addressed many years ago and is still a difficult problem (Bourgeois, 1980). We often talk about environmental forces as if they are objectively determined when in fact they may not be so. You will often find that firms in the same industry, confronting the same environment, behave differently. Some companies in the industry perform badly while other companies show an excellent performance. One reason why this occurs is that they perceive and categorize the same environment very differently. As an example, within the US airline industry Southwest Airlines has defined its competitors as customers who drive to their destinations, whereas other airlines have defined their competitors purely in terms of other airlines. In this way, Southwest Airlines perceives and categorizes its environment very differently than, say, Delta or American Airlines.

Why is that? One reason could be the cognitive capacity of the individuals in the firm that allows one firm to understand the environment much better than the other. Or it could be that the environmental scanning is done much better in one company than in the other. Or the differences could be deliberate intentions of management. As an example of the latter, Southwest has always assumed that it must compete with the low price of driving to a destination; thus, the airline has undercut fares of competing airlines by huge margins, even when the industry was expanding. In the 1980s when other airlines were offering discount fares from Dallas, Texas to Houston, Texas for $76, Southwest priced their fare at $17, because this fare was less than the cost of driving. Southwest management deliberately defined its competitive environment in terms of the low cost of driving from Dallas to Houston; whereas other airlines defined their environment in terms of the prices of what other airlines charged to fly the same route, which was $76 or more. Thus, different airline companies in the same market defined their environments very differently and pursued different strategies.

In order to survive, organizations continually monitor their environment. You may be able to predict much more precisely a firm's environment by talking to customers, or suppliers, or politicians, or specialized research firms. By going to trade shows or following basic research activities you may be able to predict technological developments. By tracking industry information you may be able to predict industry trends. By meeting with government officials you may be able to anticipate or influence political events. One thing is for sure: knowing more allows you to better understand your firm's environment and anticipate its impact on the firm.

To describe an organization's environment, we use two dimensions: complexity and unpredictability. *Complexity* is measured as the number of factors in an organization's environment and their interdependency. Environmental complexity increases as the number of factors increases and/or the interdependency among the factors increases. *Unpredictability* is lack of understanding or ignorance of the environment in terms of the nature of the factors and their variance; greater variance means less predictability. Consider the example of General Electric (GE), where the environmental factors for its thirteen product groups are relatively independent. (For instance, the market for jet engines is independent of the market for lighting.) In addition, some markets are more predictable than others. (For example, the market for lighting is easier to forecast than the market for jet engines, which is subject to new airplane orders and the global market for air travel.) GE's environment has a large number of relatively independent environmental factors, some of which are difficult to predict.

The two dimensions of complexity and unpredictability were chosen because they can be related to a vast literature of empirical studies of organizations, and they fit well with our information-processing view of organizational design. An increase in each of the environmental dimensions increases the demand for information-processing capacity in a firm, but in different ways. Greater environmental complexity increases the amount of information to process, as there are more issues of importance to the organization. Greater unpredictability requires greater capability to forecast or adjust to the changing environment. Neither necessarily increases the amount of information, but each does require a different response from an organization. An organization must either project what will happen or adjust quickly to the environment. The former is forecasting, and the latter is adapting to feedback. Many organizations use a combination of both; for example, a firm with uncertain sales will forecast and also adjust quickly to actual sales.

The two environmental characteristics are general attributes. Complexity refers to the number of powerful forces affecting an organization. If a firm has only one or two major competitors it faces low complexity; whereas if a firm must continually adjust to numerous conditions – competitors, prices, labor pool, new products – it faces high complexity. Unpredictability is the degree of uncertainty about the forces that impact a firm. The higher the environmental unpredictability, the less accurate the forecasts are and the more

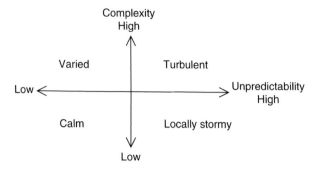

Figure 3.1 The environment space.

uncertain management can be about the future. Consider a consumer products firm with operations in the United States and Russia. The number of variables, or forces, influencing the firm's strategy may be similar across the two locations. Hence, complexity is about the same. But there is likely to be more environmental uncertainty today for the units that operate in Russia than those that operate in the US. This is due to the nature of the market and political context of Russia today, as compared to the US. Some may argue that the recent US financial crisis has made the US less predictable. For the design of your firm you should work with your perception of the environment as that influences your information-processing demand and capacity.

Applying the complexity and unpredictability dimensions to describe the environment, we get four types of environments: a calm environment, a varied environment, a locally stormy environment, and, finally, a turbulent environment. We will discuss each of these environments.

Figure 3.1 shows the complexity and unpredictability dimensions with the four environmental categories: calm, varied, stormy, and turbulent. Generally, there are increased information-processing demands on the organization as we move from a calm environment to a turbulent environment. An organization has more issues to consider and coordinate as the complexity and unpredictability of the environment increase.

Each of the four environmental categories is a different combination of complexity and unpredictability. If a firm is in a calm environment, then the environment is low in complexity and is predictable. The firm has few factors to consider and they are predictable; you know what is important in the environment with a good deal of certainty. There are no surprises and few adjustments are required. If a firm is in a varied environment, then the environment is high in complexity but is predictable. There are many interdependent factors, but these are well known and predictable. If a firm is in a locally stormy environment, then the environment is low in complexity, but unpredictable. There are few and usually independent factors, but they are not predictable. Unrelated surprises require many adjustments which can be dealt with one by one. If a firm is in a turbulent environment, then the environment is high in complexity and is unpredictable. There are many interdependent factors which are unpredictable. This is the most demanding environment for information processing, requiring many short-term and long term adjustments and coordinated responses on the part of the organization.

Now, let's consider these environments in more detail. Generally, we move from a less demanding environment to a very demanding one. In Figure 3.1, begin in the lower left corner, move to the upper left, then to the lower right, and finally to the upper right corner.

Calm environment

A calm environment has low complexity and low unpredictability (i.e., it is highly predictable). It is simple and known with few surprises. If a firm only has a few products and sells them into markets where the markets are predictable, we say it has a calm environment. The political and financial issues usually are not major challenges for management except if the firm is in a monopoly situation protected by the political system. Some public organizations think that they are in a calm environment. But recent unforeseen budget cuts create challenges to the assumed calm environment. Utility companies – at least those that have not yet been deregulated – may find themselves in a calm environment. Calm environments occur less and less frequently as more industries are deregulated. Further, the deregulation of the financial system, the creation of a single European market, the NAFTA agreement and similar agreements have done away with many calm environments.

If you are an executive in a calm environment you do not need to spend much time assessing your organization's environment, either to forecast what will happen or to adjust to surprises. Today's environment will be tomorrow's as well. There will be few surprises. So, you can focus on other organizational design issues, addressing more internal concerns.

It is important to recognize the risks of an executive's perception of a calm environment. First, the executive's perception can be wrong. Second, the environment can change, and with an assumption of a calm environment, it is likely that any change will be ignored or missed. So, the presumption of a calm environment by an executive is potentially risky. The CEO of Intel, Andy Grove, has a famous dictum that only the paranoid survive. This is a useful warning, especially for firms that perceive they are in a calm environment.

If you perceive that your organization is in a calm environment in the short run, you may be shocked or surprised without warning. With this perception and mindset, the time lag for needed change is likely to be long – perhaps too long for the survival of the firm. Bon Gout, an importer of specialty goods in Denmark, was in a calm environment for many years, where it had a good working relationship with Samsonite, one of its suppliers. Bon Gout sold Samsonite goods to retail outlets throughout Denmark. When Samsonite decided without consultation that it would sell directly to the retailers, the Bon Gout organization was in shock; the environment for Bon Gout instantly changed from calm to turbulent. Bon Gout was no longer in a calm environment and new action was required. Similarly, the financial crisis did away with calm environments for many smaller local banks. Suddenly the collapse of the well established interbank market turned everything upside down. The side effects were many and unexpected.

Varied environment

The varied environment is complex as there are many factors to take into consideration and they can be interdependent (i.e., they influence one another), but these factors are relatively predictable and/or they tend to change within known limits.

If a firm has many products and sells them into markets where the markets are predictable, we say it has a varied environment. Further, political and financial issues can add to the number of factors in the environment. If the markets, the politics and financial factors are all interdependent, as they are for many governmental suppliers, the environment is varied. In such a varied environment there are many factors for an organization to consider, but it is possible to predict what will occur. Market forecasts, analysis of political trends (e.g., road construction or environmental protection) are frequently applied techniques to predict the future environment. It is possible to project into the future with reasonable accuracy and understanding. The focus of the executive in a varied environment is on planning and coordination that will allow the organization to manage in the face of the interdependencies among the factors that are in its environment.

In earlier times, the toy manufacturer LEGO was in a varied environment. It operated in many countries with many different variations of its products, and there were many legal, financial, and logistic issues to take into consideration. Demand had seasonal variations but it was quite predictable. But that environment changed around 2000 to a locally stormy environment, where the sales were rather unpredictable.

Locally stormy environment

The locally stormy environment is highly unpredictable but not very complex. That is, there are a few factors in the environment which are relatively independent, but they are unpredictable. The locally stormy business environment is analogous to the prediction of rain with a 0.5 probability for a farmer. The amount of rainfall may be one of the few factors that determine a crop's growth rate, but the predictability of rain may be extremely low. Start-up companies that are dependent on a patent right or the result of a particular outcome of a clinical trial are in locally stormy environments.

In the locally stormy environment, executives are most concerned about the unpredictability of environmental factors that affect their firm. Many years ago Ashby (1956) proposed the Law of Requisite Variety, which states that a system's internal flexibility must meet the outside uncertainty for the system to survive. For purposes of organizational design, the Law of Requisite Variety means that a firm needs to be flexible so that it can meet the unpredictability of its environment. Put another way, the information processing capacity of the firm should be able to adjust when unpredictable events occur. Unpredictability means that the response time in which the firm has to react is much shorter than if the environment were predictable. In a predictable environment a firm has time to plan for the future; but in an unpredictable situation the peak information requirement is much higher as you have to do many things when the unpredictable factors in the environment suddenly become known. In a locally stormy environment the advantage is that only a few factors have to be monitored and they are relatively independent. Thus, the adjustments can be made one by one – a much simpler problem than if the environment is turbulent, as we shall see below.

Unpredictability without complexity can be dealt with on a local basis, not requiring the coordination for the whole firm. As mentioned before, GE has a different environment for its several relatively independent product groups. These markets can be adjusted one by one without concern for each other since the markets are independent of each other.

Turbulent environment

The turbulent environment has both high complexity and high unpredictability. There are many interdependent factors which are not predictable. This environment is analogous to that faced by the farmer who has not only the rain to consider but also the market price for grain, and the rain and price may be correlated; further, both are difficult to predict. For you as a manager, this is the most difficult environment in which to operate as it requires limited forecasting and also the flexibility of quick and coordinated adjustments as events become known. A turbulent environment requires a firm to have a large and fast information-processing capacity so that the firm can choose quickly among alternative courses of action for the organization. Thus, the adjustments must be made together and made quickly.

Today's global airlines confront a turbulent environment. Having emerged from a relatively calm environment of regulation, they now have many factors to consider: the ticket prices of other global competitors, the emergence of low price niche competitors, the global price of jet fuel, the global security situation, the competition from nontravel substitutes such as video conferencing, to name a few. Further, these factors may be interdependent. For example, the use of video conferencing may be related to the price of travel and also to the global security situation; in addition, global security affects the price of jet fuel. There are many interdependent factors; furthermore, it is difficult to predict their behavior.

Diagnostic questions

In the first chapter, you located your unit of analysis on the efficiency and effectiveness dimensions and thus categorized your organization's goals. In Chapter 2, you located your unit of analysis on the exploration and exploitation dimensions for your strategy. Here you should do the same for your chosen unit of analysis on the environmental complexity dimension and unpredictability dimension in Figure 3.1. Then you can categorize your chosen firm's environment as calm, varied, locally stormy, or turbulent.

1. First, assess the degree of complexity of the environment for your unit of analysis. Complexity is the number of variables in the environment and their interdependency. It refers to factors that can influence the operations and outcome of your organization. These may include the industry, the competitors, suppliers, the financial system, the human resource talent pool, new technology, prices, quality requirements, financial conditions, governmental relations, and political conditions, among many other factors. Identify external conditions that in a significant way could affect your chosen organization. These should be conditions that you constantly feel you need to scan and monitor. Examples of external conditions are:

   a. What is the number of critical factors in the organization's environment? List each factor below and then count to estimate the total number of critical factors.

   1: _____

   2: _____

   3: _____

   4: _____

   5: _____

   etc.

   b. What is the overall interdependency among these factors? That is, to what extent is this set of factors interrelated, or correlated with one another? Select an overall rating of: low, medium, or high.

   Now, using Table 3.1 overleaf, find the complexity score on the scale of 1 to 5. Find the column corresponding to the number of factors in the environment. Find the row corresponding to the extent of interdependency among the factors. Your complexity score is in the cell corresponding to the column and row for your firm.

Table 3.1 Complexity scores

Interdependency of factors	Number of factors in the environment				
	1–3	4–6	7–9	10–12	More than 12
Low	1	1	2	2	3
Medium	1	2	3	4	5
High	3	4	4	5	5

2. Unpredictability: For each factor that you have included in the firm's environment in Part 1a above, score its unpredictability on the scale from 1 to 5 as follows:

    1   2   3   4   5
very low   moderate   very high

Critical factors in the environment   Unpredictability score (1 = low, 5 = high)

1:_____   _____

2:_____   _____

3:_____   _____

4:_____   _____

5:_____   _____

etc.

Assess the total environmental unpredictability from the individual unpredictability factors.[1] Now with the firm's scores on environmental complexity and unpredictability, locate its environment in Figure 3.2. What is the environmental category of your chosen organization?

---

[1] We suggest that you use an averaging procedure of the detailed scores to get to the overall score, but you may make an overall estimate of the score if you prefer.

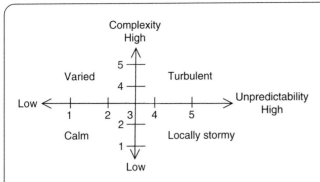

Figure 3.2 Locate your organization in the environment space by rating the levels of complexity and unpredictability.

Next, you will examine how your chosen organization's environment fits with the goals and strategy that you identified in Chapters 1 and 2.

Fit and misfits

Which goals and strategies fit well with your chosen organization's environment? Table 3.2 overleaf summarizes the best fit combinations.

As in Chapter 2 you can view the fit combinations by examining the columns. Start with column A. You see that in a calm environment a reactor strategy and nonspecific goals fit well together. In a calm environment little information processing is needed. You know what is happening; tomorrow will be like today. We can further point out that in a calm environment it does not make a lot of difference which strategy you have as all the strategic types will have an information processing capacity that will exceed the demand. In a calm environment a defender strategy will also be appropriate, although the effort needed to defend the position will be less than that required in a varied environment. Research has shown that a proper alignment of the business strategy with the environment is much more important in dynamic environments than in stable environments (Obel, 1993; Siggelkow and Rivkin, 2005). So the importance of an alignment increases as we move from column A to column D.

Table 3.2 Fit among organizational environment, strategy, and organizational goals

Corresponding quadrant in organizational design space	A	B	C	D	
Environment	Calm	Varied	Locally Stormy	Turbulent	
Strategy types	Reactor	Defender	Prospector	Analyzer with innovation	Analyzer without innovation
Organizational goals	Neither	Efficiency	Effectiveness	Efficiency and Effectiveness	

The varied environment in column B is still very predictable, but more factors can affect the organization. Planning and forecasting are the name of the game. Little new is happening, and when it happens it is at a pace that the organization can accommodate. A focus on exploitation is appropriate for this type of environment, and a defender strategy fits well here.

In column C the environment is less complex but more unpredictable. It fits well with a prospector strategy with a high degree of exploration. Here the focus has changed from efficiency as we saw it in column B to a focus on effectiveness.

In column D the environment is turbulent. The organization is affected by many factors in the environment and some, if not most, of them change in an unpredictable way. The focus in such an environment fits well with a combination of effectiveness and efficiency goals and an analyzer strategy.

Misfits occur if your assessment in Chapters 1, 2, and 3 end up in different columns. It is a common impression that the business environment changes more often and more dramatically today than earlier. As was stated above, the importance of a proper alignment is higher in unpredictable environments than in predictable environments. Thus it is a potentially dangerous situation for a firm if it has been located in a calm environment and suddenly finds itself in a locally stormy or turbulent environment. In such a case there is a need either to change the strategy or to somehow calm down the environment. Usually, the latter is not possible, or it is possible only for very large companies and is difficult to do.

If you are located in different columns based on your answers to the diagnostic questions from Chapters 1, 2 and 3, then think about how you might modify your organization so that you can obtain an alignment, with all answers in the same column of Table 3.2. Would you change the goals, the strategy, or work on the environment, or would you try to move all three to a new common quadrant?

Summary

In this chapter we have assessed an organization's environment and discussed the impact on its strategy. The elements of the environment have been discussed where complexity and unpredictability are measures of the environment. This leads to the four types of environment: a calm environment, a varied environment, a locally stormy environment, and a turbulent environment. Finally, misfits among the goals, environment, and strategy were presented.

Glossary

Calm environment: an environment with low complexity and low unpredictability.

Environmental complexity: the number of factors in the environment and their interdependency.

Interdependency: interrelatedness; the extent to which different factors influence one another or are correlated with one another.

Interrelatedness: see interdependency.

Locally stormy environment: an environment with low complexity and high unpredictability.

Turbulent environment: an environment with high complexity and high unpredictability.

Unpredictability: degree of uncertainty about the forces that impact a firm; lack of understanding or ignorance of the environment in terms of the nature of the factors and their variance.

Varied environment: an environment with high complexity and low unpredictability.

Where are you in the step-by-step approach?

STEP 1   GETTING STARTED

(1) Goals

STEP 2   STRATEGY

(2) Strategy
(3) Environment

You have now examined your firm's strategy and its environment. Just to review, there are two issues here. First, does your strategy fit with your goals? If it does not fit, reconsider your goal statement or adjust your strategy to fit with your goals. Second, does your strategy fit the environment? If not, what changes should you consider? Usually, it is more difficult to change the environment than to change the strategy. Generally you will want to move the organization's strategy to fit the environment. But you can also try to move both the environment and the strategy to a new position. To change your current environment may involve lobbying, buying out your competitor, heavy advertising, or other rather difficult changes. However, you may also change your environment by moving the firm to a new locale with a more appealing environment, by exiting a particular market, or by moving into a new market.

It is very important to assure that the organization's goals, strategy, and environment are located where you want them to be. These three items are the fundamental anchors for designing the organization and thus will strongly affect the design that you will end up with in your step-by-step analysis. Once you have your goals–strategy–environment relationships in order, you can move on to design the firm's structure.

STEP 3   STRUCTURE

The next step is to review how the organization is configured in terms of its assignment of subtasks and coordinating relationships among all the subtasks. You will then assess how this configuration operates across time and space boundaries. Further, you will want to ensure that the structure is compatible with your strategy, the environment where you operate, and your goals.

(4) **Configuration complexity**
(5) **Geographic distribution and knowledge exchange**

STEP 4   PROCESS AND PEOPLE

STEP 5   COORDINATION AND CONTROL

STEP 3
Structure

4 The configuration and complexity of the firm

Introduction

The choice of a firm's configuration – sometimes called its structure or architecture – is a critical decision for the executive (Burton and Obel, 2004). The next step in the step-by-step approach is for you to choose a configuration and decide on the organizational complexity which will enable your firm to perform well for its given goals and strategy and in its environment. A poor choice of configuration leads to opportunity losses which can be a threat to the organization's short-term efficiency and effectiveness as well as its long-term viability. As in the earlier chapters, for convenience of expression, we use the term "firm" or "organization" as the unit of analysis, but you can substitute team, department or division if that is the unit of analysis you chose in Chapters 1, 2 and 3.

A firm's *configuration*, frequently pictured as an organizational chart, tells us how the firm partitions big tasks into smaller tasks either by specialization or product, and then also indicates the formal communication patterns. As discussed in Chapter 1, organizational design of configuration involves two complementary problems: (1) how to partition a big task of the whole organization into smaller basic tasks of the subunits, and (2) how to coordinate these smaller subunit tasks so that they fit together to efficiently realize the bigger task or organizational goals (Mintzberg, 1983). Once tasks are partitioned and the smaller subunits specified, the information-processing questions for organizational design are: Who makes what decisions based upon what information? Who talks with whom about what, or what is the structure of communication (March and Simon, 1958; Galbraith, 1973, 1974)? When you have answered these design questions for your firm, you know a good deal about how it will work and can proceed to realize the goals. There are a number of choices for the configuration. Here we will consider the basic choices and how they address the fundamental questions of design.

A firm's *organizational complexity* further specifies the organizational design. For example, how many subunits are there? The number of departments should be specified as well as the number of vertical levels in the hierarchy. These are called the horizontal and vertical differentiation, which together are called the organizational complexity of the firm. More "modern" dimensions of the classic configurations include the degree of virtualization and the extent to which IT systems are embedded in the configuration. These new types of configurations are considered in Chapter 5.

Configuration

What are the dimensions for partitioning the larger task of the firm into smaller tasks such that the smaller tasks can be coordinated and work well together? In the literature on organization design two fundamental dimensions have been used to distinguish the basic configurations: *product/service/customer orientation* and *functional specialization*. The product/service/customer dimension suggests that the total firm task will be partitioned by the outputs of the firm, which give it an external focus. If the firm has divisions or departments with product or customer names, then it has an external focus and is high on this dimension. The functional specialization dimension indicates that the work will be divided by specialized activities. If the firm has departments with function names, such as production and marketing, then it has a more internal focus and is high on this dimension. These two product and functional dimensions indicate the focus of how the work will be divided and then, given this breakdown, how it must be coordinated. These two dimensions of configuration generate four basic configurations, as shown in Figure 4.1. The four basic configurations are: simple, functional, divisional, and matrix (Miles and Snow, 1978).

These four basic configurations can be combined in different patterns, and thus are the building blocks of more complicated structures depending on whether your unit of analysis is a team, a department, a division, or even the whole organization. For example, in the case of a divisional configuration, each of the several divisions of a divisional structure can be functional, matrix,

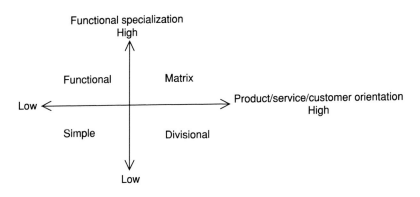

Figure 4.1 The alternative organizational configurations of the firm.

or another divisional. Thus these basic configurations may all be present inside one large organization. They should be designed using the top-down approach described in Chapter 1.

The four basic configurations of simple, functional, divisional, and matrix score differently on the product/service/customer and functional specialization dimensions. In Figure 4.1, we show the four configurations as they are located on the two dimensions: product/service/customer orientation on the horizontal axis and functional specialization on the vertical axis. The simple configuration is low on the product/service/customer dimension and also low on the functional specialization dimension. The functional configuration is also low on the product/service/customer dimension, but it is high on functional orientation. The divisional configuration is the opposite: high on the product/service/customer dimension, but low on specialization. And finally, the matrix configuration is high on both dimensions, suggesting a need for a high information-processing capacity to achieve the twin goals of efficiency and effectiveness.

Next, we discuss the four configurations, beginning with the simple configuration. In Figure 4.1, we begin in the lower left corner, move to the upper left, then to the lower right, and finally to the upper right hand corner.

Simple configuration

The *simple* configuration is: low on the product/service/customer dimension and low on the functional specialization dimension. The simple configuration is usually a small organization, consisting of an executive and perhaps a few other individuals. The executive tells the others what to do and manages the

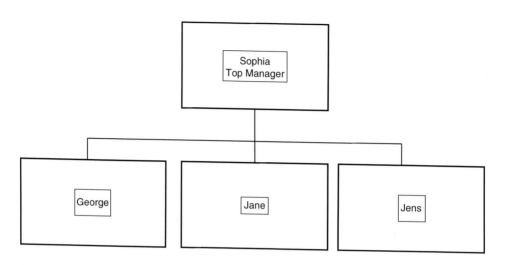

Figure 4.2 A simple configuration.

ongoing operations. The individual employees do not have specific tasks or activities to perform, nor are there well-defined job descriptions. The total task of the firm is broken down into smaller tasks and assigned to the employees by the executive on an as-needed basis; the coordination of the activities is also done by the executive. Both the task assignments and the coordination are accomplished by the executive in an ongoing and continuous manner. Little is fixed; things are very fluid and can be very flexible to adjust to the situation at hand. The executive is at the center of the information flows, makes the decisions, coordinates the activities of the employees, and controls the operations – telling others what to do. The executive is also the main contact with the market, customers, suppliers, and clients of the firm. In Figure 4.2, there is an organizational chart of the simple configuration where Sophia is the executive.

The simple configuration is usual for small firms – whether new small start-ups or older firms. In some rare situations, the executive of the larger firm may choose the simple configuration – particularly for an owner-managed firm which has grown from a small start-up to a larger firm. For all of these firms, the executive is in charge of or oversees almost everything that goes on. In terms of information processing, it can be a very demanding task.

The simple configuration is flexible but not usually efficient or effective. The efficiencies of specialization are not realized, as the employees are asked to do many tasks for which they may not be fully skilled. The simple configuration depends heavily upon the vision of the executive for its effectiveness orientation. A danger is that the focus can be narrow and not very effective for the firm's customers if needs change and vary over time. Because the executive is the focal point of all information processing in the firm, it can be difficult for this one person to take time to adjust the firm's direction or seek innovative opportunities. In brief, the simple configuration does not take advantage of the efficiencies of specialization, and its effectiveness depends heavily upon the actions of one person – the top executive.

The executive is at the center of all that happens in the simple configuration. It is the executive's show. If the executive uses time well, makes good decisions, and coordinates activities well, then the simple configuration leads to good performance. But if the executive becomes overloaded and fails on any of these tasks, the firm's performance will suffer.

Functional configuration

The *functional* configuration is: low on the product/service/customer dimension and high on functional specialization. The focus of work is based on the functional specialization – hence the name.

The functional configuration is more complex with respect to information processing than the simple configuration. In the functional configuration, there are department managers with specified subunits, each of which has well-defined jobs. The total firm task is broken down and assigned to subunits; the coordination, or putting together, is accomplished by the hierarchy, which uses a combination of rules and directives. In contrast to the simple configuration, where little is fixed (i.e., task assignment and the organizational structure can change frequently), much is fixed for the functional configuration. It is more machine-like and can accommodate large-scale organization as well as a high degree of information processing. The production flow is to hand off work from one subunit to the next, e.g., operations to marketing, which requires coordination. The executive is again at the center of the organization for information flows to and from the top, making decisions, and coordinating activities of the subunits.

Figure 4.3 shows an organizational chart that illustrates the functional configuration where the functional departments are: supply, manufacturing, and sales. There could also be functions such as operations, marketing, finance, and human resources. Operations and marketing are usually called line

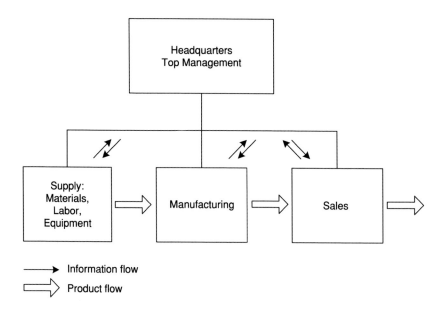

Figure 4.3 A functional configuration.

functions and departments like finance and human resources are called staff functions. The executive level coordinates the manufacturing, sales, and other major efforts and is concerned with matters such as planning and realized versus projected expectations of firm productivity. Although information flows through the top of the organization, coordination is required among the subunit activities, and each department processes information on its own, offloading some of the information-processing demand that was pushed to the executive level in the simple configuration.

The major advantage of the functional configuration is that specialization provides the rationale to assign individuals and subunits to specific tasks which they learn to do efficiently. From Adam Smith (1776) onward to this day, the economies of specialization make the functional configuration the most common configuration. The rationale is an efficient organization which is directed by the executive level. There is a strong reliance on the skill of the executive – both for the short-term coordination of ongoing operations and for the long-run choice of specialization.

A frequent question about the functional configuration is, how many subunit functions should there be? It is a question of (1) the limited time of the executive who must make decisions and coordinate the subunits (departments), and (2) the capacity of the subunits to process information. The time demands on the executive grow as the number of subunits increases, but also the coordination demands increase as the number of products increases. Unfortunately, as either the number of subunits or the number of products increase, the coordination demands increase nonlinearly with the implication that only a few functional subunits are possible (Burton and Obel, 1984). Most firms have about five subunits and rarely should they have more than seven. More formally, NK complexity theory shows that where N is the number of subunits and K is the degree of interdependent information flows going through the top, e.g., $K = N-1$, the coordination demands become overwhelming quickly as the number of subunits increases. (See Siggelkow and Rivkin, 2005 for discussion of NK theory.)

The LEGO Group has a functional organization with five functions: Markets & Products (M&P) has global responsibility for product development, marketing and sales. Community, Education & Direct (CED) is responsible for direct contact with consumers via brand retail stores, online sales, and mail order. In addition this business area handles contacts with fans and the development of new business concepts aimed directly at end-users. And it is this unit that is responsible for the Group's development, marketing and sale of educational materials. Corporate Center (CC) covers the administrative service departments: IT, Human Resources, Corporate Communications, Corporate Governance and Sustainability and Corporate Legal Affairs. Global Supply Chain (GSC) is the business area responsible for the Group's supply chain – from procurement and production to shipping and distribution to the retail trade. Finally, Corporate Finance is responsible for financial management and control as well as follow-up on business planning and strategic initiatives.

As in the simple configuration, the executive in the functional configuration is at the center of the organization and may become overloaded if the environment is not predictable. Where adjustment and change in work tasks are required, the situation can become overwhelming. The functional configuration is efficient for unchanging activities; however, that efficiency is lost when rapid change is required. The functional configuration is a good choice if you want the organization to operate with high efficiency and precision. The configuration works well for tasks that are repeated frequently and in high volume.

Divisional configuration

The *divisional* configuration is high on the product/service/customer dimension and low on functional specialization. Here the focus is not so much on the internal specialization but more on the outside products and services that the firm produces, or on the customers it serves.

There is an executive level that oversees subunits which are relatively independent of each other and have limits on their contact with the headquarters. Each subunit, which may be called a division, an SBU (strategic business unit), product business, customer business, or country business, is its own business, frequently organized as a simple or functional configuration within the subunit. Each division is externally focused and has its own markets and customers. It pursues its own destiny within the constraints and policies of the headquarters. The most important relationship is financial, where each division has its financial goals, receives its operating monies as well as its long-term investment funds (Williamson, 1975). The top executive sets policy for the divisions. These policies can be quite general, such as, "operate within the law," or they can be quite detailed including financial reporting standards, human resource policies, and innovation directives for new processes and products. The extent of involvement by the top executive can vary. At the one extreme, the headquarters is a "bank" that provides financial oversight and not much else, and at the other extreme, each division can be driven from the top. For the latter case, the headquarters is likely to become overloaded with large information flows and many decisions to make; performance suffers (Chandler, 1962). So, the divisional configuration works best when there is limited coordination from the top and each division is left to run its own business where it has resources and can coordinate its activities to focus on the market for its products, its customers, or in its region (Burton and Obel, 1984). As noted earlier, within each division, the organization can be configured as a simple or functional configuration or even another division. In Figure 4.4, the divisional configuration is shown where the product flows and information flows have been added.

The advantage of the rationale for the divisional configuration is that it aims to be effective with its external focus on the product, customer, or region. The divisional configuration is more market-responsive than the functional configuration. Because the divisions are relatively autonomous, they can make decisions on their own, meet the needs of the marketplace in creative ways, and thus foster opportunity for growth. Many firms treat new acquisitions as divisions, allowing them to operate relatively independently of headquarters so that they can continue with the success experienced prior to acquisition. Dividing the firm into product or brand groups is another way to create divisions that can grow or die depending on their success in the marketplace.

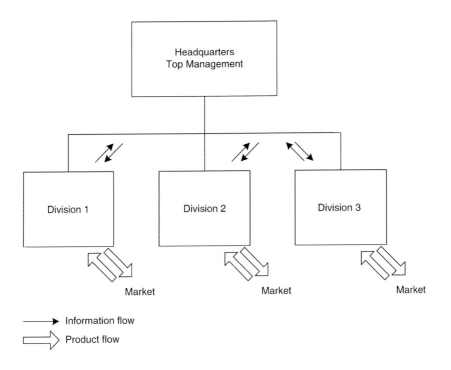

Figure 4.4 The divisional configuration with product and information flows.

The disadvantage of the divisional form is that each division is relatively independent of the other in its operations and markets. The divisional configuration does not handle interdivisional dependencies well. For example, two divisions selling competing products to the same customer or developing a new technology which requires their joint efforts will find it difficult to coordinate and/or avoid duplication of efforts. Interdependent efficiencies are lost. If a customer goes to IBM to buy both consulting services and network computers, they must deal separately with the two divisions that manage these products. The divisions have separate sales and support groups, and the customer must bear the coordination cost of dealing with the two divisions. But each division can be efficient using a functional configuration. If a division becomes less effective, it can be sold off in the marketplace, as IBM recently has done with its PC division.

At the top, the executive of the divisional configuration is responsible for the choice of the divisions and their level of activity, and more generally the overall firm performance. There is a strong reliance on the divisions and their own executives to relate to their own markets with products and services. The divisional configuration requires a top management level in which the head of each division has strong executive capability beyond those of the Chief Executive Officer.

How many divisions should a divisional firm have? Unlike the functional configuration where more functions or more products increase the coordination demands nonlinearly, additional divisions do not (Burton and Obel, 1984). In the extreme, an additional division only means choosing the divisional executive, adding one more column to the financial reports and affirming that the existing policies and information systems apply to the new division. In terms of NK complexity theory, K is very low or the divisions are only loosely connected. So, the number of divisions can be quite large, up to twenty or so. Considerably more subunits are possible in the divisional configuration than in the functional configuration. For example, General Electric has fourteen businesses, which include: aviation, healthcare, lighting, energy, finance, water, among many other diverse products and customers. As is evident, it is a diverse set of different businesses, products, services, and customers.

For the divisional configuration, the top executive is the center for corporate finance and policy. If divisional interdependencies are abundant, then the executive can become overloaded resolving interdivisional issues. The goal is to have divisions with minimal interdependency.

Matrix configuration

The *matrix* configuration is high on both dimensions: product/service/customer and functional specialization, suggesting a need for a high information-processing capacity to achieve the twin goals of efficiency and effectiveness. There is both the functional hierarchy and the divisional hierarchy for the same firm. The top executive is responsible for both the functional and divisional dimensions – to set policy, set priorities and resolve conflicts among the subunits. The top executive is not involved in the details of operations, but does oversee the entire firm. Most of the difficult coordination problems are handled by the matrix managers, i.e., those that act as a link between the lateral divisions and the functional hierarchy. Matrix managers make multiple variable tradeoffs which involve both the function and the division. Figure 4.5 illustrates a matrix in which functional specialization is combined with product orientation to yield coordination of functions across the product groups. As shown in Figure 4.5, the matrix configuration requires simultaneous coordination of the functional specialties across the projects, products,

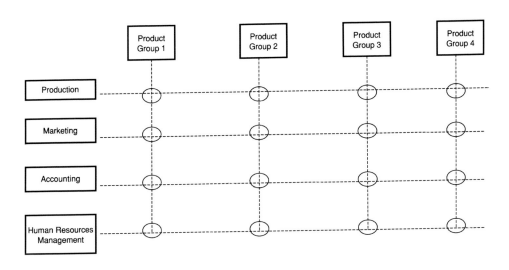

Figure 4.5 A matrix configuration.

services, or customers that the firm services. When there is a change in the timing of an activity, it ripples across the whole of the firm – called the *jello effect*.

The matrix can be very flexible, dealing with new information and adjusting to the new situations quickly to utilize limited resources to meet firm priorities. In general, a matrix organization can handle much more information than other organizational configurations. The advantage is that the matrix can realize both the efficiency of the functional form and the effectiveness of the divisional form – overcoming the limitations of both forms. When it works well, both efficiency and effectiveness result. Complicated tradeoffs are considered; decisions are made; and the firm moves on. But when the matrix is not well managed, it can be neither efficient nor effective. The challenges of managing a matrix include reconciling conflicts between the lateral and vertical subunits, information overload, excessive meetings, and decision delay. The firm does not move. The matrix configuration requires managerial skills that include a focus on the entire firm as well as one's own function or division, the acceptance of uncertainty, the willingness to consider complicated tradeoffs and negotiate realistic solutions, and a focus on results. These benefits must exceed the additional costs of coordination if the matrix is to be justified beyond the functional or divisional configurations.

The matrix configuration has many two-dimensional names in practice: function and product, function and project, specialty and industry customer, product and customer, product and region or country, basic technology and product – to name a few. There are also three-dimensional matrices, as many multinational firms have function, product, and country or regional dimensions. Procter & Gamble has a four-dimensional matrix of: global functions, global business units, regional products and the fourth, global customers (Galbraith, 2010). Matrix relations go beyond setting up the matrix configuration reporting relationships. Management must invest in developing cross-organizational coordination. This is realized in many ways: lateral relations, liaison roles, various coordinating committees – all of which consider issues which are not dealt with well or quickly within the hierarchy. Combining the matrix configuration together with its various other cross-organizational relations, it is quite possible to have eight dimensions: function, product, region, customer, technology development, basic research, human resources, and inter-country finances – perhaps more to be managed and involving complicated tradeoffs and coordination. Most firms are not so complicated; yet, many modern firms have an array of matrix relations, or cross-organizational mechanisms to coordinate across the dominant hierarchy in the firm.

How big can a matrix be? The matrix has both a functional and divisional dimension to manage simultaneously, so the size is the number of functions multiplied by the number of divisions. Given the jello effect, or more formally in NK theory where N is the number of subunits and K, the degree of interdependency, we suggest that the matrix can include only a small number of subunits, say four or five on each dimension. However, the big Swedish-Swiss multinational firm ABB at one time had a matrix configuration where there were over 100 separate SBUs along one dimension. They used an additional middle level of management in the matrix to support the complexity of interdependency to be coordinated. Still, the matrix was too complex to manage and was eventually dismantled and replaced with a simpler configuration. Yet quite recently, IBM has adopted a multidimensional and reconfigurable organization which yields both the multidimensional coordinated and also a continuing reconfiguration; it goes beyond even the four dimensions. Perhaps more important is the reconfiguration aspect which permits it to adjust to an ever changing environment (Galbraith, 2010). It should be emphasized that the coordinating units do not span all of the dimensions of the organization as found in a two-dimensional matrix. The capacity to reconfigure the matrix is paramount here. In turbulent environments, it is not likely that one configuration of the matrix will work well for an extended time, it must be reconfigured regularly. It is both the matrix configuration and its capacity for reconfiguration that are needed – not a static matrix configuration.

When both efficiency and effectiveness are needed, the matrix configuration is an appropriate choice. The matrix is usually more costly to manage than a hierarchy as there are more managers, more information, and more complicated coordination to be done. Further, the managers must consider and deal with many considerations that simultaneously have overall effects as well as effects on the subunit. Individuals who have been successful in a hierarchy may not be comfortable or successful in a matrix configuration. The matrix must be justified in terms of the strategy and the firm's environment.

The top management in the matrix has a focus on both efficiency and effectiveness – attempting to obtain both. The top management cannot direct the organization but must rely heavily upon the functional and divisional managers for the detailed, ongoing coordination adjustments in order to meet the firm priorities. Yet, the executive has much to do: set priorities, resolve differences among the subunits, and generally oversee the entire firm.

It is important to emphasize that the matrix can also lead to poor performance. The dual coordination across the functions and the divisions can lead to conflicts of priorities between the managers of subunits. If conflict management requires great involvement by the top executive, a major advantage of the matrix has been lost. The telltale signs of a matrix in trouble are, again: overload of decisions at the top as the managers are not able to solve problems; problems are not dealt with at all and opportunities are lost; budgets are exceeded; operations are not coordinated and resource utilization is lost or inefficient; employees are unhappy and confused; subunits are spending excessive time on coordinating with other subunits to the detriment of subunit performance; and opportunities are lost. When the matrix works well, it can achieve efficiency and effectiveness. But when things go badly, they can be very bad.

The organizational configuration is not the whole story; the organizational complexity is another property of the organization which can be designed to meet the goals of efficiency and effectiveness.

Organizational complexity

The organization's *complexity* (not to be confused with environmental complexity, discussed in Chapter 3) is a property or characteristic of the organizational structure. Organizational complexity is the vertical and horizontal differentiation of task management in the firm. It is how the firm's configuration is broken down into its several subunits. Roughly, it is the width and

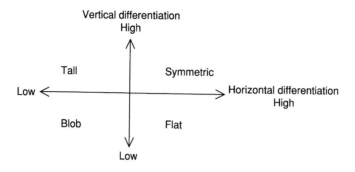

Figure 4.6 The organizational complexity space.

height of the hierarchy. The two organizational complexity dimensions are: the horizontal differentiation, or width, and the vertical differentiation, or height. The *horizontal differentiation* is the degree of task specialization across the hierarchy; the *vertical differentiation* is the depth of the hierarchy – top to bottom. Each of the configurations we discussed above can have high or low horizontal and vertical differentiation; it is a property of the organization. The practical design questions relating to organizational complexity include: the width of specialization for the firm, the span of control for the firm, the delayering of the firm to eliminate middle management, the scope in a divisional configuration, and the limitation on the number of functions and divisions in the matrix configuration. Again, these design choices are to be made in terms of efficiency and effectiveness goals.

As shown in Figure 4.6, choices regarding the degree of a firm's horizontal differentiation and vertical differentiation result in four types of organizational complexity. The organizational complexity is classified as: blob, tall, flat, and symmetric. These are not ideal types of configurations but rather archetypes that show how information processing will be conducted in the firm based on how work is allocated among subunits.

Next, we discuss four complexity types on the horizontal and vertical dimensions: blob for low and low; tall for low and high; flat for high and low; and symmetric for high and high, respectively.

Blob

If the firm does not formally divide its work into subunits, then it is like a *blob*. It is undifferentiated; it is low on both horizontal and vertical differentiation.

The blob has little specialization of task; the firm can be quite flexible and quick to respond to ongoing changes. Job descriptions are very loose, or may not exist. This lack of definition of who is to do what is very demanding on the executive, requiring decision-making for new situations on a continuing basis, where the executive can become overloaded and not be able to give adequate attention to the activities. The blob can also be confusing to customers or to newcomers who join the organization, since it is not clear who does what, or where one should go for specific types of information.

Tall

The *tall* firm is low on horizontal differentiation and high on vertical differentiation. The tall firm has a large middle management which focuses on information processing – taking directions and information from the top and making it precise for lower levels in the hierarchy; and taking detailed information from the bottom and summarizing and interpreting it for the top executives. The multilayered middle management connects the executive to the specialized task level, e.g., the top executive to the factory or service worker; the CEO to the programmer. The middle management takes directions and orders from the executive and breaks them down into smaller task implications which then must be coordinated across the subunits. For example, the executive of an auto plant may set the production plan at 100 automobiles, which must be broken down into plans for many subunits and coordinated among the subunits so that all of the functions work together to meet the plan.

From the bottom, the middle management summarizes what is happening at the bottom and passes it up the hierarchy, where the information is aggregated as it goes up, so that the top can deal with simpler, but relevant, information for decision-making and control. Both the down and up processes involve a good deal of information processing; it takes managerial time and can lead to delay. The span of control is limited as the information processing demands on the middle managers can be quite high. The inter-level vertical information transferal is usually large, involving frequent interaction of detailed information. If an additional function is added, it must be coordinated across all the functions, and thus the addition of one more function increases the information processing demands nonlinearly. This limits the number of direct reports to a few; most firms have five to seven functions.

Recently, many firms have shortened their hierarchy, eliminating middle-management levels in the firm. This is frequently called "delayering." On the organization chart, it can be simply the removal of a level, but much more is involved. A simple removal creates a mismatch and miscommunication between the two remaining levels. When a level is removed, the connections between the level above and the level below must also be changed. So, the information and communications must be redesigned, usually from top to bottom. Without the informational assessment and modification, the newly delayered firm will initially struggle. With more advanced information technology, it is now possible to achieve quickly the vertical coordination with a shorter middle management, but it still requires a redesign of the organization and its use of information. It is not simply a matter of removing a layer in the hierarchy and seeing what happens.

Flat

The flat firm is high on horizontal differentiation and low on vertical differentiation. There are fewer middle managers (or subunits) to coordinate between the top executives and the lower levels in the organization. Usually, these middle managers do not focus on detailed operations which take lots of time and attention. They focus instead on resource allocation, general policy, and finance. Other issues can be innovation, R&D, human resources – all of which involve policy and strategy. The information is aggregated and minimal. Short-term information exchanges focus on financial goals and cash flows. The long-term information exchanges focus on capital budgets and technology planning. If your firm is flat in its structure, the scope of the firm work across subunits can be quite varied, especially if there are no operational connections among them. The span of control can be wide if the focus of information flow is on policy, not detailed operations. Put another way, the information flows are minimal if exchanges focus on general policy but grow quickly for detailed operations.

A major advantage of the flat organizational structure is that each unit has autonomy to focus on its own work. Subunits can attend to the needs of customers or suppliers or new products – whatever is their particular charge, in terms of focus of work. On the other hand, the executive level of the organization bears the burden of coordinating among these subunits, and they can get out of synch, lack coordination, leading to inefficiencies for the firm as a whole.

Symmetric

The symmetric firm is high on horizontal differentiation and high on vertical differentiation. This means that the organization's work is broken down into many task specialties as well as many vertical reporting levels. Horizontally breaking down tasks into smaller tasks means that work can be done simultaneously in the horizontal subunits. Parallel processing of work, ability of each to deal with customers or others in the marketplace, and the opportunity to work independently all help to facilitate organizational effectiveness. To overcome the problem of the flat organization, in which the executive level must process information generated by each of the task-based subunits, a middle level (or perhaps multiple middle levels) are created that aggregate work from bottom to top and facilitate information flow from top to bottom. The symmetric organization tries to hit the ideal balance of vertical and horizontal breakdown of work into subunits. Middle levels help to coordinate work to yield efficiencies and so that each unit can concentrate on its activities for high effectiveness. The information-processing requirements of the symmetric organization are very high because the coordination demands are high both horizontally and vertically throughout the firm.

Diagnostic questions

For your firm, you can examine the two dimensions: product/service/customer orientation and functional specialization in Figure 4.7. Locate where you are in the figure. Then you can categorize your firm as: simple, functional, divisional, or matrix. To begin, answer the diagnostic questions overleaf.

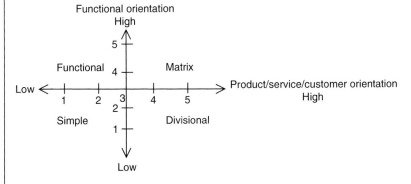

Figure 4.7 Locate your firm in the configuration space.

1. What is your unit of analysis that you chose in Chapters 1, 2, and 3? Use this unit of analysis as the organization when answering the questions below. The questions below will help you locate your organization on the functional orientation dimension and the product/service/customer dimension. For each item within question 2 and question 3, use a 1 to 5 rating scale to score your organization as follows:

       1   2   3   4   5

   very low   moderate   very high

2. Product/service/customer orientation
   a. Is the focus of your activities on internal operations of the organization (1) or, are you more focused toward products, services, and/or customers (5)?
   b. To what extent do you form subunits to organize work around your customers, (1)–(5)?
   c. To what extent do you form subunits to organize work around your firm's products or services, (1)–(5)?
   Now mark your organization's location on the horizontal axis in Figure 4.7.[1]

3. Functional specialization
   a. To what extent does your organization create subunits based on specialties or skills of its workers, (1)–(5)?
   b. Is your orientation toward specialization of functions and clear definition of jobs, i.e., high on functional specialization, or is your orientation low on specialization, (1)–(5)?
   c. To what extent does the firm have clearly defined roles and responsibilities for various subunits, (1)–(5)?
   Now mark your organization's location on the vertical axis in Figure 4.7.

4. You can now locate your organization on Figure 4.7. What is your firm's configuration?
   Next consider the organizational complexity. In Figure 4.8, the firm's horizontal differentiation and vertical differentiation are the dimensions. Here are questions which will help you locate your firm as blob, tall, flat, or symmetric:

[1] We suggest that you use an averaging procedure of the detailed scores to get to the overall score.

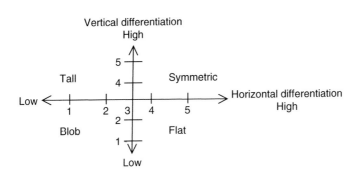

Figure 4.8 Locate your firm in the organizational complexity space.

5. Horizontal differentiation

   At the lowest level of your firm, how many subunits are there across the firm (where many subunits indicate a high horizontal differentiation and a few indicates low horizontal differentiation), few (1) or many (5)?

   If there are more than five subunits, your organization is high in horizontal differentiation.

6. Vertical differentiation

   How many levels are there from the top of the firm to the bottom, few (1) or many (5)?

   How many levels are there between the lowest-level employee and the CEO, few (1) or many (5)?

   Roughly, if there are more than five levels, assign a rating of 5 (high vertical differentiation). If there are four or five levels, assign a rating of 4. If there are three levels, assign a rating of 3. If there are two levels, assign a level of 2. If there is one level, assign a rating of 1 (low in vertical differentiation). You can now locate your organization on the figure; what is its complexity?

 # Fit and misfits

What is a good configuration for your firm, and what is an appropriate organizational complexity? What is a good fit? Here we add fit for the configuration and organizational complexity to the goals, strategy, and environment

Table 4.1 Fit among configuration, organizational complexity, environment, strategy, and goals

Corresponding quadrant in organization design space	A	B	C	D	
Organizational complexity	Blob	Tall	Flat	Symmetric	
Configuration	Simple	Functional	Divisional	Matrix	
Environment	Calm	Varied	Locally stormy	Turbulent	
Strategy types	Reactor	Defender	Prospector	Analyzer with innovation	Analyzer without innovation
Organizational goals	Neither	Efficiency	Effectiveness	Efficiency and Effectiveness	

you assessed in the prior chapters. This is shown in Table 4.1. In each of the columns A, B, C, and D, the fit relations can be read vertically from top to bottom. Misfits are any set of relations which do not fall within one column. There are a very large number of possible misfits. The critical issue is the limited attention and time of the top management. Any of these misfits can overload the executive management and lead to diminished performance for the firm. The telltale signs are: decision backlogs where the adjustments are not timely; individuals are either not told what to do or not given activities that are coordinated one with the other; or the executive works excessively long hours, but it is not enough.

In column A there is a fit among: the blob, a simple configuration, a calm environment, a reactor strategy, and ill-defined goals. The executive has the time and can devote attention to handling the relatively low information-processing demands of the configuration. If the strategy or the environment requires more information processing, then the executive can quickly become overloaded with undesired consequences. The simple configuration has a misfit with any condition or combination of conditions, which generates excessive information-processing demands for the executive: the firm is large; the strategy is a defender or analyzer which requires time-consuming planning and control; and the environment is not calm, which also requires adjustments and changes.

For a simple configuration and blob type of complexity, the reactor strategy is a good fit. This strategy lacks focus on the goals and usually is reactive to the situation at hand. The simple configuration is well matched for a reactor strategy as the executive can read the situation and then adjust to the market and the customers. The simple configuration could also work well for the prospector strategy where there is a narrow projective strategy. Here, rapid adjustment is not required until a survival threat emerges. The simple configuration is not a good fit for a defender strategy where efficiency is very important or for an analyzer strategy where longer-term planning is the norm.

In column A the corresponding environment is the calm environment. At first glance, the opposite turbulent environment may seem the better fit. The simple configuration can adjust quickly, which may not be needed for a calm environment which is predictable and not complex. But with all the information-processing demand centered on one individual, the demand on the executive quickly becomes overwhelming – especially when both the operational, tactical, as well as the strategic decisions are located with one individual. Nonetheless, the simple configuration can quickly adapt to operational changes but usually has great difficulties adapting to strategic changes. Therefore, the simple configuration works well for the calm environment, as there are fewer adjustments required. With limited attention and time, the executive finds the calm environment less demanding. The critical factor is the attention and time limitation of the executive.

Moving to column B, there is a fit among: the tall complexity, the functional configuration, the varied environment, the defender strategy and the efficiency goal. The information-processing demands have increased considerably, but the functional configuration and tall structure can handle a large amount of information which is predictable within known variations. Detailed and involved coordination can be realized. However, if the environmental unpredictability increases requiring additional information processing, then the functional configuration is not suited to making large coordinated changes quickly – a misfit situation.

For the functional configuration and tall complexity, the defender strategy with a focus on efficiency is a good fit where the defender strategy maintains the firm's position in its product/service market. Customers and clients are usually continuing, frequently with deep relationships. The marketing/sales function maintains strong ties with the customer. There is little emphasis on innovation in new products or services; however, there can be an emphasis on process innovation to reduce costs. The tall firm with a large middle management can focus on the efficient use of resources with detailed coordination of operations. The focus is continuity of operations based upon detailed plans. The firm can vary its production quantities efficiently within narrow limits, but larger variations in quantity or new activities compromise that efficiency. The tall firm is a misfit with the innovation-focused strategies. The defender wants to keep things as they are and the functional configuration fits it well. For other strategies, the functional configuration fits less well. It fits the analyzer without innovation reasonably well as planned change is possible. But for the analyzer with innovation or prospector, the functional configuration is too slow to be effective.

The corresponding environment for the functional configuration and tall complexity is the varied environment which is predictable and has high complexity. The emphasis is on predictability where the executive can anticipate what will happen in the future. The executive can deal with the complexity of the environment via rules and standard procedures that have been developed and learned over time. But when the environment becomes unpredictable – turbulent or locally stormy – then the functional configuration loses its efficiency as quick adjustments are needed and it cannot adjust quickly; it can perform the wrong activities as well. Frequently executive managers will try to take on this additional burden of driving change and become overloaded. The telltale signs of overload are backlogs of decisions and changes that are not coordinated across the whole of the organization.

Column C describes the firm that has a flat complexity, a divisional configuration, a locally stormy environment, a prospector strategy and an effectiveness goal. Each division has its own environment, which is stormy but largely independent of the others. The executive can create independent divisions to deal with the local conditions. Then the high-level executive can deal with policy and financial issues – limiting the information-processing demands. If, however, the environment becomes interdependent, such as two divisions competing for the same customer, the executive can become overloaded with coordinating details – again, creating a misfit. The tall firm is a misfit for the divisional configuration. It would be impossible for the top executive to become involved in the detailed operations of the firm, which would only lead to overload and its inefficient consequences.

For the divisional configuration and flat complexity, the prospector strategy with a focus on effectiveness is a good fit. The divisional configuration fits well the corporate strategy of prospector, where each division's own strategy is not specified from the top but is developed within the opportunities of the division's own markets and resources. The flat firm with a minimal middle management can focus on the efficient allocation of resources across the divisions using financial criteria. The divisional mix may include a defender strategy for one division and a prospector for another. The flat firm is a misfit with the intense information and high subunit coordination needed by a defender or analyzer.

The divisional configuration and flat complexity are a good fit with a locally stormy environment which can be highly unpredictable, sub-environment by sub-environment. Each sub-environment should closely match the division boundary. That is, for a product division the environment for each product can be unpredictable but not interdependent among the products. For General Electric (GE), the jet engine market is quite independent of the appliance market, but each market and technology might be unpredictable. Here, the top executive has partitioned the environment into independent segments, where the divisional executive can deal with it. The flat firm does not deal well with the highly coordinated operations which involve great detail; here there will be opportunity losses from the poor coordination.

In column D, the firm has a symmetric shape, a matrix configuration, a turbulent environment, an analyzer strategy and the dual goals of efficiency and effectiveness. The information-processing demands are very large, and detailed coordination of new situations is required (Galbraith, 1973, 2010). The firm cannot be broken down into relatively independent divisions, nor can a tall hierarchy handle all of the changes required.

The matrix configuration is a misfit with the following conditions: there is not a dual focus on efficiency and effectiveness which justifies the costs of additional management with particular managerial skills for coordinating up and across the hierarchy; the strategy is defender or prospector, which can be achieved with a single hierarchy; the environment is not complex or is predictable, which can be managed with a single hierarchy. When a single hierarchy configuration is sufficient for the desired goals, then the matrix adds cost without justification. When the strategy has a dual focus and the environment is turbulent, requiring large information processing to deal with the difficult ongoing coordination to achieve efficient use of resources, then the matrix configuration is appropriate.

The analyzer strategy, both with and without innovation, is a good fit for the matrix configuration and symmetric complexity. The analyzer operates in two domains of symmetric complexity. The first is the exploitation of the existing business, where efficiency is important; and, the second is exploration of innovation or technology enhancement, where the effectiveness of new ideas and products is paramount. The matrix configuration brings the two together to realize the needed changes in a timely manner. The matrix configuration fosters a dual focus on exploitation and exploration. It can work well in a turbulent environment where there are a large number of issues and problems to consider which are highly unpredictable, requiring the firm to adjust quickly. Together, there is a very large requirement for information processing to coordinate on an ongoing manner so that timely decisions can be made and action taken. The matrix configuration can deal well with the turbulent environment, and where there are many activities to coordinate across the entire firm. The functional managers and the divisional (product, project, or customer) managers are the coordinators both within their own subunit and across all of the subunits of the firm. There are ongoing adjustments and task changes due to the unpredictability of the environment. The information exchanges are very large and detailed. The span of control can be wide when the matrix managers work together and make the needed adjustments themselves, i.e., when the matrix is working well. When the matrix is not working well and many decisions move up to the top management, then the span of control can be quite limited. The key is the amount of information processing that the top management must deal with to achieve the coordination. The growth of the matrix is quite limited if the top management is involved in the details of operations. If the top management is not so involved, growth can be larger but is limited because the coordination difficulties grow nonlinearly as each new matrix dimension adds many coordination interfaces (Burton and Obel, 1984). The symmetric complexity is not a good fit unless the environment is both unpredictable and complex. If one of these conditions holds and not the other, the simpler tall or flat firm is sufficient.

If your firm is located in different columns based upon your answers to the diagnostic questions of these four chapters, then you should think about what you might do to bring all elements of the firm's organizational design into fit in the column that meets the firm's goals. But also think about what is involved to move to a different goal and thus a different column.

Summary

In this chapter, you have assessed your organization's configuration and organizational complexity and considered how these relate to your firm's strategy, environment, and goals. There are four configurations: simple, functional, divisional, and matrix; and there are four complexity types: blob, tall, flat, and symmetric. We discussed how your firm's configuration and complexity should be designed so as to improve the likelihood of the firm reaching goals, given the environment and your firm's strategy. If there are misfits among the design components, then you should consider how these might be changed in order to bring them into alignment.

Glossary

Blob complexity: an undefined organization in the sense that there are no formally specified subunits.

Configuration: assignment of work to units of the organization; indicates the hierarchy of responsibility; represented pictorially as an organization chart; an icon of the organization; sometimes called the structure or architecture of the organization.

Divisional configuration: tasks are assigned to relatively independent divisional units by product, customer, region; or other externally oriented focus; each division relatively self contained; executives make policy and financial decisions; organizational chart represents the divisions reporting to the headquarters.

Flat complexity: an organization with many jobs at the bottom and few levels bottom to top; high horizontal differentiation and low vertical differentiation.

Functional configuration: tasks are assigned by specialization of work; tasks are grouped by skills requirements.

Functional specialization: the primary partitioning of the firm's task into smaller specialized tasks and the efficient completion of each task.

Horizontal differentiation: the degree of task specialization across the hierarchy.

Jello effect: the situation where a small change in one part of the organization requires change and adjustment throughout the organization. E.g., in a matrix configuration, a change in one function or project frequently requires adjustments in a number of other functions and projects.

Matrix configuration: a combination of a functional and divisional form; a dual focus; a dual hierarchy.

Multi-dimensional matrix: a matrix organization with more than two dimensions.

Organizational complexity: the vertical and horizontal differentiation dimensions of the organization; the shape of the organization.

Product/service/customer orientation: the primary partitioning of the firm's task into smaller tasks by the output orientation and their effective completion.

Simple configuration: tasks or work activities are specified on an ongoing basis rather than in advance; an organization where one individual, the boss, is responsible for all activities; the organization chart usually shows all employees reporting to one person.

Span of control: the horizontal complexity or width of the organization, usually measured as the number of individuals reporting to a manager.

Symmetric complexity: an organization with a balance of specific jobs and levels; neither tall nor flat; high on both horizontal and vertical differentiation.

Tall complexity: an organization with a large number of levels from bottom to top; low horizontal differentiation and high vertical differentiation.

Vertical differentiation: the depth of the hierarchy; total number of levels, top to bottom.

5 Distributed organizations

Introduction

In the previous chapter you described the organization in terms of its basic structure. Today many organizations operate in multiple locations and use variants of the basic organizational structures presented in Chapter 4. Distributed organizational designs enable firms to coordinate work across national and other geographic boundaries and meet the knowledge needs of our increasingly service-oriented economy.

This segment of our step-by-step approach consists of two analyses. First, we will assess your organization's approach to organizing across geographic boundaries. Second, we will assess the organization's approach to organizing for knowledge exchange. The variants in structure described in this chapter are sometimes called "new organizational forms" because they represent new twists on classic ways of organizing (DeSanctis and Fulk, 1999; Heydebrand, 1989). The variants described here represent options for designing your firm to meet the demands of today's global, information-intense organization.

When an organization is founded, it typically starts by doing business in one locale. That locale services a particular neighborhood, city, or even an entire country. As the executive managing a business centered in one locale, you become an expert in doing business in that environment. You know the people, the culture, and the general setting in which your firm operates. Your firm becomes highly knowledgeable about that one locale. This allows you to build efficiency and effectiveness based on local knowledge. In addition, doing business with partners, that is, managing relationships with suppliers, distributors, government regulators, and other entities, is relatively straightforward when all are co-located. You share a common language, laws, customs, and ways of doing business.

As your business expands to include operations or sales activity to regions that are geographically distant from your home locale, you face significant organizational challenges. These relate to managing people and processes across distance and cultures. The challenges are important whether you are managing a large organization or a small work team. Should you organize around the talent (expertise) or function, regardless of locale, or should you organize based on geographic location? To what extent should you allow various locales to operate independently versus enforce standard ways of doing things across the firm? Should you own or directly manage operations in distant locales, or would it be better to form partnerships or alliances that permit local units to organize as they see fit? To what extent should you rely on information technology, versus travel and face-to-face meetings, to link people together?

As an example, consider the European appliance manufacturer Merloni Elettrodomestici, an Italian-owned company with headquarters in Paris. Initially limited to regional operations in Italy, the company began exporting its products in 1972. The company soon had a sales force distributed across Europe and later acquired or built facilities in Germany, France, the UK, Spain, Portugal, Holland, and Belgium (Bower, 2001). The firm then faced the challenge of how to organize a growing, distributed enterprise. Merloni first created country-based organizations, all coordinated through the Paris office; later the company consolidated by product line, creating several centers of excellence that coordinated all operations for a given product throughout Europe. By 1994 a matrix reporting structure was added to link research and development activities with brand-based activities. In more recent years the firm has created a "developing markets division," with country-based organizations in Russia and China, while maintaining product-line organizations in Europe. Merloni's experience illustrates the kinds of design choices that firms have to make as they expand their businesses around the world.

Similar design decisions must be made by managers of small work teams. Consider an energy engineering firm operating within a large multinational enterprise. The large company may operate in a divisional fashion, but any one division may have engineering teams with research expertise in Germany, design expertise in the US, and production expertise in Malaysia. How should the team organize? All work could be coordinated through one locale, such as the US facility, or, instead, team members in each of the three countries could do their work autonomously and simply link tasks together on an as-needed, project-by-project basis. Team members could complete all task demands on their own, or they could hire external parties to work as contractors, passing routine or specialized work to the contractors and leaving core work tasks for the regular team members. The team could designate liaison representatives in each country to coordinate with team members in the other countries; or teams could set up a matrix system in which specialists from each locale regularly communicate with all parallel specialists in the other locales.

Every day you face these kinds of design decisions in your organization. As an executive, you decide how work is to be allocated and coordinated across place and space. When workers are in different time zones, speak different languages, have different holiday schedules, work habits, and skill sets, the work allocation and coordination challenges escalate. Worldwide distribution of work creates access to resources to accomplish the organization's mission, and it can bring your company close to the customers and suppliers with whom you do business; but distribution of work also creates immense challenges in how to design work processes for the greatest efficiency and effectiveness.

Let us begin by assessing an organization's approach to organizing across geographic boundaries. Next, we will assess the organization's approach to organizing for knowledge exchange.

Structures for spanning geography

A simple and powerful way to describe a firm's approach to managing across distance is in terms of the extent to which it locates based on optimal sourcing versus a particular geographic boundary, and the extent to which it locates to yield local responsiveness versus global standards and economies of scale. Other dimensions could be used as well; however, we focus on these because they relate to theory and research and provide simplicity within our step-by-step approach.

Optimal sourcing refers to the decision to locate operations in the place in the world that brings the greatest advantage to the firm in terms of customer contact, cost efficiency, human resource skill need, or other objective. For example, a software company may choose to locate in California's Silicon Valley or Sophia Antipolis on the Côte d'Azur of France in order to be close to programmers and engineers with needed technical skills for new product development. Alternatively, if the firm seeks low-cost, high-skilled labor, it may locate one or more facilities in Hyderabad or New Delhi. In order to reach customers in developing markets of Russia, the company may locate offices in Novgorod, Kursk, or Vladivostok. If a firm locates work based on placing it as close as possible to the resource supply, then the firm is placing high value on optimal sourcing. Alternatively, if a firm locates work based on other factors, such as being conveniently close to headquarters or in a particular city, country, or geographic region where the company has existing business or operations, then optimal sourcing is low.

Local responsiveness refers to the decision to distribute work in many locales versus consolidating work in one or a few centralized locations. Distributing work to many locales maximizes your firm's flexibility to complete work tasks any time, any place. A highly distributed workforce, perhaps consisting of an army of mobile salespersons, software programmers, or service operators, exemplifies this extreme. These workers may be organized by country or region if the firm is very large; but the key is that the locally responsive firm tries to distribute work as much as possible, thus enabling close contact with customers or suppliers and the ability to anticipate and respond to their needs. Consolidation of operations reduces local responsiveness, although it brings economies of scale, the opportunity to standardize work practices, and a general increase in managerial control over the work.

Optimal sourcing and local responsiveness represent tradeoffs in organizational design that correspond to the firm strategies of exploitation and exploration discussed in Chapter 2. To the extent that your firm pursues exploitation, you should organize work to be high in optimal sourcing. To the extent that the firm pursues exploration, you should organize work to be high in local responsiveness.

The tradeoffs associated with organizing for optimal sourcing and local responsiveness yield four basic options for structuring the distributed organization. The following typology is based on the seminal work of Bartlett and Ghoshal (1998), who studied how multinational companies develop strategy and marketing worldwide. Bartlett and Ghoshal described their categories in broad terms and multiple dimensions. The typology we present here is strictly based on two dimensions and focuses on organizational structure (and not the broader strategy and marketing issues). Our typology descriptions diverge somewhat from theirs, but we stick with the fundamental assumptions of their theory.

Figure 5.1 displays the organizational design space of optimal sourcing and local responsiveness along with the four types of distributed organizational design that relate to these dimensions: (1) global, (2) international, (3) multidomestic, and (4) transnational.

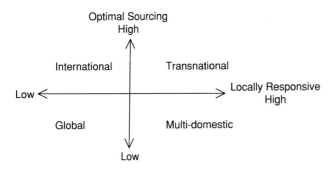

Figure 5.1 The organizational design space of structures for spanning geography.

These four approaches to organizational design across geography correspond to the four classic organization configurations described in Chapter 4,
with global corresponding to the simple configuration, international corresponding to the functional configuration, multi-domestic corresponding to the
divisional configuration, and transnational corresponding to the matrix. As
with the classic configurations discussed in Chapter 4, the typology illustrates
major design approaches. Variations are possible, and firms sometimes combine these approaches, perhaps using different designs at different levels of
the firm; or there may be variation across business units, with some units
designing globally, for example, and other units taking an international or
transnational approach. Consistency in design up-and-down or across the
multinational firm is not imperative. More important is that you choose a
configuration that is consistent with your organization's goals, strategy, and
environment.

Global

If your organization is not organized to be locally responsive or to yield
optimal sourcing but instead concentrates its work activities in one locale
(usually the place of your firm's founding, i.e., its corporate headquarters),
then it is *global* in design. The global design is a centralized approach to
organizing and thus yields the advantage of high centralization of decision-
making and work practices that are established by the "home base" of operations. A global organizational design is consistent with a strategy of offering
similar products or services worldwide, no matter where products are

ultimately sold. Work practices (the way work is done) are controlled by, and consistent with, the way corporate headquarters wants things to be done. Organizations that offer identical products or services to all markets and concentrate their upstream and support activities in one country are global in design. The global design scores low on both optimal sourcing and local responsiveness. The global design is akin to the simple configuration outlined in Chapter 4.

Consider the case of a software company that offers project management software solutions to customers all over the world. The company is headquartered in the US, in Arlington, Virginia. The management, developers, and support staff are located there. Sales representatives may call on customers throughout the world, and contract workers from locales other than Virginia may be hired to complete specific tasks. Support staff may make site visits to customers throughout the world. But the management of all these work activities is centered at the Virginia headquarters. There is little customization of work as a function of geography. Instead, work is managed from the corporate center. There may be customization of products and services to meet the needs of specific customers, but the arrangement of this work is controlled at the center, that is, in the US locale. This organization has a global design.

International

International firms move beyond the home base of operations to create "centers of excellence," or hubs for each major product or service. These hubs are located so as to maximize optimal sourcing; that is, work is located as close as possible to the resource the organization needs to do the work, wherever that may be in the world. These hubs then service worldwide markets. Local responsiveness is low as the products and services tend to be standardized rather than customized to location.

The upstream segment of the oil business traditionally has been managed using the international approach. Drilling operations are placed anywhere in the world where there is an accessible, fertile oil field. This may mean that the firm has many operations in Alaska, Malaysia, or off the coast of Western Africa, and very few operations in Europe or North America. Thus the upstream business is not balanced or bounded by geography; instead, it diffuses to "where the work can best be done."

Let's consider a modern, service-oriented business, such as the example of the software company described above. Suppose our software development firm, located in Arlington, Virginia, has grown such that its project management software products have sold to customers throughout the US, Western Europe, Japan, Taiwan, and Australia. The company now services thousands of customers in these locales. This has created a huge workload for the corporate operations; further, the company cannot find enough programmers in Virginia at sufficiently low cost to meet the software support needs of customers who are now spread around the globe. To meet customer support needs, the company may open two operations in India, perhaps one in New Delhi and one in Hyderabad, where high-quality customer relations and technical skills are available at a relatively low cost of labor. Further, these operations have sufficient labor pools to replenish workers who leave the firm in good economic times when staff turnover tends to be high. The New Delhi operation serves as a customer call center. The Hyderabad operation serves as a technical support center where programmers work on software fixes and upgrades. This is an international type of organizational design.

The international organizational design is like a functional form in that configuration is based on concentrating expertise, or skills, as a way of managing work. The organization distributes work geographically, away from corporate headquarters, but corporate headquarters maintains a great deal of authority. The organization is "tall" rather than flat; that is, the vertical differentiation is high.

Multi-domestic

If a firm takes a decentralized, geography-based approach to organizing work, then its configuration is *multi-domestic*. The multi-domestic organization customizes operations to specific countries or regions, offering unique products or services to meet local preferences. The multi-domestic is like a divisional form. Work is organized to exploit local opportunities, especially the cultural, political, and geographic opportunities associated with a given locale. Divisions or other operations are located in different locales to yield local responsiveness to customers, not to yield optimal sourcing. The multi-domestic organizational design can be very effective for the firm that is entering markets which are very different from the home locale, where management has little experience in the new locale and wants to benefit from learning about customer needs or possible ways of doing work in that locale. This type of organizational design is flat in shape rather than tall, meaning that work practices will vary as a function of locale. The locale could be a region or a country.

Consider the case of 3M in the US. As the firm entered Europe in the mid-twentieth century, it took a multi-domestic approach. At that time the company was interested in acquiring research and development expertise in Europe and in generating new business there; however, the American management had relatively little knowledge about local ways of doing work, customer needs, and so on, across the European market. Further, the European market was fragmented, with language, currencies, employee work practices, and customer tastes all varying across countries. Given these environmental conditions, along with a strategy of exploration in the European market, 3M established country-based organizations, and gave each a high degree of autonomy to manage work and grow the business in these countries (INSEAD, 1994). By the end of the twentieth century, conditions were different. The EU was established, work practices were more similar across Western Europe, and, in general, the European market became more (though not entirely!) homogeneous. With this environmental change, 3M moved to a regional-centered design, consolidating the country operations. Locale remains a cornerstone of 3M's organizational design today, with operations organized as a function of region, including the Americas, Western Europe, Eastern Europe, Russia, China, Japan, Southeast Asia, Africa, and the Middle East. Organizing by locale supports high local responsiveness. Products and services, as well as management of employees and work tasks, vary as a function of region to provide maximum local responsiveness.

Like the divisional configuration, the multi-domestic approach to structuring work supports growth via exploration of new products and services. The multi-domestic configuration is a good choice of organizational design if the source of growth is geographically based. Consider our example of the software development firm, headquartered in Arlington, Virginia. Suppose the firm seeks to grow the service side of its business, offering a variety of project management services to customers that use its project management software. If the firm assesses the environment and determines that service needs are quite different in, say, developed countries versus developing countries, and, further, that there are major differences in service needs in Asian countries versus Western countries, the firm could adopt a multi-domestic organizational design for management of its service business. The firm might establish regional operations in Japan or Singapore to service the many developed economies of Asia. It might then establish a country-based operation in mainland China to explore the unique needs of that market. Similarly, it might locate an operation in London from which it would service the Western European market, with additional offices in Moscow and Budapest, to service the unique needs of these more volatile, growing economies. The multi-domestic approach involves significantly more investment for the otherwise corporate-centered firm. This approach to organizational design requires that the firm establish local presence, develop employees to manage in that locale, and so on. But the potential payoffs for growth are great, if the locales are selected and managed well. Over time, less successful local operations can be shut down, while those that are more successful can be allowed to grow.

Transnational

The *transnational* organization blends the international and multi-domestic structures to yield both the location advantages of regional or country-based design and the economic efficiencies of optimal sourcing. In the transnational design some operations are located close to needed resources; but location decisions also are made such that the firm has presence in all areas of the world that are of strategic importance. In this way, the organization develops customized offerings by region while at the same time gaining efficiencies through worldwide centers of operation. The transnational organization takes a sophisticated approach to locating its operations. Some are centralized in the home locale; some are optimally sourced, wherever those sources are located; and others are distributed among country or regional operations.

Unilever, Procter & Gamble, and NEC are examples of companies that have adopted transnational designs (Bartlett and Ghoshal, 1998). Consider the detergent business within Unilever. Research and product development activities are located based on optimal sourcing. Basic research facilities are located in the US and Europe, in centers close to universities and ample supplies of chemists and chemical engineers. Product development groups, on the other hand, are located close to the business units that they serve, wherever that may be in the world. There are manufacturing facilities in Asia and Latin America, where natural resources are available and labor costs are relatively low, but sales, distribution, and service operations are localized, in some cases by country, or even a region within a country, to reach and respond to the needs of particular customer groups.

Why choose a transnational design? This design makes sense if the organization has diverse and conflicting strategic needs and/or high variation in the business environments the firm confronts as it moves outside of its home country. Suppose you manage the software company described earlier, with corporate headquarters in Arlington, Virginia. You might take an optimal sourcing approach to locating a technical support or call center, perhaps placing both facilities in India despite the low presence of customers in that country. At the same time you might locate sales and service operations in London, Moscow, Budapest, Japan, and China, so that you reach your major strategic markets. These facilities might operate somewhat differently, depending on the needs of customers in the regions they serve and the degree of investment your company intends to make in the particular region. The transnational approach to your organizational design means that you disperse subunits, develop specialized centers of operation, and then link these through effective management of interdependent relationships (Cullen, 2002).

The transnational is the most complex distributed design to manage because some aspects of the firm's work are region-centric whereas other aspects of the firm's work are resource-centric. Like the matrix organization, management of the transnational organization requires a combination of centralized and decentralized decision-making. Managed well, the transnational design can bring the benefits of high efficiency and effectiveness to a firm. The corporate headquarters must be very adept at knowing what work is best located as a function of sourcing and what work is best located to yield local responsiveness. Most important, once the location decisions have been made, management must be adept at coordinating among the firm's distributed operations. This means that there must be structures to support the exchange of knowledge among the various geographic locales. We now turn to the possibilities for organization of knowledge exchange.

Structures for managing knowledge exchange

A major challenge for the distributed organization is to structure so as to maximize efficiency and effectiveness of knowledge exchange. We focus on knowledge exchange for this component of organizational design, rather than the more general issue of information exchange. *Knowledge* is information that corresponds to a particular context. Knowledge exchange is the sharing of information that requires interpretation, or intelligence, to fully understand

and apply. Configuring your organization for knowledge exchange is important, because how you design for knowledge exchange will affect other aspects of your organization's design, especially the design of coordination and control systems. Structures for managing knowledge exchange constitute the infrastructure on which the basic organization configurations discussed in Chapter 4 rely as they become more distributed in design.

Structures for knowledge exchange can help the organization to increase its information capacity, that is, the amount of information that the organization can process. Consider the case of a pharmaceutical company that is continually under pressure to develop new products while controlling costs in an intense, highly competitive industry. Suppose you are the chief executive of this company. The company has subunits working on tasks related to primary care products, oncology, vaccines, neurological agents, metabolic, and gastrointestinal products. Each of these product areas has its unique research and production requirements, and each may face special scientific, legal, or other constraints as it conducts its work. Each area is continually gathering and generating knowledge to do its work, but at the same time some or all areas may benefit from knowledge processed by other groups. The potential for shared knowledge may be chemistry-based, or it may relate to the development of research platforms, testing methods, statistical analyses, production methods, sales opportunities, and the like. How can you structure your organization for knowledge exchange? What are your options? In today's modern enterprise, you can rely on two important mechanisms, virtualization and information technology, to manage knowledge exchanges.

Virtualization refers to the degree of boundary-spanning or organizational "reach" that a company uses as the basis for knowledge exchange (Davidow and Malone, 1992). Organizations that are high in virtualization look outward, linking teams, business units, or even the firm itself with parties outside the organizational boundary in order to gain knowledge. Organizations that are low in virtualization take a more inward focus, gaining knowledge by developing it inside corporate boundaries, inside specialized groups, or by acquiring knowledge externally and then harboring it inside the firm. An example of the latter occurs when one company makes an acquisition of another company in order to capture new capabilities from the marketplace. *IT infusion* refers to the extent to which a firm relies on information technology-based systems, including data processing and computer-based communication systems, to manage knowledge exchange. Although nearly all organizations today rely on IT to acquire and transfer knowledge, some firms rely more heavily on IT-based

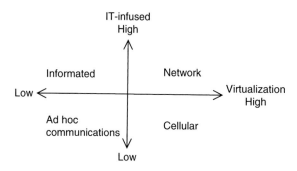

Figure 5.2 Structures for managing knowledge exchange.

systems for knowledge exchange, whereas others rely more heavily on face-to-face or manual systems to support knowledge exchange.

These two dimensions suggest four major types of organizational designs for knowledge exchange, as shown in Figure 5.2.

Ad hoc communications

Ad hoc communications are the primary knowledge exchange approach used by firms that score low on both the dimension of virtualization and IT-infusion. These organizations rely on person-to-person contacts or small groups (two to ten people) whose members are all from inside the organization (or organizational unit) to share knowledge on an as-needed basis. Small, loosely created groups of people provide knowledge-based innovation that is ground-up, meaning that it comes from the people closest to the work at hand. These informal groups typically are temporary. They come together to meet a specific task need. They usually are appointed by management, work with a fair amount of autonomy and may vary in the methods used to track their progress and share results with those outside of the group. Ad hoc communications manage knowledge exchange on an as-needed basis; members adjust the way they organize work and report to one another and their boss depending on the nature of the particular task at hand. In ad hoc communications, a leader's preferences for managing work may have a high degree of influence on exactly how the work is organized. So, there are not pre-established routines for conducting work. Instead, the organization of work – how knowledge is shared and tasks are completed – is put together on the fly, to meet the particular work needs. Ad hoc communications can be a very effective way to generate and transfer information to meet the specific knowledge needs of a given project, event, or client.

Informated

Shoshana Zuboff (1988) coined the term the *informated* organization to refer to the use of computer and related systems to manage information up and down the organization. Informated organizations are low in virtualization and high in IT infusion. The label harkens back to an earlier era of automation, or machine-based design of work, but informated implies more than automated work. Today computer technology is heavily embedded in the design and monitoring of work processes such that tasks can be streamlined, closely linked with one another, and continually managed for improvement in quality and cost control (Keen and McDonald, 2000). Most modern banks use information systems to monitor customer inquiries and call center operators to continually improve customer support and yield greater worker productivity. In a similar way, UPS, the worldwide package delivery service, links information systems inside trucks with package-tracking systems that allow customers, workers, and management to view systems operations from the time of order placement all the way to package delivery. These are examples of informated organizations. Via computer technology, events and processes are made visible and measurable, making redesign and customization of work possible. The informated organization increases the intellective demands of work, as well as the possibilities for creative ways of rearranging and linking work activities. Informated organizational design is possible in a wide range of industries from manufacturing to the service sector. Going forward, we can anticipate more informated organizational design in businesses such as hospitals, consulting, and education as they increasingly rely on intense knowledge exchange to meet client needs.

Cellular

Cellular organizational forms are characterized by small, autonomous groups or business units that largely self-govern and can grow, reproduce, and form relations with other units as needed (Miles et al., 1997). The label is based on the biological metaphor of a living cell. The cellular organization has an inward focus for knowledge exchange within teams or units, coupled with boundary-spanning across cells and into the marketplace in order to gain access to external sources of knowledge. Compared to the informated organization, which is high-tech and competes on its ability to rapidly arrange and rearrange work processes, the cellular organization competes on the ability of cells to import and export knowledge while harboring information inside for creative or competitive benefit. Furthermore, compared to informated organizations, cellular organizations will have more variability in the process of knowledge exchange within subunits. Compared to ad hoc communication-based organizations, cellular organizations develop extensive relationships with external parties for knowledge sustenance. Thus the cellular organization scores high on virtualization but relatively low on IT-infusion.

Like ad hoc communications, cellular organizations rely heavily on rich forms of interaction between people for knowledge exchange. Information technology may be used to coordinate work, but systems will not be consistent or perfected in the sense of being fully engineered for smoothness and quality control. Instead, flexibility in the way knowledge is exchanged is important. High interpersonal contact, such as conferences, seminars and face-to-face meetings, may be used to facilitate tacit knowledge sharing. The goal is to promote an entrepreneurial mindset with a focus on innovation and growth within the cell and the larger organization of which it is a part. Cellular forms tend to be suitable for research firms and divisional forms where highly varied approaches to knowledge development and exchange are needed across the subunits.

Network

The *network* organization links units within the firm with one another and, further, develops active linkages between internal units and external organizations to meet the organization's knowledge needs. It scores high both on virtualization and IT-infusion. Networks often take the form of strategic alliances, research partnerships, and consortia. Like the cellular form, the network configuration would be nearly impossible to create without the use of modern information technology. The network is similar to the traditional matrix configuration in that it is both product and specialty intense; however, unlike the matrix, it lacks symmetry or balance in its structure (Miles and Snow, 1986). Information technology is used to link units in multiple directions, not just vertically or horizontally (Boudreau et al., 1998). Theoretically, the network can operate as a ring, a star, or a web of ties among the subunits of the firm. Resources, people, and ideas flow in all directions. Specific points of exchange can be made between the subunits and with external parties "that matter" to the business need. In this way, the network does not necessarily get out of control, creating information overload. Instead, network ties are formed and managed intelligently, putting knowledge exchange when and where it's needed (Hansen and Nohria, 2004; Velstring et al., 2004). The network organization combines the information-intensity of the informed firm with the boundary-spanning approach to knowledge exchange found in the cellular organization.

Diagnostic questions

1. What approach does your chosen organization use to span geography and support knowledge exchange? Answer the questions below.[1] Use the same unit of analysis when answering these questions as you have used in the prior chapters.

   For each item within questions 2 through 4, use a 1 to 5 rating scale to score your organization as follows:

1	2	3	4	5
very low		moderate		very high

2. What is the organization's degree of local responsiveness (1)–(5)? To answer this question you may think about the following:
   a. To what extent are the units of your firm located close to corporate headquarters (1) or far from corporate headquarters (5)?
   b. To what extent does your firm consolidate work in one region of the world (1) or distribute its work to many locales (5)?
   c. To what extent are the important business decisions in your organization made with a corporate perspective in mind (1) versus a local perspective (5)?

[1] As in prior chapters, you can use an averaging procedure of the detailed scores to get to the overall score for each dimension, or you can use the questions as a general guide to estimate your firm's score on each dimension.

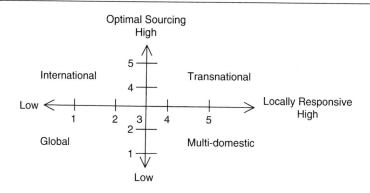

Figure 5.3 Locate your organization in the geographic space by rating its degree of local responsiveness and optimal sourcing.

d. Overall, is the firm organized to assure centralization of decision-making and consistency of work practices across subunits (1) or autonomy of local units and customization to meet local needs (5)? How does your chosen organization score on local responsiveness? Now mark the organization's location on the local responsiveness axis in Figure 5.3.

3. What is your organization's degree of optimal sourcing (1)–(5)?
To answer this question you may think about the following:
To what extent does your firm make decisions about where to locate its operations based on the following criteria:
a. close proximity to customers (1)–(5)?
b. close proximity to human resources, whether skilled or unskilled (1)–(5)?
c. close proximity to suppliers (1)–(5)?
d. close proximity to business partners (1)–(5)?
e. close proximity to resources to its ongoing business (1)–(5)?
How does the organization score on optimal sourcing, low or high? Mark your organization's location on the local responsiveness axis in Figure 5.3. Now with your scores on local responsiveness and optimal sourcing, locate the organization in the geographic design space shown in Figure 5.3.

4. What is your organization's degree of virtualization (1)–(5)?
To answer this question you may think about the following:
a. To what extent does the organization rely on internal (1) versus external (5) sources of knowledge to do its work?

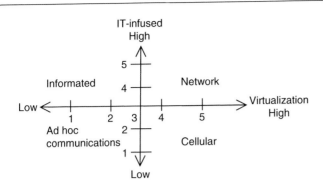

Figure 5.4 Locate your organization in the knowledge exchange space by rating its degree of virtualization and IT-infusion.

b. To what extent does the organization develop specialized groups, or centers, of expertise that are free to grow on their own (1)–(5)?

c. To what extent does the organization develop unique partnerships with other units or organizations for purposes of fostering innovation, product development, or innovative forms of service support (1)–(5)?

d. To what extent is the organization dependent on information supplied by other organizations or units in order to do its work (1)–(5)?

e. To what extent are other organizations or units dependent on information supplied by the organization or unit in order to do their work (1)–(5)?

Based on your rating for items a through e above, determine the score for virtualization. Now mark the organization's location on the virtualization axis in Figure 5.4.

5. What is your organization's degree of IT-infusion (1)–(5)?
   To answer this question you may think about the following:
   a. To what extent does the organization rely on computer-based systems to manage its most critical business activities (1)–(5)?
   b. To what extent does the organization invest in continual improvement of business processes (1)–(5)?
   c. Which tends to be more frequently used to manage interpersonal communication, face-to-face contact between people (1), or electronic communication systems (5)?

> d. Do systems of communication in the organization tend to be informal
>   and changing (1) or more formalized and prescribed (5)?
>
> Now mark your organization's location in the organizational design space
> for knowledge exchange shown in Figure 5.4.

Next we want you to examine how your firm's approach to distributed design
and knowledge exchange fits with its configuration, as well as goals, strategy,
and the other design components that you identified in the prior chapters.

Fit and misfits

Table 5.1 summarizes the four columns in the organizational design space thus
far. For each row in this table, circle the firm's type (A, B, C, or D), as selected in
this and the prior chapters. Next, review the columns. Are all of the circled
items in the same column? To the extent that the circled items fall in the same
column, the organization has good alignment, or fit, among its goals, strategy,
and structure. As before, design types in the same column tend to fit well
together.

Firms in column A are simple in structure and manage knowledge on an
ad hoc, informal basis. These organizations don't have a strong organizational
form; instead, the task design is changed to meet the needs of the work at hand.
When firms in column A "go global," that is, when they venture outside of their
own country, they tend to do well with centralized, headquarters-based management. Hence, a global approach to geographic distribution makes sense.
Headquarters can "call the shots" and manage on the fly to meet the demands
of the business. There is great flexibility in this organizational design, but its
efficiency and effectiveness are limited. Management in the home country
locale must be very adept at processing information for the firm as a whole.
As we have noted in earlier chapters, this type of organizational design works
well when the environment is stable or the organization is small. If the environment shifts in some significant way or becomes more turbulent, the global
organizational design can be very slow to adapt.

Firms in column B organize knowledge by specialty, i.e., by area of expertise,
and then use information processing to gain high efficiencies in business

Table 5.1 Fit and misfit table for geographic distribution and knowledge exchange

Corresponding quadrant in organizational design space	A	B	C	D	
Knowledge exchange	Ad hoc communi- cations	Informated	Cellular	Network	
Geographic distribution	Global	International	Multi- domestic	Transnational	
Complexity	Blob	Tall	Flat	Symmetric	
Configuration	Simple	Functional	Divisional	Matrix	
Environment	Calm	Varied	Locally stormy	Turbulent	
Strategy types	Reactor	Defender	Prospector	Analyzer with innovation	Analyzer without innovation
Organizational goals	Neither	Efficiency	Effectiveness	Efficiency and Effectiveness	

processes. These are functionally designed firms that distribute work based on optimal sourcing. The functional organizational structure does well to organize for geographic distribution using an international model, creating centers of excellence and informating to gain improvements for managing business processes and enabling cost control. Alternatively, if the firm has a divisional structure, then when it distributes globally, a multi-domestic form of organizing presents a better fit. In the latter case, each domestic locale can operate as a cell, developing creative methods to meet its unique knowledge needs. The column C approach to organizational design supports a prospector strategy.

Column D is perhaps the ideal approach to organizational design for the geographically distributed firm with high information-processing demands. This organization form should develop network forms of knowledge exchange to meet the demands of a turbulent environment. The network

approach to organizing facilitates both exploration and exploitation strategies, thus facilitating goals of both effectiveness and efficiency. As discussed earlier in this chapter, the transnational organizational design is the
trickiest to manage; a clever combination of local and global operations, and
the use of IT-infused and rich human interactions must be applied to meet
business needs. If a firm has been successful in managing a matrix design in
its home market, then it is more likely to be able to manage a transnational
design in global markets.

More than likely, not all of your organization's design components are in the
same column (i.e., they do not all fall within the same column of Table 5.1).
Where you see misfits you should ask yourself whether these misfits are
causing decrements in your firm's ability to meet its goals. If not, it may be
fine to live with the misfits. However, as you look to the future, you should
consider whether any misfits should be corrected. A large number of misfits
should give you pause for thought, and you should consider adjusting your
firm's misfits such that you bring the organizational design components of
Table 5.1 into the same column. Note that misfits that are in adjacent columns
are less of a concern than those that are in opposing (distal) columns.

As we come to the end of Step 3 in our step-by-step approach, it is important
to keep in mind that organizational design is an ongoing process, not a goal
state to achieve. Design components and their fit with one another must be
developed on a continuing basis. A firm may be informated today, but if it does
not invest in development of information systems on an ongoing basis, the firm
may lag in this design component in the future. Similarly, a firm might
implement systems but employees resist their use or find over time that they
rely on more flexible, ad hoc systems to do their work. In this way, your firm
can drift from one column to another as time goes by. Sometimes this drift is
intentional on the part of management and other times it happens due to
managerial neglect or due to changes in how people choose to do their work.
For example, if the firm is growing or is acquired, yielding a fresh labor
pool, IT-infused work that was prevalent in the past may become more
people-based if newcomers are not trained in, or accepting of, established
systems. A new manager may foster networks of relationships to exchange
knowledge, even if the organizational strategy calls for a defensive, more
inward focus on exploitation. The point is that what you see as a fit today
can migrate to a misfit tomorrow, whether planned or unplanned. It is important that management continually assess and develop fit among the organizational design components.

Summary

The modern organization embellishes basic configurations of simple, functional, divisional, and matrix to yield distributed arrangements, including global, international, multi-domestic, and transnational. Firms that are consistent in their basic (Chapter 4) and distributed (Chapter 5) organizational structures are more likely to achieve their efficiency and effectiveness goals. In this chapter we reviewed the design alternatives for geographic distribution and we described how organization structure can be used to support different forms of knowledge exchange. We now move on to the next step of organizational design, which is the design of process and people systems to support organization structure.

Glossary

Ad hoc communications: use of temporary, informal pairs of workers or work groups from inside the firm as the primary design for knowledge exchange. Virtualization and IT infusion are low.

Cellular organization: small, autonomous subunits that largely self-govern and can grow, reproduce, and form relations with other units, including those outside the firm, as needed; information technology facilitates team interaction and connections among the various "cells."

Global: a distributed organizational design in which work activities are centrally organized to yield the advantage of consistency of work practices, as established by the "home base" of operations (usually the corporate headquarters). Optimal sourcing is low.

Informated: embedding of computer technology in the design and monitoring of work processes such that tasks can be streamlined, closely linked with one another, and continually managed for improvement in quality and cost control. Virtualization is low and IT infusion is high.

International: a distributed organizational design in which work is located as close as possible to the resources the organization needs to do the work, wherever they may be in the world. Work is located close to resource inputs, not as a function of customer location or to spread operations across locales or regions of the world.

Knowledge: a higher-order notion of information; knowledge is information that corresponds to a particular context and requires interpretation, or intelligence, to fully understand.

IT-infused: the extent to which an organization relies on information technology, including data processing and computer-based communication systems, to support knowledge exchange.

Local responsiveness: the decision to distribute work in many locales versus consolidating work in a centralized location.

Multi-domestic: a decentralized, geography-based approach to organizing in which operations are customized to specific countries or regions, offering unique products or services to meet local preferences.

Networked organization: a distributed organizational design in which links of information exchange are IT-infused and established between units within the firm and between internal units and external organizations to meet the organization's knowledge needs.

Optimal sourcing: the decision to locate operations in the place in the world that brings the greatest advantage to the firm in terms of customer contact, cost efficiency, human resource skill need, or other objective.

Transnational: an organizational design that blends the international and multi-domestic structures to yield both the location advantages of regional or country-based design and the economic efficiencies of optimal sourcing.

Virtualization: the degree of boundary-spanning (reaching across the borders of the organization) that a firm uses as the basis for knowledge exchange.

Where are you in the step-by-step approach?

STEP 1   GETTING STARTED

1. Goals

STEP 2   STRATEGY

(2) Strategy
(3) Environment

STEP 3   STRUCTURE

(4) Configuration and complexity
(5) Geographic distribution and knowledge exchange

In Step 3 you described the organization's structure in terms of: configuration, complexity, geographical location, and knowledge exchange. Do these four parts of the firm's structure fit together? If not, which should be changed, and how would you go about it? Think carefully about this question. Further, review where your firm is located in the spatial graphs presented in Step 3. Do you think that the description in the figures gives a fair and reasonable representation of your unit of analysis? If not, which changes would you like to make? Would you like to see your organization move from one place on the graph to another place? Consider the accuracy and the internal consistency of your organization and, again, think about where your organization is and where you would like it to be, and your plans for changing organizational components so that they are in fit with one another.

Once you are satisfied with the organization's structure as analyzed in Step 3, then you should review the goals, strategy, and environment. Are they aligned or are there misfits with structure? If you have misfits, think about what you can and might do. Usually, if there are misfits between the strategy and the structure, the structure should be adjusted to fit the strategy, i.e., structure follows strategy.

Step 3 is complete, and you are ready to move on to Step 4.

STEP 4   PROCESS AND PEOPLE

We will examine the task design in your firm, that is, how the organization carries out its work. Then you will assess your firm's people, leadership, and climate.

(6) Task design
(7) People
(8) Leadership and organizational climate

STEP 5   COORDINATION AND CONTROL

STEP 4
Process and people

6 Task design

Introduction

How should an organization be designed to perform its work? At the most basic level, one can think of an organization as performing a very large task which must be broken down into smaller and smaller tasks in order to get the work done. Suppose you manage a software design company. Should you divide the work into processes such as design, development, sales, and service; or might it be better to divide the work according to client type: individuals, small business, large business, and government? Of course, other options are possible too. Once a firm selects a way to organize the work at the highest level (the big task), there is the question of how work should be divided inside of each of the subtasks. Within subtasks, the work is further divided, until it reaches the lowest task-level of the organization.

Task design is decomposing work into subtasks while considering the coordination among the subtasks to meet organizational goals. Prior to the information age, task design was sometimes called "technology design" by organizational designers. In the traditional setting of manufacturing, technology design was a matter of figuring out whether work should be arranged sequentially (as in assembly lines), in parallel (as in custom building), via teams that continually passed work back and forth among members, or in some other way. Today the word "technology" has broader meaning, so we use the simpler label of task design; but the essential design question remains the same, which is how the big task of a firm is broken down into smaller tasks and how these smaller tasks interconnect with one another so that the big task is successfully completed.[1] As we shall see, a firm's approach to task design is related to its choice of efficiency and effectiveness goals, as well as the structure and strategy of the firm. Task design determines the coordination requirements for the firm's work, and thus it is vital that there is fit between task design and the other components of organizational design. Given a firm's strategy and structure, some approaches to task design will fit better than others.

Researchers have described the approaches to task design in several different ways. Woodward (1965) in her classic studies of organizations categorized tasks as: unit, mass, and process production, where each had a different task design. Unit is more craft-like; mass is assembly line; and process is automated. These represent distinctly different ways of organizing and managing work. She found a nonlinear relationship between task design and other components of the organization's design. The unit and process approaches had many components in common, whereas the mass production approach was different. Compared to mass production, the unit and process production had higher skilled workers, lower organizational complexity, lower formalization, and lower centralization. The work pace of mass production was very precise and so required more detailed coordination than the less clock-driven unit production and the maintenance-oriented process production. Woodward's studies were the first to link task design to other dimensions of organizational design. Thompson (1967) categorized the relationship between tasks as: sequential, pooled, or reciprocal. Sequential tasks are coordinated by standardization of the tasks; pooled tasks are coordinated via planning and task allocation; and reciprocal tasks are coordinated by mutual adjustment. Carroll et al. (2005) examined the dynamics of changing these task relationships and found in a project setting that transforming sequential tasks into parallel and reciprocal tasks decreases project time initially, but increases project time over time as more reciprocal tasks demand much greater coordination and costly mutual adjustments.

Scott (1998) described task design along three dimensions: complexity of items requiring simultaneous consideration, uncertainty, or unpredictability, and interdependency, where a change in one requires a change in another item. (Note that these task design characteristics are similar to the environmental characteristics described in Chapter 3.) Greater complexity, greater uncertainty, and greater interdependency all require greater information processing to obtain the coordination required to get the work completed.

---

[1] There are two complementary task-design approaches. We begin with the total organizational task and examine its decomposition into smaller tasks. The complementary approach is to begin with the individual works tasks and aggregate them into larger tasks (Sinha and Van de Ven, 2005). For both approaches, coordination of the subtasks is a central issue.

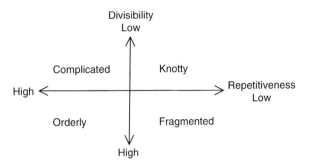

Figure 6.1 Task design space.

Summarizing the above discussion, an organization's task design can be categorized along two important dimensions: *repetitiveness* and *divisibility*. If a task is well defined such that it is undertaken again and again, then it has higher repetitiveness. Notice that standardization in execution of the task enables repetitiveness. If the task is not standardized and varies in how it is done, then it has low repetitiveness. A highly repetitive task has low uncertainty, whereas a task low in repetitiveness has a higher uncertainty. When a bigger task is broken down into subtasks which require little coordination (i.e., the subtasks are independent), it is highly divisible. On the other hand, if the subtasks require high coordination with one another (i.e., they are interdependent), then the task has low divisibility. Note that this definition of divisibility is related to Thompson's categories of sequential, pooled and reciprocal interdependency. With these two dimensions, we have four basic task designs which we call: orderly, complicated, fragmented, and knotty. The four task design categories are shown in Figure 6.1.

We will discuss the four categories briefly before considering each in detail. The *orderly* task design is highly divisible and highly repetitive; it requires relatively little coordination among the subtasks to accomplish the work. The *complicated* task design is not very divisible but is highly repetitive. It requires more coordination of the connected and repetitive tasks. The *fragmented* task design is highly divisible, but not very repetitive. It requires a different kind of coordination to adjust to ongoing variations across the subtasks, but adjustments for connectedness among subtasks is not required. The *knotty* task design is neither divisible nor repetitive; it is the most difficult to coordinate as adjustments to both connectedness and non-repetitiveness are required simultaneously.

For your unit of analysis try to think about the highest-level task that must be designed in your organization. How is it defined? How is it currently designed? For example, if your chosen organization is a bank, the work of the bank could be divided into subtasks based on specialization such as handling investments, money transfer, lending, etc. Alternatively, the work of the bank could be defined in relation to customer groups: private customers, institutional investors, small business customers, etc. The bank may define the work so that it can be repeated, by standardizing transactions for all specializations or customer groups. Alternatively, it may take pride in customizing the work, deliberately avoiding standardization so that interactions with customers or others are managed uniquely. When we talk about task design we are thus talking about the overall design, not just the design of the individual subtasks. The coordination requirements are very different in the two task designs just presented. Task design is also related to business process re-engineering as well as process management methods and philosophies, such as just-in-time and supply chain management. The particular tasks and their design are also highly influenced by modern information technology. For example, many routine tasks in banks are now either done electronically or the task is performed by the customer from a home banking system. This influence of information technology is similar in all industries. So with new information technology, some tasks may disappear and new tasks may emerge. Part of task design is highly related to choice of information system. A careful analysis of work flow and flow of information and decision-making is therefore an important part of the design of the organization. Basu and Blanning (2000) present a formal approach to workflow analysis. They integrate the informational entities involved in the process, the structure of these entities, and their interrelationships. Further, they take into account which tasks are being performed and what informational elements are involved in these tasks. Additionally, which agents/resources are involved in each task, where information entities are stored, and what communication is needed between agents/resources are also incorporated.

Next, we consider the four task designs in more detail. In Figure 6.1, we begin in the lower left corner for an orderly task design and move to complicated, fragmented, and finally knotty task design.

As we go through these task types, it is important to keep in mind where we are in the organizational design process. Task design follows design of strategy and structure. As an executive, you have a choice about how to design the work of your firm. The choices described below may be more or less appropriate, depending on your firm's strategy and structure.

Orderly

If you choose an orderly task design, then you are organizing your firm's work so that it is highly divisible and highly repetitive. You break up the work into pieces so that you can direct each work unit to perform independently of other units. When each unit completes its work, the results flow back up to the executive level, and then you assign a new piece of work to that unit. Units that experience problems or difficulties turn to you to resolve problems. An obvious advantage of this task design is that slowdowns or other difficulties in one unit don't prevent other units from continuing progress on their tasks. Within each unit the tasks are standardized as much as possible so that they can be readily repeated. To the extent that workers in each unit are able to develop skills to do the tasks assigned to their unit, the specialization of tasks can yield very high efficiency.

When tasks are designed using the orderly approach, there is almost no coordination required between units performing the subtasks of the organization and no need for them to adjust to one another. Piece work, whether in manufacturing or service industry, has these characteristics. The work of a law firm could be organized in this fashion too. As clients contact the firm, they may be assigned to an attorney who handles their case independently. Once a case is closed, the attorney is assigned another case. The attorneys operate independently, processing cases, taking as much time as needed before moving onto the next case. As another variation on the orderly approach, the attorneys might be grouped by specialty such that customers with family law needs are assigned to the family law group, clients with criminal law needs are assigned to the criminal litigation group, and so on. Again, the work of the organization is divided across units such that individual units perform their work independently of the others, completing the entire task assigned to them (low divisibility). Completing the "big task" work of the firm is accomplished as the work is more or less standardized and the individual units gain expertise to do their assigned work in an efficient manner. As another example, consider mill workers who do hand sewing and are given an inventory or list of things to do. Each worker takes an assigned garment to sew and places finished items in an out-basket. These in-process inventories help create the divisibility of work. The worker may have fixed productivity targets to meet, and these are monitored at the executive level. The executive has little to coordinate, except to assure that assignment and completion of work is done in a satisfactory manner. Further, in the orderly approach it is the executive level that brings in the work to the organization; the workers or subunits do not typically solicit work on their own. It is the executive-level responsibility to assure that each unit or worker has something to work on.

Complicated

If you choose to design your organization's task so that it is low on divisibility yet remains highly repetitive, then you have a complicated task design. Complicated tasks require a high degree of coordination due to low divisibility; that is, the subtasks can be performed by different units of the firm, but they are interdependent to get the work done. As an example, suppose you manage a hospital emergency ward. You might divide the work into four subtasks: (1) admissions, (2) triage screening, (3) focused care, and (4) release. Patients move sequentially through these processes, with different groups of people (subunits) responsible for each of the four subtasks. The work processes are repetitive and the services remain quite standardized (at least at the level of the "big task" design). The complicated task design suits processing of large volumes of work. There are many examples of a complicated task design in manufacturing, the most classic being the automobile assembly line. McDonald's is an example in the restaurant industry. The subtasks of order processing are highly repetitive but not divisible, as the completion of an order for a customer requires that each part of a meal is assembled correctly. Every order is unique within a limited set of possibilities so that the tasks become very repetitive.

Mass production requires not only the skills of orderly production but also precise coordination among the units responsible for the subtasks. The production processes must be timed to avoid bottlenecks and to meet efficiency goals in which inventories between processes are minimized. A well-designed complicated task requires that these work processes are repetitive and ongoing. The executive level overseeing the firm's work focuses on the coordination of the connected processes, which require continuous attention. Given the low divisibility, a breakdown in any one small task can shut down the whole operation, which can be very costly. Detailed and ongoing coordination requires a high level of information processing. Advances in operations research, along with the embedding of information technology into manufacturing processes, have increased managerial success in using complicated task designs. Firms that use these designs can compete based on their ability to process work with great speed and sophistication.

Fragmented

If you choose to design your organization's task so that it is high on divisibility yet low on repetitiveness then you are using a fragmented task design. Fragmented tasks require less coordination than complicated tasks due to their high divisibility. By reducing coordination needs, each subunit can process work at its own pace; it doesn't have to wait for other units to complete their work in order to proceed. Further, the subunits can take creative approaches to completing their tasks, perhaps soliciting their own customers or clients, since bottlenecks are not a concern. By breaking down the big task of the firm, the subunits are likely to be more innovative and aggressive. Some may outperform others or contribute more to the firm's overall work completion.

Consider a technology development firm, such as a software developer, that is trying to grow its business. The needs of its customer base (individuals, small business, large business, and government) are quite different, that is, they are not repetitive. The work of each subunit is conducted independently. Alternatively, the firm might divide the work according to type of software, such as desktop software and network-based software. In either case, if the big task is treated as highly divisible and with low repetitiveness, then the task design is fragmented. Within each subtask, the work could be further fragmented, or another task design might be selected.

The fragmented task design means that the firm divides its work so as to accommodate the varied nature of its business. Although it is tempting to think that task design is inherent in the work itself, it is important to recognize that in many cases the same work might be designed in different ways. Thus task design is a matter of managerial choice. Suppose your organization is an investment bank. You might choose a fragmented approach, dividing your big task into subtasks such as investment counseling, trust services, and estate planning. Each group is free to solicit its own customers and design its services to meet customer needs. There may be repetitive work within each of these subunits, but at the level of the big task design of the bank, there is low repetitiveness; that is, customers are directed to one group or another, and work is accommodated to meet their unique needs. The nonrepetitiveness approach to task design requires lots of adjustments (i.e., execution of work is not standardized); but as these adjustments are not connected, the coordination requirements are quite minimal. To manage a fragmented task design, the executive needs to ensure that the subtasks (i.e., the subunits) have resources and a reading on the environment, but the executive need not be involved in detailed coordination. In the case of the investment bank, the fragmented design may not be the ideal choice, especially if customers prefer that the subtasks be coordinated, e.g., if they want their estate planning to involve their trust accounts. This is the downside of designing tasks to have high divisibility. The investment banker might consider a knotty task design instead.

Knotty

The knotty task design is low on both divisibility and repetitiveness. If you choose a knotty task design for your organization, then you will have to invest in ways to coordinate work among the subtasks and at the same time support the nonrepetitive approach to doing the work. Knotty tasks are not standardized. This approach to task design encourages those responsible for subtasks to develop innovative ways to do their work, accommodating the unique demands of each customer, while at the same time those performing subtasks must integrate their work with other units in the firm. Knotty tasks are likely to lead to the greatest customer satisfaction since production is customized, but they are the most demanding type of task to manage.

When products are new, the knotty approach to task design is often favored by managers. High technology innovative products and services are illustrations – such as a new and short-lived video game, a biotech entity, or a new global financial instrument. The executive focuses on the coordination of the connected processes, which are continually changing. Given the low divisibility, a breakdown in any one small task can shut down the whole operation, which can be very costly. Given the nonrepetitive approach to task design, the information-processing demands increase greatly. Taken together, the information-processing demands go up nonlinearly with executive overload. Therefore, this task design is the most demanding on management.

New product development (NPD) in automobiles at Toyota or Renault, pharmaceuticals at Eli Lilly, or household products at Unilever, requires high coordination and adjustment of the tasks to the emerging technology. NPD tasks are often designed according to a knotty approach, but a knotty approach can be applied in more routine industries for competitive advantage. For example, a gourmet restaurant may create new food offerings each day, with each new offering requiring unique production and high coordination among the kitchen staff. Since the task is designed to be nonrepetitive – providing a new dining experience each time customers visit the restaurant – the organization must have highly skilled staff that can continually innovate and coordinate with perfection.

Diagnostic questions

How is the task designed in the organization you have chosen to design? As in prior chapters, use the same unit of analysis that you selected in Chapter 1 to answer the following questions. In answering these questions, it is very important to take a top-down approach and limit the analysis of the task to the "big task" of your unit analysis. (Remember, subtasks, once created, have their own designs.)

Note that the rating scales for task design are reversed, so that 1 = high and 5 = low.

1. What is the degree of repetitiveness of the task in the firm, i.e., high to low?
   a. Does the firm treat each work task as unique (low)?
   b. Does it execute the task today much as it did yesterday (high), or is there a good deal of variation (low)?
   c. To what extent does it standardize the task (high) rather than customize it (low)?

   Score the repetitiveness on a scale from 1 to 5 as follows:

1	2	3	4	5
very high		moderate		very low

2. What is the degree of divisibility of the task in the firm, i.e., high to low?
   a. Does the firm divide its big task into subtasks that are independent of one another (high), or are the subtasks connected, requiring a lot of coordination (low)?
   b. Does it manage the task as a set of specialized independent functions (high) or as a process flow (low)?

c. To what extent are the units that perform the subtasks free to design their work as they wish (high) rather than as instructed (low)?
Score the degree of divisibility on a scale from 1 to 5 as follows:

1	2	3	4	5
very high		moderate		very low

You can now locate your firm on the graph in Figure 6.2. What is the firm's task design?

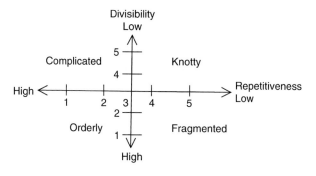

Figure 6.2 Locate your firm in the task design space.

 ## Fit and misfits

Table 6.1 is the table from Chapter 5 with the task design row added. Again, there is fit among the design elements of your chosen firm if the entries for each row fall into the same column. Misfits are deviations from a common column.

The orderly task design is appropriate if your firm's goal is neither efficiency nor effectiveness. There can be some efficiencies in the orderly task design due to its repetitiveness, and for this reason, managers may find this approach to task design to be appealing. The orderly task design approach works well so long as the environment is calm and the corresponding strategy is a reactor which is also unfocused. A simple configuration works well for the orderly task design as it breaks the total task into smaller tasks which require very little coordination from the executive. Knowledge can be exchanged on an ad hoc basis. So long as things are calm, the organization with the simple

Table 6.1 Fit and misfit for task design

Corresponding quadrant in organizational design space	A	B	C	D	
Task design	Orderly	Complicated	Fragmented	Knotty	
Knowledge exchange	Ad hoc communications	Informated	Cellular	Network	
Geographic distribution	Global	International	Multi-domestic	Transnational	
Complexity	Blob	Tall	Flat	Symmetric	
Configuration	Simple	Functional	Divisional	Matrix	
Environment	Calm	Varied	Locally stormy	Turbulent	
Strategy types	Reactor	Defender	Prospector	Analyzer with innovation	Analyzer without innovation
Organizational goals	Neither	Efficiency	Effectiveness	Efficiency and Effectiveness	

configuration using the orderly task design creates minimal information-processing requirements. The executive is not overloaded with detailed coordination problems – unless the environment changes. The risk for the firm occurs if new business causes a shift in the type of work needed such that high repetitiveness is not possible. Then the orderly approach is a misfit and the task design inappropriate. Organizing work so that it is divisible and can be executed as independent subtasks puts a high load on the manager if there is any change in the environment.

If your organization adopts an orderly task design approach then you should be aware that this is a misfit with an efficiency strategy of a defender or an effectiveness strategy of a prospector. Any deviation from a calm environment creates difficulty as adjustments will be required. Functional, matrix, and divisional configurations are more costly and are not needed to achieve the required coordination for the highly divisible and highly repetitive task. For most organizations, an orderly task design is not sustainable except for the most routine operations, making these types of tasks good candidates for automation or outsourcing.

The complicated task design is focused more on efficiency than on effectiveness. The corresponding strategy is a defender where the efficiency of repetitiveness helps achieve profitability through low cost. The varied environment, which is complex but predictable, is a good fit for the complicated task design. So is the functional configuration since it has the capacity to coordinate detailed and standardized processes which rely heavily on rules and procedures.

The complicated task design is a misfit with an analyzer strategy, which requires innovation and introduces nonrepetitive processes. Similarly, turbulent and stormy environments require adjustments which are extremely difficult to make if you have designed your organization using a complicated task design. The executive will be overloaded with the coordination details.

The fragmented task design is focused more on effectiveness than on efficiency. This approach to task design works well if you are pursuing a prospector strategy, seeking high degrees of effectiveness and continual innovation. If your firm faces a locally stormy business environment, i.e., high unpredictability, then it makes sense to design work so that it is high in divisibility and low in repetitiveness. The divisional configuration is a good fit; here management focuses on providing resources and policy but not detailed coordination. The cellular configuration is also a good fit.

The fragmented task design is a misfit if your firm has the dual goals of both efficiency and effectiveness. Fragmented task design breaks the big task into subtasks which are relatively independent and optimal in the use of resources. It is therefore hard to achieve efficiencies for the big task if the fragmented task design is adopted.

The knotty task design is appropriate if your firm has the dual goals of both effectiveness and efficiency. The turbulent environment, which is complex and unpredictable, is a good fit. The corresponding strategy is an analyzer with innovation. The matrix configuration is a good fit because it emphasizes coordination across multiple dimensions and ongoing coordinated adjustments of the work to meet organizational goals. The knotty task design customizes work and so, if done well, can yield high customer satisfaction for a range of customer demands. As we shall see in the next chapter, conducting the knotty task requires highly skilled employees and management that can simultaneously support autonomy, control, and learning as tasks are executed.

The knotty task design is a misfit with any strategy, environment or configuration which has a dominant focus on either efficiency or effectiveness. If your chosen firm is pursuing a defender or prospector strategy, then you should avoid the knotty approach to task design because it is too complex and expensive and so not the best fit for your goals.

Summary

This chapter on task design further completes the description of a firm to find a design that fits with its goals, strategy, and structure. In this chapter you described an organization's task design in terms of repetitiveness and divisibility, and categorized it as: orderly, complicated, fragmented, or knotty. If the organization's current approach to task design does not fit its organization's goals, strategy or structure, it should consider adjusting the task design so that the task design is aligned with the other dimensions. Next we turn to the human resource requirements that are needed to support a firm's task design.

Glossary

Complicated task design: an organizational task design in which work is organized in a way that it is not very divisible but highly repetitive; usually requires a high degree of coordination among the subtasks.

Divisible task design: a task which can be broken into subtasks that are relatively independent of one another with respect to resource utilization and dependency of operations.

Fragmented task design: an organizational task design in which work is organized to be highly divisible but not repetitive; usually requires less coordination compared to complicated task design.

Knotty task design: an organizational task design in which work is organized in a way that it is neither divisible nor repetitive; usually requires not only coordination among subtasks but also support for the nonrepetitive nature of subtasks.

Orderly task design: an organizational task design in which work is organized in a way that it is highly divisible and highly repetitive; usually requires relatively little coordination among the subtasks.

Repetitive task: a task which is well-defined (i.e., standardized) so that it is executed again and again.

Task design: decomposing work (the big task) into subtasks and then coordinating among the subtasks to meet organizational goals.

7   People

Introduction

"An enterprise is its people," so stated the famous Japanese industrialist Matsushita Konosuke. Like many successful business leaders, Matsushita believed that effective management of people was an essential ingredient to a firm's ability to reach its goals (PHP Institute, 1994). From an organizational design perspective the question for the executive is: what is the best way to manage people, given the organization's goals, strategy, structure, and task design? As is the case for other dimensions of design, multiple approaches are possible. Deciding among these approaches depends on two critical factors: the number of people in the organization and their professionalization. The organization and the people must fit together. Depending on the design choices you have made with regard to goals, strategy, structure, and task, different approaches to managing people are recommended.

We will deal with the people dimension of organizational design in two ways. In this chapter you will describe the size and capabilities of a firm's workforce. These dimensions affect the firm's information-processing capacity. In the next chapter you will assess the leadership and organizational climate of the firm. These dimensions affect the ability of people to handle information, cooperate and make decisions.

We defined the organization in Chapter 1 as a social entity, so it follows that how you manage the people in your firm depends on how many people you employ and the kinds of capabilities they bring to the organization. Managing people is a complex matter, and many factors might be considered. Here we want to focus on the most fundamental factors that relate to organizational design. So we take a minimal approach in this chapter, focusing on (1) the size of the labor pool, and (2) the degree of professionalization. In the next chapter we will address the attitudes of top management and employees as they are important as well with respect to understanding the relationship between people and the organizational design.

Depending on the relative size of the firm's workforce and its professional capabilities, different managerial approaches are appropriate. Our attention to these two factors fits with our information-processing view of the firm. Most of the information processing in a firm is done by the individuals in the firm. People represent the intellectual capacity of the firm. This is especially true in today's knowledge-intense enterprise.

Although people bring skills and intellectual resources, having more people is not necessarily a better state from an organizational design standpoint. Large organizations (i.e., those with more people) must be designed differently than smaller ones (Burton, Minton and Obel, 1991). For example, larger firms are usually more decentralized. If there are only two people in a firm, then the decision-making, communications, and coordination are easy. As the number of people increases, communication becomes very problematic. People generate information as they do their work, and they also require information as inputs to their work. So there is a growing need for information exchange as the size of the firm increases. If each person talks to everyone else, then the communication links grow quickly and exponentially with the number of people (Burton and Obel, 2004). It is not a practical solution for General Motors to have all of its 300,000 employees talking with one another. Even for much smaller firms or subunits, communications are limited. Electronic communication systems may make transmission of information relatively easy, but, as we know from information-processing theory (Chapter 1), each person's attention is limited and costly. This is also true for the subunits in which people are organized. Information-processing capacity is limited. So we need ways to limit information and focus it on the goals and tasks. The configurations we discussed in Chapters 4 and 5 limit communications and direct them along the hierarchy in the functional and divisional configurations or across units in the matrix. Indeed, one of the major reasons to form configurations is to manage the otherwise extraordinarily high information flow in the firm. Depending on the organizational configuration, one person communicates with a small fraction of the total workforce in the firm. The firm is able to coordinate its activities across a very large number of people.

As you design your organization, you must decide not only whether to employ many people or a few but also what types of people are needed, given your strategy and structure. The professionalization of the workforce is a measure of its skills, knowledge, and capacity to both generate and process information. If your organization has a more professional workforce, then individuals can perform tasks that are more complicated, lengthy, and cognitively difficult. Education, training, and experience increase the professionalization. In turn, how people are managed can affect their professional development. Organizations that are not designed to benefit from and enhance the professionalization of their workers are less likely to meet their efficiency and effectiveness goals. The individual's knowledge is the basis for what he/she can do. In this sense, it is the realized skill. This knowledge may be explicit, which means it can be codified. Or it may be tacit, which means it is not readily documented. Explicit knowledge is easier to capture and transfer around the organization to others; tacit knowledge is far more difficult to transfer and requires rich forms of social interaction in order to be shared. The more professionalization that exists inside the firm, the greater is its capacity to exchange tacit knowledge.

Whether explicit or tacit, knowledge is the basis for the skills and other aspects of the professionalization level, as well as the routines and other capabilities people apply in doing the work of the organization. It is important to note that individuals are "boundedly rational," which means that we are limited in our capacity to process information (March and Simon, 1958). It seems obvious that each of us cannot do all things perfectly and instantaneously. We have imperfect information, which we interpret reasonably but imperfectly; and we communicate only a fraction of what we would like to communicate and, again, imperfectly. The bounded rationality of people is at the heart of why we need an organization. At the most fundamental level, we need configurations, task designs and information systems to permit us to reach large goals in the face of our bounded rationality. Even with high professionalization, individuals are boundedly rational, and the organization is a way to cope with that limitation while at the same time harnessing the skills and capabilities that people collectively offer in performing work tasks.

The number of people in an organization and their professionalization measure the basic characteristics of the people dimension of the organization's design. The *number of people* is simply a count of all individuals in the firm (i.e., unit of analysis). *Professionalization* is the collective skill level of the individuals and a measure of their capabilities for the work tasks at hand.

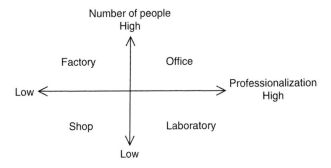

Figure 7.1 The people space.

Professionalization depends upon employees' education, training, and experience, i.e., their knowledge base, whether accumulated prior to their hire or on the job.

In Figure 7.1, there are two dimensions: professionalization on the horizontal axis and the number of individuals on the vertical axis. Depending on these two dimensions, there are four general approaches to people management. Beginning in the lower left corner, there is the *shop* where the number of people is low and professionalization is low. Moving to the upper left corner, we have the *factory*, which has a large number of people, but relatively low professionalization. In the lower right corner professionalization is high, but there are few people, which we call a *laboratory*. Finally, in the upper right corner there are many people with high professionalization, which we call an *office*. Each category describes a different approach to designing the people component of organizational design. We will now look into each of the four categories.

Shop

The shop approach to managing people involves employing few people who are low on professionalization. The shop design works well if the individuals have not had specialized training or if their experience has not given them extensive skills. Examples of such organizations are small stores that employ people who are only given a few days of training. In this design, the information-processing capacity of the employees is low. Routines must be simple with only a few steps; they must be easily understood and easy to learn. The manager of the shop must be "hands on" in directing people in order for the shop to run smoothly. Coordination requirements are low so long as there are few people, particularly if the task design is fragmented.

The shop is not focused on efficiency or effectiveness. People are generally not efficient due to low skill and are expected to wait for direction from management. People are not encouraged to develop skills, make decisions, or advance significant change to improve the organization.

The shop design is appropriate if tasks are orderly and the available work-force is small and low-skilled. In this case, the manager can give individualized instructions and change the instructions as work comes into the organization. Difficulties arise, however, if a large number of people or those with profes-sional skills are managed via the shop approach. If management tries to "micro manage" in the sense of directing a large number of people on what to do on an individualized basis, then the organization will be inefficient. If management tries to micro manage professionals on what to do on an individualized basis, then the organization will be ineffective. For larger organizations, or for those with a professional workforce, management should consider a factory, labora-tory, or office approach.

Factory

The factory approach to managing people involves employing many individ-uals who are low in professionalization. Here the assumption is that people have relatively little specialized expertise and the routines are relatively simple, meaning that their work tasks can be executed repetitively following training. Employing a large number of individuals means that there are very high coordination requirements. Thus, the factory is focused on efficiency, which requires detailed coordination for a large number of individuals. To run a factory, you need many people, and you need focused skill sets rather than broad professionalization.

The assembly line is a classic example of the factory. To build an automobile, the total task is broken down into hundreds of small tasks each of which is relatively low-skilled. But the overall coordination is extremely high as the matching fender, wheel, engine, and hundreds of other items must come together exactly on the assembly, where task design makes it routine to put the pieces together. Today's modern call center manages people as a factory. Large numbers of people are employed and given focused, repetitive tasks to perform as they place or receive large numbers of phone calls. People with low professionalization are ideal for such work. Another example is a large hotel, where there are a large number of low-skill jobs, and tasks are designed in an orderly fashion with high repetitiveness.

If workers have high professionalization, then the factory approach to managing people is less desirable, since the design does not take advantage of the knowledge and skill capacities of professionals.

Laboratory

The laboratory approach to managing people involves employing a few people, each with high professionalization. Professional routines which are obtained through extensive education, training, and experience permit relative independence among the individuals or among small collections of individuals (such as those working together in a cellular configuration). High professionalization facilitates worker autonomy rather than strict supervision, so each one can work alone and the manager's job is to support the individual. A good example could be a university faculty where independent scholarship is the norm. Other examples include a financial research group, salespeople who seek their own clients, and high-tech software design groups. In the laboratory design detailed coordination of activities is not required; in fact, it may be considered intrusive in the sense that directive management can stifle knowledge production and discovery of innovative ways of doing things. Motivation and incentives are the important means for coordination.

The laboratory is focused more on effectiveness and high quality than on efficiency. Each individual, or subunit of professionals, can work with relative autonomy and achieve the purpose for the organization. There are many high-level work routines for the individuals, but these routines are varied and largely under the control of the individuals, not the organization. The routines are very complex and include many tacit aspects which cannot be codified but have high-quality requirements. Detailed coordination is usually not required. Instead, workers coordinate in small groups for intense information sharing, and these groups then build directed knowledge exchange with the specific clients, subunits, or other sources needed to accomplish their tasks.

3M is a good example of a company that uses a laboratory approach to managing people. Individuals and subunits are encouraged to create new products and services with relative autonomy. It is a cellular configuration where there are relatively few individuals in each cell, but it replicates itself into a very large corporation.

Office

The office approach to managing people involves employing many people with high professionalization. Again, professionalization comes from education, training, and experience. Due to the large number of people to manage, the need for coordination is very high. The organization must process lots of information and support extensive communication. High-level work routines are very important as they help define and manage work for efficiency and effectiveness.

Large consulting organizations have highly skilled professionals who must be coordinated in complicated detail to meet the needs of the client. These organizations often manage people as an office. Employees are given autonomy to do their work but they also engage in heavy communication with others as they develop client projects and meet customer needs. Consultants may be organized into subunits which, in turn, are managed as an office, meaning that the subunits operate with a combination of autonomy and inter-unit coordination. Many large-scale engineering construction firms and new product development projects within pharmaceutical firms are managed in this way.

Deciding whether to organize as an office – like deciding about other components of organizational design – is a matter of managerial choice. The office approach is recommended if a firm has large numbers of people with high professionalization. Note that the communication demands of the office are larger than in the laboratory. Workers are given autonomy to find, process, and produce knowledge; but they also are expected to engage in intense knowledge sharing with others who are dependent on them to do the work of the organization. The interdependent nature of work is higher in an office than in a laboratory. Subunits have more people, though they are managed as professionals. Again, the office consists of a large number of highly skilled people who work together to accomplish the simultaneous goals of efficiency in using work routines to execute tasks and effectiveness in meeting organizational goals.

Diagnostic questions

For your firm, you can examine the two dimensions, number of people and their professionalization, and locate where the firm is in Figure 7.2. Then you can categorize the firm's design of people as: shop, factory, laboratory, or office. To begin, answer the diagnostic questions below.

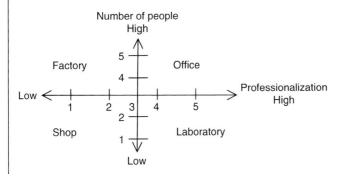

Figure 7.2 Locate your organization in the people space.

1. What is your unit of analysis that you chose in earlier chapters? Use this unit of analysis as the organization when answering the questions below. The questions below will help you locate your chosen organization on the number of people and professionalization dimensions.

2. Number of individuals

   How many people are there in the firm? Normally, we mean the number of employees. The measure is the actual count of individuals who are working in the organization, whether full time or part time.[1]

   Here is the mapping for the actual number into the scale in Figure 7.1.

   Less than 100 employees – 1
   101–500 employees – 2
   501–1000 employees – 3
   1001–2000 employees – 4
   More than 2000 employees – 5

---

[1] It is important to include all people, not just full-time equivalents, as it is the number of individuals that determine the coordination requirements.

3. Professionalization

What proportion of employees hold advanced (university) degrees or have many years of specialized training and experience?

    0 to 10% – 1

    11 to 20% – 2

    21 to 50% – 3

    51 to 75% – 4

    76 to 100% – 5

4. You can now locate your organization in Figure 7.2. What would you call the people mapping of the firm?

 ## Fit and misfits

What is a good fit between management of people and other dimensions of an organization's design? Here, we discuss the fit and misfit relations. In Table 7.1, we add fit for the people to earlier dimensions. In each of the columns A, B, C, and D, the fit relations can be read vertically from top to bottom.

As before, misfits are any set of relations which do not fall within one column. There are a very large number of possible misfits. The misfits arise from the size of the workforce or their professionalization. A critical issue is the limited time and skill of the individual as well as the limited attention and time of management. These misfits can overload the executive oversight of people and lead to diminished performance for the firm. The telltale signs are: individuals are not aware of what to do, or are given directives that hamper rather than facilitate their coordination; decision and communications backlogs increase; adjustments are not timely; or all work excessively long hours without results.

For column A, there is a fit for the shop with a reactor strategy, a calm environment, a simple configuration, and orderly task design. In the shop setting people can do their jobs following a rather limited direction and coordination. There are relatively low information-processing demands on everyone, except on the manager who oversees the shop. If the strategy or the environment requires more attention and time, then the individual's tasks need to change and the executive can quickly become overloaded. The individual's activities

Table 7.1 Fit and misfit for people design

Corresponding quadrant in organizational design space	A	B	C	D	
People	Shop	Factory	Laboratory	Office	
Task design	Orderly	Complicated	Fragmented	Knotty	
Knowledge exchange	Ad hoc com- munications	Informated	Cellular	Network	
Geographic distribution	Global	International	Multi- domestic	Transnational	
Complexity	Blob	Tall	Flat	Symmetric	
Configuration	Simple	Functional	Divisional	Matrix	
Environment	Calm	Varied	Locally stormy	Turbulent	
Strategy types	Reactor	Defender	Prospector	Analyzer with innovation	Analyzer without innovation
Organizational goals	Neither	Efficiency	Effectiveness	Efficiency and Effectiveness	

quickly become misaligned with the new challenges. One approach to handle these new challenges is significant professionalization of the employees.

The potential misfits are numerous in the shop setting. If the environment becomes more uncertain and requires changes involving a new strategy that is not just reacting to the events in the environment, it is very likely that the nonprofessional people inside the shop will either resist change or lack the skills or experience for change. Alternatively, if the workforce is professional or very large and managed via one-to-one directives by the manager, the shop becomes very ineffective and inefficient.

Moving to B, the factory is a fit for an efficiency goal, defender strategy, varied environment, a functional configuration, and a complicated task design. The information-processing demands have increased considerably as there is a large number of individuals to coordinate. For many variations, a tall functional configuration can handle a large amount of information needed for detailed and involved coordination. However, if the environmental unpredictability increases and thus requires additional information processing, then the functional configuration is not suited to make large coordinated changes quickly. In such a misfit situation, the individuals will require greater professionalization. Use of automated systems can help reduce the need for greater professionalization, as computer-based routines and information substitute for adding skills and experience to the workforce. It is for this reason that call centers are sometimes criticized as technology-based sweatshops. Technology substitutes for increasing the professionalization of the workforce. Efficiency is enhanced, but the knowledge capacity of the people is not enriched.

The higher-level routines and formalized rules between and among jobs and individuals help to coordinate the total set of activities for the factory. High organizational complexity with a large number of low-skill jobs and a tall organization for coordination works well, but change is difficult. The functional configuration is a good fit for the detailed operational coordination of the factory. A varied environment where changes are small and anticipated is a good match as well. The complicated task design of low divisibility and high repetitiveness fits the factory, because there are a large number of people who are managed at low skill level.

The potential threat for managing people in a factory setting is change that may involve a higher degree of decentralization and a flexible response to changes.

For column C, the laboratory is a good fit for: a flat complexity, a divisional or cellular configuration, a locally stormy environment, a prospector strategy, and an effectiveness goal. In a laboratory the individuals are very skilled and can deal with variation derived from environment and innovation. The executive can create independent divisions to deal with the local conditions. Each division has its own environment which is stormy but largely independent of the others. As the number of subunits increases, the coordination issues will become problematic and will eventually create a misfit. Alternatively, if the environment changes such that two divisions compete for the same customer, the executive can become overloaded with coordinating details – again, creating a misfit. The tall firm is a misfit for the divisional configuration. If the top executive becomes involved in the detailed operations of the firm, cognitive overload, neglect of important issues, and poor firm performance will occur.

The cellular configuration is a good fit where there is relative independence between cells – not necessarily within a cell. On a larger scale, the divisional configuration is similar; there can be relative independence between divisions – not within divisions. A prospector strategy which develops new things in a locally stormy environment is a good match. High skill permits exploration. These tasks can be fragmented with high divisibility and low repetitiveness.

For column D, the office is a fit for a symmetric complexity, a matrix configuration, a turbulent environment, an analyzer strategy and dual goals. This requires highly skilled individuals to work together so as to realize the needed coordination. The information-processing demands are very large as detailed coordination is required by new situations (Galbraith, 1973). The firm simply cannot be broken down into independent divisions, nor can a tall hierarchy handle all of the changes required to effectively adapt to a turbulent environment. The executive can create divisions to deal with the local conditions, but the matrix configuration is a good match when the task design is knotty and the environment is turbulent. A large number of skilled individuals will help to execute knotty tasks and deal with continual change and coordination across the matrix. Departures from the alignment lead to costly misfits.

The matrix configuration where there are two or more reporting dimensions (but fewer than where all individuals can talk with each other) is a midrange solution to limiting information processing and obtaining the needed coordination. The focus here is both efficiency and effectiveness. An analyzer strategy with innovation in a turbulent environment is a good match. Further, the task design can be knotty with high divisibility and low repetitiveness.

If your chosen firm is located in different columns based upon your answers from these four chapters, then you should think about what you might do to bring the firm into fit in the column that meets your goals. But also think about what is involved to move to a different goal and thus a different column.

Summary

In this chapter, we have outlined the people component of organizational design, which should fit together with other design components to meet your firm's goals. There are four categories: shop, factory, laboratory, and office, which are located on two dimensions: the number of people and their professionalization. The idea of choosing the two dimensions is related to the task of processing information, where the degree of professionalization is a proxy measure for the individual's ability to process information. Taken together with the number of people, we thus have a measure of the information-processing capabilities embedded in the human capital of the firm. We also discussed misfits. These misfits were developed from the idea of information processing given the setup of the 2×2 model. For example, a defender strategy with its high volume of standardized activities does not fit a laboratory with few people with a high degree of professionalization.

Glossary

Factory: supporting the firm's strategy and structure with many people who have low skills. Their work routines are designed to be as simple as possible and easily learned.

Laboratory: an approach to people grouping which has few people, where each one has high professionalization or a high level of skill which was obtained through extensive education, training, and experience.

Office: an approach to supporting the firm's strategy and structure with many people with high professionalization, where the skills incorporate a high level of knowledge obtained from education, training, and experience.

Professionalization: the skill capability of the individuals in the firm, depending on employees' education, training, and experience (i.e., knowledge base) accumulated either prior to their hire or on the job.

Routine: a set of processed tasks which together accomplish a higher level unit of work or task.

Shop: supporting the firm's strategy and structure with few people who are not highly skilled. People have had little specialized training or experience.

Size: for organizational design purposes, the total number of people in the firm who are working on the firm's big task; includes full-time, part-time, temporary, and volunteer workers.

8 Leadership and organizational climate

Introduction

Leadership style and organizational climate are two of the most widely used, debated and researched concepts in management. Everyone can make a list of great leaders. We know good leadership when we see it. What is a leader?[1] Does a good leader stand alone, or must there be a good fit with the firm's culture and climate?[2] What is a good climate? What climate is needed to be successful in an organizational change process? Leadership and organizational climate are important issues to take into account when you design an organization. A firm's leadership style and organizational climate are the two sides of how the people in the organization think and act. In your approach to designing an organization you should focus on analyzing the leadership style and organizational climate. The *leadership style* is the predominant mode used by the top management of your unit of analysis to manage employees. This is the top management of the entire organization if your unit of analysis is an entire company or firm. It is the department head or team leader(s) if your unit of analysis is a department or team. Top management is the individual or group of people at the highest level of your unit of analysis. The *organizational climate* is the internal environment or working atmosphere as experienced by organizational employees. The organizational climate for your unit of analysis may

---

[1] We use leader both generically and also as one of the four leadership styles. The context should make it clear which usage is appropriate.

[2] We focus on the organizational climate in this book. There has been a long discussion in the literature about the difference between culture and climate (e.g., see Denison, 1996).

or may not be consistent with the climate of the broader organization. So let us get on with these two important concepts. We start with the leadership style and then continue with the organizational climate.

Leadership style

Theory X and theory Y leadership descriptions (McGregor, 1969) are widely used in management conversation as contrasting styles. A theory X leader is direct-ive, short-term and control-oriented whereas a theory Y leader delegates, is long term and motivates through inspiration. Autocratic versus democratic leaders as described by Likert (1967) and managers versus leaders as described by Kotter (1988) capture contrasting styles. Building upon Cyert and March (1963), Burton and Obel (2004) argue that these contrasting styles can be summarized as decision-making preferences that are a function of a leader's preference for delegation, on the one hand, and the tendency to avoid uncertainty, on the other hand. Håkonsson et al. (2008b) found empirical support for such a categoriza-tion. Preference for delegation follows from Cyert and March (1963)'s idea of problemistic search. The managerial propensity to delegate serves as a decision-making heuristic whenever the executive finds delegation to be efficient due to their limited attention and time availability. Similarly, Cyert and March's notion of uncertainty avoidance incorporates several executive desires: preference for detail, tendency to be reactive rather than proactive, short-term versus long-term decision-making, and ability to motivate via control rather than inspir-ation. To illustrate, one way an executive can avoid the uncertainty of long-run anticipation and commitments is to provide detailed directions to employees based on short-run feedback. This means solving pressing problems rather than developing long-run strategies. It also means avoiding having to anticipate the business environment or otherwise negotiate change within the organization to meet major environmental shifts. Some executives tend to provide detailed instructions to employees and avoid the uncertainty of managing for the future. Other executives are the opposite – they embrace the "big picture," let employees find their own direction, and take risks for the future despite the uncertainties involved. Of course, there are gradations in between, as we shall see.

We use the two dimensions, preference for delegation and uncertainty avoidance, to analyze leadership style. Together, these two dimensions measure how managers influence organizational efficiency and effectiveness, i.e., how managers contribute directly to organizational performance through their

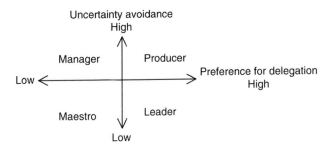

Figure 8.1 The leadership style space.

leadership. *Preference for delegation* is the degree to which the top management encourages lower-level managers or other employees who are their direct reports to make decisions about what and how work is to be done in the organization. Preference for delegation is high if top management relies on lower-level managers and employees to work autonomously and make decisions without top-management approval. Preference for delegation is low if top management prefers to make decisions about how and what work is done and to direct activities in a close-handed way. *Uncertainty avoidance* is the degree to which the top management shuns taking actions or making choices that involve major risk. Uncertainty avoidance is low if your top management tends to be risk-taking, whereas uncertainty avoidance is high if your top management tends to be risk-averse.

The two leadership dimensions are shown in Figure 8.1. Uncertainty avoidance is on the vertical axis and preference for delegation is on the horizontal axis. This provides us with four leadership style categories: maestro, manager, leader, and producer. The maestro prefers little delegation and accepts uncertainty. The manager, similar to theory X, prefers little delegation and avoids uncertainty. The leader, opposite of the manager and similar to theory Y, accepts uncertainty and delegates decision-making to subordinates. And finally, the producer avoids uncertainty and has a high preference for delegation. The manager and leader are well-known contrasting styles; the maestro and producer are new style descriptions. We now describe each in more detail.

Maestro

The *maestro* has a low preference for delegation and low uncertainty avoidance. The maestro will intervene directly to assure that decisions are made congruent with his or her own desires. At the same time, the maestro does not avoid the uncertainty of long-term decisions and their implications for the firm.

The maestro can become overly involved and overly burdened with too much to do when the lack of delegation creates a bottleneck for decision-making and a barrier to action. Decisions are not made; projects are not started; products are developed too late for the market. Further, we can see that the effective maestro requires great expertise – expertise for knowing how and when to take risks and how to lead people to make great progress for the organization.

The maestro leadership style fits well with the small start-up company, while for the large mature corporation a reactive strategy taking unnecessary risk may be the situation. The maestro leadership style may be appropriate in a crisis or at a time of major change like a merger.

The maestro's attention on ongoing decisions and uncertainty avoidance leaves top management open to longer-term vulnerabilities. If the top management takes a maestro approach, then it reacts better than it anticipates. Environmental and innovation changes can be missed or observed too late for reaction. Making change in an organization that is led with a maestro style will be difficult, particularly in the time frame when change is needed. Thus there is an explicit focus on neither efficiency nor effectiveness.

Manager

The *manager* has high uncertainty avoidance and a low preference for delegation. Avoiding uncertainty is realized again by making reactive and short-term decisions with a fine level of detail. The manager focuses more on the control of operations than on strategic decisions. The manager does not delegate decision-making authority but instead uses formalized rules to manage subordinates. The manager knows what is happening in detail and can react quickly to undesired activities, i.e., bring things back into control. The manager achieves the goal of efficiency in operations where the utilization of resources is very important.

If the top management adopts a manager style of leadership, then it has excessive attention to detail that can make an organization vulnerable to those issues that, for one reason or another, are overlooked or receive little managerial attention. There can be little attention to the longer-term strategy of what to do or the "bigger picture" of work to be done. Thus, some vital details may be missed. And if the environment becomes less predictable, the firm is likely to miss the opportunity for change, which can harm overall effectiveness. Further, the manager approach to leadership gives little attention to innovation, except for efficiency-related innovation that threatens the technology base of the firm. In general, the manager leadership style has a short-term orientation that tends to overlook issues that make the firm viable for the longer term. The primary focus of a manager is on efficiency.

Leader

The *leader* has a high preference for delegation and low uncertainty avoidance. The leader is confident that others can make good decisions for the firm and thus finds delegation an efficient way to save time. Moreover, the leader does not avoid long-term uncertainty but instead embraces its challenges by attending to more strategic decisions. If the top management takes a leader approach to managing people, then it spends much time thinking about the long term, taking risks and avoiding the time-consuming task of detailed control. The leader encourages new ideas, initiatives and projects, both its own and those of subordinates. The leader explores new ideas and actions. And with the confidence to let subordinates make decisions and take actions, the leader can focus on more strategic considerations of the long term.

A leader has a focus on effectiveness and is willing to take substantial risk in order to achieve ambitious goals. The leader is vulnerable to weak following behavior in the process of implementation. If the subordinates do not live up to the confidence of their leader, then organizational performance can suffer – perhaps for an extended time period. Lack of attention to detail can create large problems for the organization. Further, the leader can take on risky projects which turn out badly for the firm and the leader.

Producer

The *producer* has a high preference for delegation and scores high on uncertainty avoidance. The producer focuses on both efficiency and effectiveness. If your firm's top management adopts a producer style of leadership, then the organization is likely to be well positioned *vis-à-vis* its competitors. The producer assures that new products and services are developed and introduced. The focus of attention is a dual one: short term and long term; operations and strategy; products and innovation; internal activities and the environment reading; hands-on management and letting others act independently; and efficiency and effectiveness.

The producer wants to know what is going on, assigns work to others, but does not need to make each and every decision the organization confronts. To avoid uncertainty, the producer has a long-term forecasting and planning focus. The producer exploits the subordinates' managerial resources well, delegating to be efficient in use of time, especially when others make decisions consistent with his or her preferences. The producer style is delegation with detailed oversight and a focus on the short term to avoid uncertainty. The strength of the producer's leadership style is the delegation to others, but the producer does this with an oversight that can assure decisions are made according to his or her preferences and that those actions are coordinated across the subordinates.

Organizational climate

Organizational climate is the "relatively enduring quality of the internal environment of an organization that a) is experienced by its members, b) influences their behavior, and c) can be described in terms of the values of a particular set of characteristics (or attitudes) of the organization" (Tagiuri and Litwin, 1968, p. 27). Climate is a characteristic of an organization which is experienced by its members. It is a psychological measure of the organization. Whereas leadership style refers exclusively to top management, organizational climate refers to all members of the organization, including superiors and subordinates.

Zammuto and Krakower (1991) measured organizational climate using many dimensions: trust, conflict, morale, rewards, resistance to change, leader credibility, and scapegoating (that is, blaming others for mistakes or problems in the organization). In a study of 246 Danish service firms, Burton et al. (2004) found that these seven dimensions could be reduced to two: tension and resistance to change. Here we treat tension and readiness to change (the opposite of resistance to change) as the two most fundamental design dimensions for organizational climate. Håkonsson et al. (2008a, 2008b) argue that organizational climate captures affective events, which in turn influence shared employee emotions and consequent information-processing. The basic argument is that employees within a given organizational context will perceive experiences as affective events (captured here as the psychological climate). This perception will lead to particular emotions, which serve as informational filters in their information-processing. Employees share these information-processing biases/filters, and they are not likely to change easily. The biases/filters do not change easily because experiences with affective events are stored in a shared organizational emotional memory (Damasio et al., 1996). This shared organizational emotional memory serves as a double-edged sword. First, it allows employees to relate to new information with a basis in their previously acquired experiences, but makes short-run change more difficult. Second, it biases their information-processing.

Tension is the degree to which there is a sense of stress or a psychological "edge" in the work atmosphere. Tension incorporates a combination of organizational factors as experienced by insiders, including trust, conflict, morale, rewards, leader credibility, and scapegoating. When tension is high, trust is low, conflict is high, morale is low, rewards are perceived as inequitable, leader credibility is low and there is a tendency toward scapegoating. Low tension is the opposite: trust is high, conflict is low, morale is high, rewards are perceived as equitable, leader credibility is high, and there is little or no scapegoating. High-tension climates will be characterized by unpleasant emotions and low-tension climates by pleasant emotions. At first glance, high tension sounds like a bad state for an organization. How could it be healthy for an organization to have low trust, high conflict, low morale, etc.? Although any one of these dimensions may have negative consequences, in combination they can bring an intensity and vigor to the organization – especially if they do not occur in the extreme. Extremely high conflict and low morale, etc., may be disastrous, but some degree of these in combination with the other factors mentioned above can spur effectiveness, especially if they occur in combination with the other design factors for managing people and processes, as we discussed in Chapters 6 and 7. Some degree of tension in the organizational climate is stressful, yet it increases the pace of work and movement toward efficiencies. Imagine the transition period of IBM in the late 1980s as Lou Gerstner took charge of moving the company from being a leading, established but old-style computer company to a more high-tech savvy software and service-based enterprise. Tension was high during this transition, but tension enabled the insiders to confront the challenges at hand and to mobilize to cut costs and move towards efficiency.

Readiness to change is the degree to which the people in the organization are likely to shift direction or adjust their work habits to meet new, unanticipated

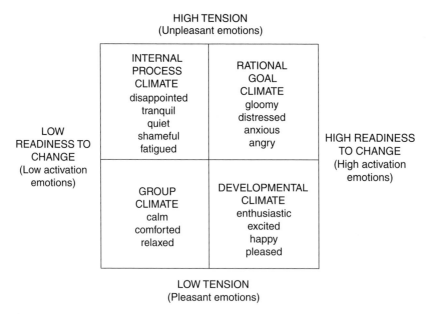

Source: Håkonsson et al. (2008b), based on Burton and Obel (2004), and Huy (2002)

Figure 8.2 Categorization of organizational climate and its effect upon emotions.

challenges. High readiness to change climates will be associated with high-activation emotions, and low readiness to change climates with low-activation emotions. High or low activation depends on whether employees believe they have the resources to deal with change. Ongoing norms and practices, or routine ways of doing things, can be an asset to an organization, in that they provide a sort of social skill set for getting work done. But ongoing ways of doing things also can be a liability if people are set in their existing routines of work and resist change. Readiness to change, to discover, and adopt new work habits and practices is vital if an organization is to be effective over time.

Climate can then be categorized into four climate types: group, internal process, developmental goal, and rational goal, as shown in Figure 8.2. The group climate has a low tension and low readiness for change – pleasant and low activation emotions; it is a quiet place. The internal process climate tends to be more mechanical with a low readiness for change and relatively high tension – low activation and unpleasant emotions. The developmental climate is more externally oriented with relatively low tension and a high readiness for change – pleasant and high activation emotions. The rational goal climate is also externally oriented to succeed with high readiness for change, but with relatively high tension – high activation and unpleasant emotions.

Group

The *group climate* is characterized by low readiness to change and few events of high tension. Based on cumulative experiences with such events, this is a climate characterized by emotions such as calmness, comfort, and relaxation, with open and free flow of information – pleasant and low activation emotions.

It is a pleasant place to work where individuals trust each other, conflict is low, rewards are perceived as equitable, and there is little readiness to change. Here, the individuals are comfortable with the situation as well as with each other and see no need to consider any change. The group climate can be stressful for the leader, who must make decisions about how work is done and maintain the status quo, but it is pleasant for employees generally. A group climate usually has a low degree of conflict. If conflict exists, it is constructive and tends to strengthen the organization, rather than destroy it, i.e., there can be disagreement on the group purpose itself. This is usually coupled with a high or moderately high degree of employee morale. Individuals feel that they belong to and are part of the organization. Rewards need not be equally distributed, but there must be a sense of fairness where the basis for the distribution is understood and accepted by the individuals in the organization.

If an organization has a group climate then it will find that managing information flow is relatively easy. Information is more likely to be "broadcast" than "channeled." "Need to know" is replaced by "everybody knows," or informal communication among specific parties who need to share knowledge. There are few secrets. The group climate can handle complex sets of information.

Although things are pleasant in the group climate, people do not have a high readiness for change. There is a high degree of trust and little scapegoating and the leader likely enjoys a high degree of credibility with the subordinates. However, getting people to embrace change is nonetheless a challenge in that the group climate has a consistent pattern of beliefs and attitudes about desirable behavior that are not readily adjusted as circumstances change.

Internal process

The *internal process climate* is characterized by high tension and low readiness to change. These are climates in which organizational work situations are experienced affectively as relating to high conflict, low morale, low leadership credibility, i.e. unpleasant emotions. Similarly, the low-activation emotions are likely to be related to disappointments in dealing with change, and employees no longer believe they have the adequate resources to deal with change. Prevailing emotions are disappointment, tranquility, shame, and fatigue. In terms of information-processing, internal process climates are likely to lead to little sharing and openness, little spontaneous information, and limited shared information within rules and according to procedures, and closely associated with the job or task. The unpleasant, low-activation emotions characteristic of this climate will lead to an internally driven, top-down, and systematic style where perceptions and judgments are less ambitious (Forgas and George, 2001; George and Zhou, 2002). It is a less pleasant place to work, where individuals are less trusting, have more conflict, perceive rewards as inequitable, and yet there is little readiness to change.

Compared to the group climate, the internal process climate is characterized by lower trust. There is not a sharing and open atmosphere among the individuals, as each is more inward and guarded. Conflict can be high in the organization and so people may disagree over both means and ends (i.e., work methods and goals). Rewards are perceived to be given inequitably. As a result, employee morale can be low.

In the internal process climate people tend to focus inwardly on how work is done, i.e., the work methods or processes. This can be very important to gaining organizational efficiency. So, such a climate is not necessarily destructive for the organization. The managerial challenge is to keep people focused on work processes without letting trust, conflict, perceived inequities, and so on, become so low that they obstruct organizational success. Managed carefully, an internal process climate can bring organizational benefit. As an example, consider the popular Six Sigma programs (Hahn, 1999), which emphasize a culture of measurement, excellence, confrontation of conflict, and rewards based on continual error reduction. A Six Sigma program will tend to promote an internal process climate. The managerial challenge is to nurture the internal process climate in such a way that it does not spin into a downward spiral of negativity by employees but instead promotes the value of excellence, achieving organizational efficiencies, and error control.

If your organization has an internal process climate then it will observe that there tends to be a low readiness to change. Perhaps this is not intuitive as it might be argued that a change, or any change, would be welcome in such a climate. But the evidence suggests that an intense process-orientation on the part of people goes along with a preference to keeping that orientation rather than engaging in activities that could lead to a different situation. Perhaps it is the reduced level of trust in these organizations that helps explain this reluctance. There is less faith in the leadership and more faith in processes themselves, so resistance to change tends to be high. A higher than ideal level of scapegoating seems consistent with this story about the internal process organization.

The internal process climate does not possess the capacity to process a lot of information through informal means. There is not a norm of sharing and openness. Instead, the organization structure must supply the requisite information-processing capacity. Information tends to be private and within the role or specific job scope of those who need the information. Information is passed on within prescriptions and according to procedures. It is closely associated with the job or task, or "a need to know." Spontaneous information links are largely missing, or not utilized.

Developmental

The *developmental climate* has low tension and a high readiness to change. Since these are the typical affective events that employees are experiencing, these are likely to create a feeling of having the adequate resources to deal with change (high activation) as well as having the feeling that new events are generally pleasant. Subsequent emotions therefore are: enthusiasm, excitement, and happiness. Such climates will be characterized by optimistic perceptions and judgments along with a bottom-up, flexible, and generative style (George and Zhou, 2002; Forgas and George, 2001).

It is a pleasant place to work, where people generally trust each other; conflict is relatively low; rewards are perceived as equitable, and people are quite willing to engage in change. People in the developmental climate are comfortable with each other and welcome new opportunities.

Some of the characteristics for the developmental climate are similar to those of the group climate. For both, trust is high, conflict is low, and morale is high, with relatively equitable rewards. The significant difference is the readiness to change, which tends to be low in a group climate but high in a developmental climate. If an organization has a developmental climate, you will find that there generally is a great focus on the growth of the individuals and their quality of work life. So although there is a focus on growth of the organization the tension is rather low. This is the basis for the high readiness to change. In the developmental climate, rewards can be more individually based than in the group process climate with less attention to the impacts on perceived equity. Individual contribution to the organization is more important and, in a well-functioning developmental climate, this is accepted by employees. Compared to the group and internal process climates, the developmental climate is more externally oriented. People believe and act based on an assumption that success is realized more outside the organization.

There are also small differences with respect to leader credibility and the level of scapegoating. The developmental climate has different information characteristics as compared to the group climate. The group climate will focus more heavily on internal information, whereas the developmental climate focuses more on external environmental information. Environmental information is likely to have more value for development and growth. Additionally, compromise is important (Quinn and Kimberley, 1984).

Rational goal

The *rational goal climate* has high tension and a high readiness to change. Emotional reactions to such climates are: anger, anxiousness, and distress. However, this is a climate in which employees believe they have the adequate resources to deal with change. The openness towards change is based on distress with respect to the current situation. This is also a climate characterized by unpleasant emotions; it is a competitive climate where employees are not likely to have experienced positive emotions, e.g. in admitting mistakes and obtaining rewards. Rational goal climates are characterized by a private view of information, where sharing and exchange of information does not occur spontaneously, but is job-related. The unpleasant, high-activation emotions will thus lead to less ambitious judgments and perceptions and at the same time an externally-oriented and bottom-up style (George and Zhou, 2002; Forgas and George, 2001). It is goal-driven and the individuals are a bit on edge as the tension is high, but at the same time tension is not so high that it is detrimental to performance. In fact, tension helps to drive performance as people deal with fluctuations in trust, conflict, and so on. People are willing to change and accept new challenges and opportunities if they believe goals can be met.

The rational goal climate is closer to the internal process climate than to the developmental climate, although they are different. The main difference is the readiness to change. The rational goal climate is structured with an emphasis on planning, productivity, and efficiency (Quinn and Kimberley, 1984).

Information processing in the rational goal climate is similar to internal process climate but with a greater emphasis on environmental/external information. The low level of trust, high conflict, etc., leads to a private, or customized view of information; sharing and exchange of information does not occur spontaneously, but information is shared if it is goal-oriented. Put another way, people do not share information for its own sake but rather to meet specific needs related to their work tasks. In this way, information sharing is tempered rather than fully open. The rational goal climate is a very competitive environment to work in. It is not to be expected that the employees will be loyal to the organization in the sense that high turnover can be expected. Rewards are performance-based. The organization may work hard to keep the most valued or skilled employees but not worry too much if others are unhappy and leave. With the high readiness to change, reorganization of personnel level can be expected, with very tough competition for the prestigious jobs.

Diagnostic questions

For your organization you should first examine the two dimensions in Figure 8.3: preference for delegation and uncertainty avoidance. Locate where the top management leadership style is along these two dimensions and then categorize the leadership style as: maestro, manager, leader, or producer. To begin, answer the diagnostic questions below.

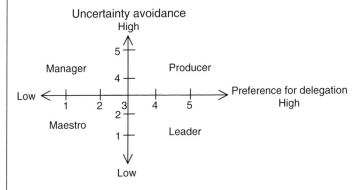

Figure 8.3 Locate your organization's leadership style.

1. For your unit of analysis, what is the top management that you
   are describing here? It may be a single executive or a set of people
   (such as an executive group or board) who oversee your unit of analysis.
   Use this top management level when answering questions 2 and 3 below.
   Note that if you are the executive in charge of your unit of analysis, then
   these questions are about your leadership style.[3]
   The questions below will help you locate your top management
   on the preference for delegation and uncertainty avoidance
   dimensions.

2. Preference for delegation
   a. To what extent does top management maintain control themselves
      (1), or encourage others to take on responsibility for managing work
      tasks (5)?
   b. To what extent does top management allow its direct reports to make
      important decisions and take actions for the organization (1 = low,
      5 = high)?
   c. Overall, for your unit of analysis, what is top management's preference
      for delegation, (1) low or (5) high?
   Score the preference for delegation on a scale from 1 to 5
   as follows:

1	2	3	4	5
very low		moderate		very high

3. Uncertainty avoidance
   a. To what extent does top management concern itself with the "big
      picture" (1), rather than the detail (5), in decision-making?
   b. Does top management tend to be aggressive (1), or cautious (5), in its
      decision-making?
   c. How risk-embracing (1), versus risk-avoiding (5), is the top
      management?
   d. To what extent is top management control-oriented in the
      management of its direct reports: low (1) or high (5)?

[3] As before, you can average your scores for the items within each question to create an overall score for
each design dimension, or you can use the questions as a guide to assign an overall score for each
design dimension.

Score the uncertainty avoidance on a scale from 1 to 5 as follows:

1	2	3	4	5
very low		moderate		very high

4. You can now locate your organization on Figure 8.3. What is its leadership style?

Now, consider the organizational climate. Remember to include the entire unit of analysis as you answer these questions. In Figure 8.4, the firm's readiness to change and tension are the dimensions, and the organizational climate is then categorized as: group, internal process, developmental or rational goal. Here are questions which will help you locate your chosen firm.

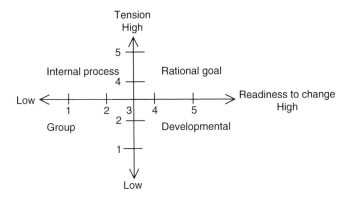

Figure 8.4 Locate your firm in the organizational climate space.

5. Readiness for change – activation emotions

   a. To what extent do people prefer old ways of thinking and doing things (1) versus embrace new ways of thinking and doing things (5)?

   b. To what extent do people tend to shift direction or adjust their work habits to meet new, unanticipated challenges, low (1) or high (5)?

   c. Overall, what is the organization's level of readiness to change, low (1) or high (5)?

Use a 1 to 5 rating scale to score your organization as follows, 1 = low to 5 = high:

1	2	3	4	5
very low		moderate		very high

6. Tension – pleasant/unpleasant emotions
   a. What is the level of distrust in the firm, low (1) or high (5)?
   b. What is the level of conflict in the firm, low (1) or high (5)?
   c. To what extent do people perceive rewards not to be equal across employees, low (1) or high (5)?
   d. To what degree do people question the credibility of the organization's leaders, low (1) or high (5)?
   e. What is the level of scapegoating, or blaming, of people for problems, low (1) or high (5)?

Use a 1 to 5 rating scale to score your organization as follows, 1 = low to 5 = high:

1	2	3	4	5
very low		moderate		very high

You can now locate your chosen organization on Figure 8.4. What is your firm's climate?

Fit and misfits

What is a good leadership style for a firm, and what is an appropriate organizational climate? What is a good fit? In Table 8.1, we add fit for the leadership and organizational climate to the goals, strategy, environment, configuration, and task design for your chosen firm. In each of the columns A, B, C, and D, the fit relations can be read vertically from top to bottom.

Misfits for leadership and climate pose a particular difficulty from the point of view of organizational design. Although you may be able to change the goals, strategy, or the configuration of your chosen organization, it may be very difficult for an executive to change the leadership style. You may have no control over this design factor. Therefore, managing the fit between leadership style and other design components can be problematic. To change the

Table 8.1 Fit and misfit to include leadership style and organizational climate

Corresponding quadrant in organizational design space	A	B	C	D	
Organizational climate	Group	Internal process	Develop-mental	Rational goal	
Leadership style	Maestro	Manager	Leader	Producer	
People	Shop	Factory	Laboratory	Office	
Task design	Orderly	Complicated	Fragmented	Knotty	
Knowledge exchange	Ad hoc com-munications	Informated	Cellular	Network	
Geographic distribution	Global	International	Multi-domestic	Transnational	
Organizational complexity	Blob	Tall	Flat	Symmetric	
Configuration	Simple	Functional	Divisional	Matrix	
Environment	Calm	Varied	Locally stormy	Turbulent	
Strategy types	Reactor	Defender	Prospector	Analyzer with innovation	Analyzer without innovation
Organizational goals	Neither	Efficiency	Effectiveness	Efficiency and Effectiveness	

leadership style may require a new executive and/or other members in the top management roles. Similarly, organizational climate is a relatively enduring property of the organization and cannot be easily changed in the short run. So if there are misfits with the leadership style and climate, it may be easier to adjust to them rather than to change them in a significant way. Of course, if this means changing to a different and less satisfactory strategy for your chosen organization, it may be necessary to take a long-term view and take on the difficult actions necessary to bring the organization's leadership style and climate into alignment with goals, strategy, and configuration. To align the leadership style and climate is however very important (Håkonsson, 2008b) for the performance of the organization as well as the alignment with other contextual and structural elements of the organization (Burton et al., 2002; Burton and Obel, 2004; Jung et al., 2008).

As Table 8.1 suggests, in column A there is a fit among the maestro, the group climate, the blob organizational complexity, a simple configuration, a calm environment, a reactor strategy, and ill-defined goals. The organizational climate is pleasant and non-threatening. It usually is not very fast-paced. A new executive with a new style can quickly become a threat to the individuals and create a misfit with the group climate. If the firm is not performing well, there may be good reason to create a misfit, spurring the opportunity to redesign the organization. A new organizational design can be introduced and brought into alignment, bringing the various components together into a new quadrant of the organizational design space over time. In this way the organization can achieve firm goals of efficiency and effectiveness. We will discuss the process of misfits and change management in more detail in Chapter 11.

Moving to column B, there is a fit among the manager, the internal process climate, the tall, functional configuration, the varied environment, the defender strategy, and the efficiency goal. The information-processing demands have increased considerably, but the manager takes a more hands-on approach with less delegation and more detailed monitoring. The commensurate climate has high tension with less trust and leadership credibility, and is less pleasant. Generally, this climate is less difficult to establish but it takes a longer time to reduce the tension. At the same time, the firm's efficiency goals can be realized, but innovation is less likely.

For column C, the firm has a top management with a leader style, a developmental climate, a flat, divisional configuration, a locally stormy environment, a prospector strategy, and an effectiveness goal. The executive lets others make decisions but accepts the uncertainty. The climate has low tension and a high readiness for change. Many individuals would find the organization with the profile of column C to be an exciting place to work due to high trust and executive support. It fits well with a prospector strategy and an effectiveness goal. If there is a desire to focus on short-term efficiency, the executive may

become more control-oriented and directive, which is a threat to the developmental climate. Then the executive can become quickly overloaded with the
details, which may further threaten the developmental climate rather than
resolve it. The leader style and developmental climate work best when innovation is valued and the organization pursues a prospector strategy with subunits organized as independent divisions or cells.

For column D, the firm has a leadership style that acts as a producer, a
rational goal climate, a symmetric, matrix configuration, a turbulent environment, an analyzer strategy, and pursuit of the dual goals of efficiency and
effectiveness. The producer leadership style means that top management delegates with high information processing but also tries to avoid uncertainty. The
climate has high tension but also has a readiness for change. The organization
in this quadrant is performance-driven, aiming to achieve both efficiency and
effectiveness of innovation. It is a demanding place to work, where tension is
high, but some individuals find it exciting and embrace a high readiness for
change. The organization in column D is a good fit with the turbulent environment and analyzer strategy of innovation and change. Coordination needs are
high in this type of organization and quick change is required to meet organizational goals. As such, the goal-driven matrix configuration with large
information-processing capacity is a good fit.

If your chosen firm is located in different columns based upon your answers
to the diagnostic questions in this chapter, then you should think about what
you might do to bring the organization into fit in the column that meets your
goals. But also think about what is involved to move to a different goal and
thus a different column and what should or could be done both in the short run
and in the long run. In the next section[4] we show such an approach.

Adapting for better performance in the short run

Climate is a main source of inertia as well as an effective means to guide
innovation. Leaders, by creating a clear vision, can reduce the ambiguity
surrounding employees. This creates a shared sense of the world that guides
employee actions for better organizational performance. Hence, the role of the
leader is not simply one of formulating a vision, but rather one of understanding

---

[4] That section and the one that follows it are an adaption of Håkonsson et al. (2008a).

employees' emotional boundedness, and supporting it. This creates difficulty at two levels. First, the leader needs to be aware of the direct short-term and long-term effects that his leadership style has on the climate. Second, he needs to be aware of the indirect effect his actions on the other contingencies have on the climate. This overview and balance is easy to maintain in stable and short-term environments, but much more difficult in the longer term. This will be explained in the following section, using imaginary scenarios.

As an example, consider the scenario where the climate is an internal process climate (quadrant B). Furthermore, this type of climate is in fit with the other system components (i.e., the organization is positioned in quadrant B). The internal process climate is a climate in which employees, due to previous bad experiences in sharing information, are reluctant to do so again willingly. At the same time, employees are resistant towards change and generally they do not focus on new and disconfirming information. Because these information processing behaviors will fit the organizational goal of efficiency (quadrant B), the manager should support this type of climate by keeping his focus on the internal organization and ensuring that information is transferred. One way is to keep decision authority at close hand (low preference for delegation), while keeping the focus on the short term and making low-risk decision opportunities (high uncertainty avoidance) – i.e., a manager leadership style (quadrant B). In this situation, because the climate fits the rest of the situation (i.e., all system contingencies are positioned in quadrant B), the managerial job is "simply" that of supporting the climate and maintaining it through his leadership style. Moreover, because climates are conceptualized as affective events, the climate will serve to stabilize employees' information-processing behaviors. This is because the organizational events (i.e., the strategy, leadership style, design, etc.) will serve to confirm affective events. These affective events will serve to maintain the employees' emotions, confirm emotional memories and, consequently, serve to maintain employees' information-processing behaviors. However, consider the case where the internal process climate described previously is in misfit with the other system contingencies. The other system contingencies are positioned in quadrant C (i.e., prospector strategy, locally stormy environment, etc.). The internal process climate might become a problem in locally stormy environments, where the need for new developments is high and the focus should be on maintaining effectiveness and adjustments. One way for a leader to support employees' information-processing boundedness in this situation will be to make sure that the decisions made are long-term, and that they contain elements of high risk (low uncertainty avoidance).

Simultaneously, it is necessary for the leader to delegate low risk decisions to make sure they are made quickly (high preference for delegation). In other words, the appropriate leadership style in this situation is a leader leadership style. It will serve to complement the boundedness of employees' information-processing that seemed inadequate to meet the demands of the situation. What this shows is that leaders may complement, in the short run, causing a situation of fit, even though the organization is in misfit. This requires a leader who is fully aware of employees' emotions and consequent information-processing biases. When this is not the case, leaders will not be able to compensate employees' biases through their own information-processing profiles. The above-mentioned examples relate strictly to short-term implications only. They illustrate how leaders in periods of fit, with no external pressures for adaptation, can support climates effectively through their own leadership styles. In this manner, they can use climates as an effective means to support organizational goals. In fact, climates may even represent an effective emotional inertia serving to maintain the system in fit. The requirement is for the leader's perception of the climate to be correct and for him to be continuously aware of how his actions relate to the other contingencies and how they will affect the climate. When this is not the case, or when the need for change is more immediate, achieving this balance becomes much more difficult.

Transforming climate in the longer run

In the previous section, we indicated that climates can be changed, as a reaction to both the leadership style and the other system components, or work events that also shape the climate. Yet, when conceptualizing climate as affective events, we have an understanding that climates may not be as effective in periods of transformation. This is because the affect and emotion-based nature of climates entails that climates, because they represent shared emotional memories, are not likely to change quickly. Adaptation is only relevant in situations of misfits. We will discuss how to manage climate in adaptation through two examples: one in which management is aware of misfits, and one in which they are not. Consider the scenario discussed above. In other words, the organization's internal process climate (quadrant B) is problematic in relation to the other system contingencies (that are all positioned in quadrant C). The leader is aware of this and is interested in changing the climate. As discussed above, the appropriate leadership style to complement the internal process climate is normally a manager (quadrant B). In this particular situation, however, the appropriate leadership style is not the manager leadership style but rather the leader leadership style, as this fits with the contingencies of quadrant C. The expectation is that a leader leadership style, through high motivation, high equity in rewards, and high delegation, would lead to a change in climate, yet this will only occur over a long-term period because actions such as delegation will not be associated with pleasantness until the emotional memories of employees change. The reason for this is that the executives' actions would be perceived through the old information-processing filters, and therefore even acts of motivating employees will not be perceived as positive. Moreover, acts of delegating decision-making authority will not be trusted. Employees will be hesitant towards such actions because of previous experiences in an internal process climate. Thus, climate cannot change swiftly even in a situation where an executive is aware of a misfit. It will require consistency in managerial actions over longer periods of time in order to change employees' views and emotional memories. Alternatively, there may also be situations of misfit, which leaders have not realized and in these situations the consequences of climates are even more serious. To illustrate this, consider the situation where all contingencies, except the strategy, are situated in quadrant B. The strategy is in quadrant C. In other words, this is another example where the strategy (in this case the prospector strategy) does not match the rest of the organization. Because climates and their subsequent emotions are experience-bound, employees will be influenced by strategy as a work event. This will impact the affective events and, again, employees' emotions. Hence, the climate will change in reaction to the misfitting strategy. This is because employees' behaviors will not be validated with respect to the strategy dimensions. In this particular case, the prospector strategy and its high focus on newness and exploration will make mistakes difficult to avoid. Affective events are likely to arise, which are related to positive forgiveness. Such events will decrease tension in the organization (through lower scapegoating), and, over time, the climate is likely to become characterized by more pleasant emotions. If the leader is not aware that the climate has changed and, accordingly, does not complement the new climate well, his actions will have little effect because they are aimed at the wrong type of emotional boundedness. These situations are likely to be followed by a period of change in many work events, i.e., leading to situations of transformative change. What is particular about these situations is that the process has been initialized from within the system but that the leader has very little control over it. Climate in that way constitutes an internal dynamic in relation to misfits between the contingencies, a dynamic which cannot be easily controlled in situations of misfit. Such situations are only likely to occur when the leader is not aware of misfits and consequently does not act on them. When misfits are dealt with in a timely manner and hence are not persistent over longer time periods, climates are not likely to change in reaction to misfitting contingencies. The overall conclusion is therefore that misfits need to be dealt with in a timely manner.

Summary

In this chapter, we have included the leadership style measured as preference for delegation and uncertainty avoidance and organizational climate measured as tension and readiness for change to the set of relations which should fit together to meet a firm's goals. There are four leader styles: maestro, manager, leader, and producer; and there are four climates: group, internal process, developmental, and rational goal. We then discussed fit and misfit possibilities. Finally we showed how to make short run and long run changes to address misfit situations. Next we move on to consider approaches for managing coordination and control in your organization.

Glossary

Affective events: affective events theory (AET). AET demonstrates that employees react emotionally to things that happen to them at work and that this influences their job performance and satisfaction.

Developmental climate: an organizational climate characterized by low tension and a high readiness to change.

Group climate: an organizational climate characterized by low tension and low readiness to change.

Internal process climate: an organizational climate characterized by high tension and low readiness to change.

Leader: a leadership style in which top management accepts uncertainty and delegates decision-making to subordinates (similar to theory Y).

Leadership style: the predominant mode used by the top management of your unit of analysis to manage subordinates, which is measured in terms of preference for delegation and uncertainty avoidance.

Maestro: a leadership style in which top management orchestrates the work of others through a combination of direct involvement and high tolerance for uncertainty.

Manager: a leadership style in which top management prefers little delegation and avoids uncertainty (similar to theory X).

Organizational climate: the internal environment or working atmosphere of the organization as experienced by all employees, including the leader and subordinates.

Preference for delegation: the degree to which the top management of the organization encourages lower-level managers or other employees who are their direct reports to make decisions about what and how work is to be done in the organization.

Producer: a leadership style in which top management avoids uncertainty through short- and long-term planning and has a high preference for delegation, but with detailed oversight.

Rational goal climate: an organizational climate characterized by high tension and a high readiness to change.

Readiness for change: the degree to which the people in the organization are likely to shift direction or adjust their work habits to meet new, unanticipated challenges.

Tension: the degree to which there is a sense of stress or a psychological "edge" in the work atmosphere; it incorporates a combination of organizational factors as experienced by insiders, including trust, conflict, morale, rewards, leader credibility, and scapegoating.

Uncertainty avoidance: the degree to which the top management shuns taking actions or making choices that involve major risk with short-term, reactive decision-making; low uncertainty avoidance means management is risk taking with longer-term focus.

Where are you in the step-by-step approach?

STEP 1   GETTING STARTED

(1) Goals

STEP 2   STRATEGY

(2) Strategy
(3) Environment

STEP 3   STRUCTURE

(4) Configuration and complexity
(5) Geographic distribution knowledge exchange

STEP 4   PROCESS AND PEOPLE

(6) Task design
(7) People
(8) Leadership and organizational climate

Here, you focused on the work of the firm and the people who do the work. First, you designed the tasks, then you considered the number of people and their skills, and, finally, you examined the leadership style of the top management and the climate where everyone works. A good organizational design includes fit among all of these elements: the tasks, people, leadership, and climate. Before moving on, it is important to review how well these fit together in your organization. Identify misfits and consider what steps you might take to improve fit. When you are satisfied that there is a fit among the processes and the people, you should review how they fit with the goals, strategy, and structure of your firm. If there are misfits, think about what you can and will do to bring these organizational design components into alignment. Then move on to the next step, design of coordination and control systems.

STEP 5   COORDINATION AND CONTROL

Next we examine the coordination and control components of your firm including the information systems and the incentives.

(9)   Coordination, control, and information systems
(10) Incentives

STEP 5
Coordination and control

9 Coordination, control, and information systems

Introduction

Once you have designed the processes and people-based systems to support your chosen organization's structure, the next step is to design coordination, control, and information systems to manage the linkages between the various parts of the organization. Along with people and processes, coordination, control, and information systems are important to assure smooth working-together among the organizational components, so that all move in a common direction toward strategic goals. Coordination, control, and information systems support integration of the organization, and they also provide monitoring and support for decision-making so that managers can anticipate and react to internal and external changes that require organizational adjustment.

In this chapter we consider the range of devices that managers can use to coordinate and control the organization's work. Prior to the development of computer systems, coordination and control systems were entirely manually based. Today, of course, these systems are both computer-based and manually based. Some systems are visible, in the sense that they are stated as tangible rules or can be seen in the form of reports or established routines. Others are invisible and operate in the informal ways that people think and act. These systems may even be created "on the fly," i.e., on an as-needed basis to meet unanticipated needs. Considered together, coordination, control, and information systems constitute the *infrastructure* of the firm, that is, the underlying pathways for information sharing. A vibrant, well-designed infrastructure can facilitate healthy integration of the organization's structure, the functioning of its business processes, and interactions among its people.

We will consider two major aspects of organizational infrastructure in this chapter: coordination and control systems, and information systems. *Coordination and control systems* are methods for linking together the otherwise disparate elements of the organization's structure and supporting responsiveness to changes in the environment or task demands. In other words, these are systems that integrate, or tie together, the various subunits of the organization. *Information systems* are methods for providing meaningful data to decision makers. As noted above, information systems may be computer-based, but this is not necessary. Information systems also can be based on paper memos, conversations, or informal meetings. Whether manually or computer-based, information systems serve as conduits for the flow and processing of meaningful data throughout the organization. Similarly, coordination and control systems can be computer-based and/or manually based.

Information systems provide the data necessary for coordination and control systems to operate. In fact, the distinction between information systems and coordination and control systems is largely conceptual. The two are (or should be) intricately intertwined to facilitate the work of management. They should not be designed separately but rather together.

As we discuss these systems it is important to keep in mind that we are talking in very general terms about the guiding principles, or philosophy, that drive systems design in an organization rather than the specifics involved in setting up a particular coordination/control system or an information system. Specific design of systems is a major undertaking requiring much detailed attention. The executive's highest-level concern is with choosing basic principles, or guiding dimensions, for systems design. This is our concern here. We lay out the major options along important dimensions for systems design. Once you decide where you want your organization to be along these major dimensions, then you can proceed to the detailed design of your organization's infrastructure. Though our discussion is general and high-level, choosing where you want your organization to be on the dimensions outlined in this chapter is not a trivial exercise. These are some of the most important design decisions you must make as an executive, and so they deserve careful attention. We urge you to think through each dimension described below with care, as the choices you make will set the tone for the development of your firm's coordination, control, and information systems infrastructure.

Coordination and control systems

Early on in the development of professional business organizations, managers gave dominant attention to developing control systems, or methods for assuring quality and efficiency of information flow between the highest and lowest level of the firm. The role of middle management was to assure control – to pass information up and down the hierarchy between top management and workers. Control systems monitor and measure the performances of subunits and their people, providing feedback to managers about compliance of these units. Budgets, production measurement systems, and performance reviews are examples of control systems. As organizations have become flatter and more distributed, there has been increasing emphasis on coordination, including the lateral flow of information among the subunits. Coordination systems support flexibility and adaptiveness within and across departmental or divisional boundaries. Coordination systems "let the right hand know what the left hand is doing," so to speak. Cross-functional teams and committees, as well as project management systems, are examples of coordination systems. Today, control and coordination systems are inextricably intertwined. Systems such as Movex, Navision, SAP, and People Soft, which provide support for management of inventory, people, and projects, are examples of large-scale coordination and control systems. Smaller-scale coordination and control systems include liaison roles, committees, formal and informal rules, job descriptions, statements of procedures, codes of ethics, employee or customer survey systems, statistical sampling systems, and generally accepted "ways of doing things" in the organization. As you can see, coordination and control systems embrace a myriad of possible methods for directing, monitoring, and assuring adaptiveness and flexibility of the firm.

To design coordination and control systems it is useful to begin by making two fundamental choices. First, how formalized do you want these systems to be? Second, how centralized should control and coordination be? Formalization and centralization are the two fundamental design dimensions that underlie the design of coordination and control systems.

Formalization is the degree to which the organization specifies a set of rules or codes to govern how work is done. One of the simplest ways to coordinate work is through formal rules and regulations that govern how work is to be done, who is to do it, and under what circumstances or constraints. Formalization is high if these rules are very detailed and consistently communicated to organizational members. Formalization is high if rules are recorded in policy statements, such as in classic bureaucracies, where written codes are formulated and published for all to see and share; or if computer or other programs are written to monitor and provide feedback. Monitoring and feedback systems serve to reinforce the formalization process. As we shall see, it is possible for formalization to be high even if rules are not "written down." Rules can be communicated through training procedures, modeling of behavior, or verbalized codes of working that people are expected to learn over time. As an example of the latter, consider an organization with high ethical standards that everyone knows and follows, even if the ethical guidelines are not written into a document. The guidelines are taught, practiced, and followed; everyone knows about them, and so they are visible even if not on paper. The important thing to note about formalization is that it bases coordination and control in very strong expectations of how work should be done, with monitoring and feedback mechanisms in place. In highly formal organizations there are penalties for breaking rules.

Formalization is low if there is not a set of strongly written or accepted rules or codes of conduct. Where formalization is low, there is high variance, and hence flexibility, in the methods and procedures used to govern the organization's work. Rules are likely to change over time and vary across circumstances. In the extreme, an organization with no formalization is chaotic, and an organization with very high formalization is bureaucratic and stifling of creativity. Most organizations operate somewhere in between, with relatively high or relatively low formalization.

Centralization is the degree to which coordination and control are managed by a core person or level of the organization, usually corporate headquarters. In the small start-up firm or the traditional bureaucracy, centralization is usually high. Many modern firms have moved toward more decentralized approaches to coordination and control. Hence, it can be more meaningful to think about the degree of decentralization you want in your firm's coordination and control systems. *Decentralization* is the degree to which responsibility for coordination and control lies in the subunits of the firm and individual managers, rather than corporate headquarters or one specific level of the hierarchy. Decentralized systems accommodate the diverse needs of the more distributed enterprise and allow more local responsibility for firm actions. The centralization–decentralization distinction especially applies to operational kinds of decisions. If strategic decisions are made at the top level in the firm but operational decisions are made by the subunits, the organization is more decentralized than

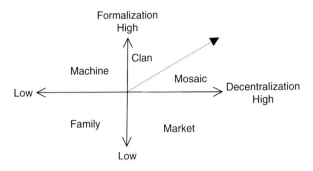

Figure 9.1 Coordination and control space.

a firm in which operational decision-making is located at the top. Put another way, coordination and control systems are more concerned with the design of work process than setting strategy or policy. In today's knowledge economy managing work processes means managing how people interface with one another to complete the organization's tasks. There is a strong human aspect to systems design. The choice of centralization vs. decentralization also affects the dispersion of information in the organization (Burton and Obel, 1984, 1988; Alonso et al., 2008).

We use the dimensions of formalization and decentralization to summarize the design options for coordination and control systems. Together, these two dimensions suggest five basic approaches to the design of coordination and control systems. You can think of these as different guiding paradigms, or models of managing work processes. They range from being very simple to being quite elaborate.

Figure 9.1 summarizes the five design options using the dimensions of formalization and decentralization.

Family

If both formalization and decentralization are low, then coordination and control systems are designed to rely on informal and centralized means of control. We refer to this as a *family-based* model. There are few written rules and procedures, and people know what to do based on what they are told by a centralized source, probably the CEO or, in the case of a business unit or department, the head manager. The organization operates like a family where the head(s) of the household dictate(s) what is to be expected and how work is to be done. The head of the household directs the show and others following along because they believe in him/her. In the family model, control and coordination are ad hoc, in the sense that rules are developed as needed. So long as people comply with directives from the central source, this approach to systems design works reasonably well. Further, low decentralization and low formalization allow flexibility. However, troubles arise if new members are added (e.g., the family grows), the head of household changes (e.g., a new CEO is appointed), or other disruptions occur that make reliance on informality and centralization ineffective for managing the work of the organization. The well-known Walt Disney, founder of the Disney Corporation, was famous for managing his company as a family operation, with Walt acting as the family patriarch. Employees were expected to work together like family members, helping each other out as needed, following directives from the top, holding strong loyalty to the founder.

Entrepreneurs often run start-up ventures using a family model. Coordination is informal and centralized. People pull together to get work done, relying on the boss for direction. Coordination using a family model can be effective if the leader is competent, and the members are cooperative, but this form of coordination also lends itself to becoming dysfunctional, if members or the family leader are incompetent, the leader changes and is not viewed with the same respect as the prior leader, or people don't "get along." These types of challenges tend to require more formality and decentralization of control in order for the organization to do its work.

Machine

If an organization adopts a *machine model* for coordination and control, then the emphasis is on a high degree of formalization and a high degree of centralization. Unlike in the family model, where authority rests in a central, core place, such as corporate headquarters, the CEO, the auditing department, or some other center of power in the organization, the machine model systems are designed with documentation of rules and procedures in mind. Considerable attention must be given to specifying how work should be done, how it is to be monitored, and how the feedback and correction systems should be designed. Machine-based organizations can tend toward bureaucracy with many rules and procedures to govern work processes, but this does not mean that such organizations are inefficient. On the contrary, coordination and control systems can help the organization to operate as a smart/intelligent machine. Just-in-time inventory management, Six Sigma quality control systems, and 360-degree feedback are examples of control systems that are designed with a machine-based model in mind. The organization makes high use of information to build efficiencies and adapt to changing demands by modifying rules so as to make the organization dynamic, not fixed. As we shall see, excellent data processing will facilitate the success of the machine approach to coordination and control.

Wal-Mart is a good example of a company that has built excellent coordination and control systems that allow the company to monitor all aspects of its business, from hiring and employee development to inventory management, sales, distribution, and forecasting. Many hospitals likewise adopt a machine type of model when designing coordination and control systems. In a hospital setting, a disciplined approach to information tracking is needed to assure a high level of patient care. Job descriptions and detailed procedures for doing work are critical. Reporting and accountability systems are important for managing both large and small tasks.

Of course, the downside of the machine model is that it can lack creativity and flexibility. Old systems have to be replaced with newer ones on a regular basis; otherwise, the existing systems are likely to keep the organization entrenched in the past, rather than changing to meet new environmental or other demands.

Market

The *market model* for the design of coordination and control systems emphasizes low formalization and high decentralization. Some coordination and control systems may be formalized, such as budgeting and performance reviews, but overall there is an emphasis on more informal sources of control, such as the value of sharing information or a culture in which people are encouraged to "speak up" and report problems. Informal approaches to setting expectations and detecting difficulties occur through training, custom, and everyday interaction of people. A key aspect of the market model is that there are variations in coordination and control across different departments or subunits of the organization, because it is difficult in a decentralized, informal approach to develop consistent ways of doing work and monitoring effectiveness. Standardized approaches to systems design and use are shunned in favor of letting subunits police themselves and/or work with other subunits as driven by informal norms.

If done well, the market approach can be an effective approach for managing coordination and control, especially for promoting innovation and customizing coordination and control needs to particular subunits of the enterprise. Nokia (Nokia, 2003) has taken a market-based approach to innovation, relying heavily on informal norms to foster innovation throughout the company. Governance is similar to a confederacy or federation, with pockets of control residing in product lines or regional groups rather than corporate headquarters.

In the market model governance is relatively decentralized, meaning that groups or business units oversee themselves with high autonomy relative to corporate headquarters. A market organization is risk-taking, tactical, and innovative. With few stated rules, things may seem chaotic to the newcomer who is trying to figure out "the rules" and "how to get things done." But for those who work inside the organization, low formalization and high decentralization foster innovation. Of course, the downside of the market approach is that all subunits may not police themselves equally well, and there can be a tendency toward conflict if the various units develop quite different ways of executing work tasks.

Clan or mosaic

When decentralization is high and formalization is high, there are two possible approaches for designing coordination and control systems. Though these have common attributes, they are sufficiently different approaches to coordination to warrant separate discussion. The *clan model* tends toward somewhat greater formalization and less decentralization. The clan model uses strong norms to guide how work is done, and these norms are deeply embedded in the hearts and minds of employees no matter where they reside in the organization. Employees are selected based on their likelihood of conforming to norms, which then are communicated through training manuals and other formal means. In addition, rules for coordination and control area are communicated via extensive modeling by both workers and managers and in discussions of "the way we do things" during the everyday life of the organization (Ouchi, 1980). There are strong expectations, and attention is given to designing systems that communicate these norms on an everyday basis. Written rules and procedures establish a minimal set of necessary standards from which people can design work routines on an as-needed basis to meet changing work demands. In this way, the clan model tends to be more flexible than the machine model.

Southwest Airlines with its colorful CEO, Herb Kellerher, developed a very successful clan type of model on which highly efficient and effective coordination and control systems have been built. The firm is famous for selecting happy, fun-loving employees who interact well with customers and value high efficiency and high quality of service that continually improves over time. The airline is widely distributed across the US and operates in a disciplined but not bureaucratic fashion. Employees are well versed in a minimal, basic set of guidelines from which they can then make decisions that meet customer needs. The firm insists on high quality standards, and there is also a high degree of consistency that results from formalization of rules and procedures. People work together as a strong community with common values (Gittell, 2003). These common values provide the basis for coordination and control systems.

The success of a clan depends heavily on having leaders who communicate a strong set of norms and values that underlie how work is to be accomplished, and on selecting and training employees who are versed in those norms. At the same time, the people inside the clan don't feel trapped or suppressed. Instead, they are loyal to the organization and work together for high efficiency and effectiveness. The Swedish furniture giant IKEA is another example of an effective use of a clan model for coordination and control. It developed "the IKEA way" of doing business, which consists of a written set of principles for doing business. These are standard throughout the world and strictly enforced, yet there is also managerial and employee freedom to take needed steps to meet customer needs that vary across countries and around the world.

The *mosaic model* for coordination and control tends toward somewhat greater decentralization and less formalization than the clan model, although it remains high on formalization and decentralization relative to the models reviewed earlier. In the mosaic model there is a greater tendency for heterogeneity (rather than similarity) of systems than in the clan model. Coordination and control systems – including the rules that they embed – are not identical throughout the organization. Instead, they vary as a function of the subunit. Again, this is a matter of degree. The company may have one inventory system for all its operations worldwide, but if it is a mosaic, then it does not attempt to have all of its coordination and control systems (e.g., accounting, human resources, performance measurement, knowledge-management systems) standardized throughout the firm. Instead, common standards are minimized, and all remaining standards and methods of monitoring are customized to meet the needs of subunits. To allow effective coordination across the firm as a whole, the organization attempts to keep disparate systems as compatible as possible; the various coordination and control systems are not loose or scattered; instead, they fit together into a meaningful whole, much like a mosaic.

Unilever takes a mosaic approach as it fosters heterogeneity across countries/regions and product lines, yet it integrates its disparate systems with a strong managerial infrastructure of interdependency. Hence there is a holistic quality to the organization – it is more than a collection of cells or business units that operate with their own coordination and control systems.

Using the mosaic model, if the organization decides to change its coordination or control systems in one area of the firm, it is not necessary that the entire firm change its systems too. The mosaic approach allows disparate systems across the enterprise to change much like a kaleidoscope. The pieces move together. Although the change process may appear blurry, it is nonetheless systematic. As you can see, a mosaic model for systems design is difficult to achieve. The approach requires what Powley et al. (2004) described as a dialogic democracy, that is, extensive two-way communication across subunits of the firm to assure that the needs of the whole are met even as the customized coordination and control systems are developed for subunits.

Information systems

In addition to coordination and control, information systems are vital components of the infrastructure of the organization. Whereas coordination and control systems are methods for governing how work is done, information systems are methods for providing meaningful data to decision-makers. We use the term information systems in the broad sense to include all systems that collect, store, and process information within the enterprise. The supplier or user of information systems may be outside the firm (e.g., customers or a government agency), but the systems themselves operate under the control of the organization. Thus, the design of information systems is integral to the larger process of organizational design. Information systems may be computer- or telecommunications-based, but this is not necessary. In fact, person-to-person passing of information is vital to some organizational designs, as we shall see.

Many types of information systems are possible. Which are the most vital for an organization? What types of systems should be the priority? Although many factors can be used to determine the design of an organization's information systems, here we focus on two critical dimensions: the amount of information and the tacit nature of information. Think about an organization's dominant, overall information-processing needs when considering these dimensions. The goal is to design information systems that can optimize an organization's information capacity.

Amount of information is the overall volume of data that an organization must collect, process, and store on a regular basis. To some extent, this dimension is a function of firm size; larger organizations tend to have greater information-processing demands. But amount of information is more closely related to the kind of work that a firm does, and to the design of work tasks (per Chapter 6), than to organizational size. If tasks are repetitive and executed hundreds or thousands of times throughout the day (such as in a large retail chain or a bank), then the information-processing demands are huge. Here we would say that the amount of information that must be processed is large. On the other hand, if tasks are one-time tasks and there are relatively few and they may be general, fragmented or knotty, that is, there is variety in how tasks are done, then the amount of information to be processed is smaller.

Note that a low amount of information to be managed does not imply that information processing is an easy matter! Collecting, processing, and disseminating information in a low-volume setting can be just as difficult as in a high-volume setting. The amount of information has implications for the approach management takes to information systems design, rather than for the degree of difficulty of developing the systems.

The second critical dimension for information systems design is the *tacit nature of information* that is exchanged within the organization. Tacit knowledge is characterized by causal ambiguity and difficulty of codification (Choo, 1998; Polyani, 1966). Tacit information is not readily articulated as a set of facts or rules, and so is difficult to transfer (Sorenson et al., 2004). This is in contrast to explicit knowledge, which can be expressed formally as a system of symbols and facts, and therefore more readily communicated (Nonaka and Takeuchi, 1995). Of course, all organizations must process both tacit and explicit knowledge. The question is which type is more critical to the everyday functioning of the organization; that is, which is more important to executing tasks and getting work done. If exchange of high amounts of tacit information is critical to an organization's everyday work, then its

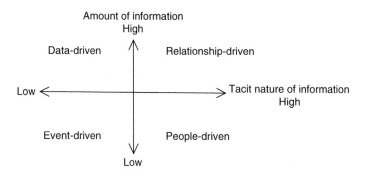

Figure 9.2 Information systems space.

approach to information systems design will be more people- or relationship-based, rather than event- or data-based.

The two dimensions of amount of information and tacit nature of information suggest four general approaches to information systems design. These are summarized in Figure 9.2.

Event-driven

If the overall amount of information processing in a firm is low and the tacit nature of information is low, then the information systems of the firm can be designed using an *event-driven* model. This means that systems are designed to process information associated with specific occasions or results as they occur. Event-driven systems are reactive to needs as they arise. Examples of event-driven systems are factual meetings, announcements, and communication of directives from one location in the firm (usually a manager or CEO) to another. Email and telephone calls communication, or other systems, can also be event-driven. Systems are set up to communicate information as needs arrive, with information flowing from the source to the destination, hopefully in the smoothest possible way and with maximum clarity.

Event-driven systems require little forethought or planning to implement, except for purchasing and installing the technologies (e.g., an email system) that provide the necessary conduits for passing information and alerting employees to be responsive to information that flows through the system. Investment in sophisticated search and retrieval systems is not a priority, since the amount of information to be processed is relatively low, and the primary objective of systems design is to pass information on on an as-needed basis.

Use of systems for sophisticated data analysis, interpretation, or long-term planning is not a priority. So long as the tacit nature of information is low (that is, the meaning of information is clear and readily interpretable), event-based systems do not present a problem for the organization. Event-driven systems make sense in small, reactive organizations.

Data-driven

As the amount of information to be processed increases, information systems design should become more data-driven. Systems can no longer be based on a reactive model and instead require ongoing capture, analysis, and transfer of vital information. The *data-driven* approach is appropriate for organizations that must process high volumes of information, and do so in a systematic and intelligent manner in order to increase the firm's information-processing capacity. The data-driven approach assumes that information is codifiable, that is, it can be readily captured and stored. The low tacit nature of information is key to the efficiency of the data-driven approach. Data-driven information systems increase the information processing in the firm by bringing timely, detailed information to decision makers, who can then act quickly and precisely to meet organizational goals.

If a firm adopts a data-driven model for information systems, then it can expect to invest in large transaction-based systems, databases, and enterprise-wide systems such as SAP or PeopleSoft. These types of systems are critical to the data-driven organizational design as they make it possible to manage huge amounts of information for purposes of inventory management, performance measurement, forecasting, quality control, and so on. The data-driven approach goes along with the machine-based model for developing the firm's coordination and control infrastructure.

People-driven

Firms that process highly tacit information that is relatively low in volume should rely on a people-driven model for information systems design. A *people-driven* approach emphasizes capture, processing, and transfer of data that is embedded in the minds and actions of people. It presumes that the vital information of the organization is difficult to codify in a routine way, and therefore the priority of systems should be either to bring people together face-to-face so that they can share tacit knowledge, or to use computer- or telecommunications-based systems that readily support subtle, rich knowledge transfer. Face-to-face meetings are a classic type of information system for sharing of tacit knowledge. If face-to-face meetings are not possible, then intense phone conversations can suffice, or decision-support systems and other rich online media, such as video conferencing, are options for information systems.

Although you may not think of meetings or conferences as information systems, they are just that – if they are thoughtfully designed with effective knowledge transfer in mind. Organizations can take systematic steps to design people-based information systems, and they should do so if the amount of information to be exchanged is not extremely high and the tacit nature of the information to be shared makes structured, routine types of systems inappropriate or impossible to implement.

People-driven systems work well so long as the volume of information to be exchanged is not too high. Consider a company that has developed a new venture in a line of business that is unfamiliar to most involved, such as the recent acquisition of the IBM PC product line by the Lenovo Group, a Chinese company. As Lenovo and IBM undertake their merger, the newness of the business model and its setting require exchange of information that is not readily processed through a database, simple announcements, or other standard information systems. Knowledge of new markets, products, culture, and the creation of new ways of doing business together in a novel context demand many one-to-one personal exchanges among members of both organizations. Online discussion groups and other unstructured ways of exchanging ideas and designing methods of working together as a new company are needed. A people-driven approach to information systems design is appropriate in the formative stages of this new organization.

The people-driven approach makes sense wherever the tacit and relatively unique nature of information requires a high degree of interpersonal interaction in order for information to be effectively transmitted. Development of more routine, or standardized, information systems are not worthwhile because information is not readily codifiable and can be expected to change over time. Laboratory organizations and customized consulting are other examples of settings where a people-driven model is appropriate. The people-driven approach fits well with the market model for developing the firm's coordination and control infrastructure.

Relationship-driven

The most complex model for information systems design is also the one with the greatest potential for promoting firm efficiency and effectiveness. The *relationship-driven* approach to information systems design emphasizes capture, processing, and transfer of data that is embedded in the links, or relationships, between people and data. This is an appropriate design model if the overall amount of information to be processed is high and the tacit nature of information is high. Relationship-driven systems integrate hard (codifiable) data with soft (interpretational) data to yield rich results for organizational decision-making.

The most well-known relationship-driven systems today are so-called customer relationship management (CRM) systems. CRM systems capture large, quantifiable data about customers but also provide interactive capabilities so that two salespeople, for example, can exchange unstructured observations or comments about their experiences and implications for meeting new customer needs. Video conferences in which, for example, physicians can talk to one another at a distance while both view and interact with a patient's MRI or CT images, are another example of relationship-driven systems; the physicians may add comments or suggestions to the medical record which are then visible, along with the more quantifiable data, later on in the patient care process.

Relationship-driven systems are complex to develop because they include both data-driven and people-driven elements. Well-designed relationship systems include up-to-date transaction and database information as well as softer, interpretive information that arises as people use the quantifiable data. In this way the systems are not simply "updated" over time but instead continually grow in their knowledge capacity as they are used. Sophisticated searching algorithms and natural language interfaces are important to the ongoing success of relationship-driven systems.

Organizations that process high volumes of information but also highly tacit information cannot rely solely on a machine-based model because too much of the information that they process is non-codifiable. Similarly, they cannot rely exclusively on a people-driven model because, although effective for processing tacit information, the people-driven approach is inefficient when the volume of information to be processed is high. The relationship-driven approach fits well with either the clan or mosaic model for developing the firm's coordination and control infrastructure. If there is a clan form of governance, then the information systems will tend to be similar in design throughout the enterprise. If there is a mosaic form of governance, then the relationship-management model should vary to meet particular subunit needs.

Diagnostic questions

Consider your unit of analysis as a whole in answering these questions. Think in terms of the dominant, driving needs of your organization's work as it pursues its business goals. For each diagnostic question, use a 1 to 5 rating scale to score the organization as follows:

1	2	3	4	5
very low		moderate		very high

1. First, examine the two dimensions in Figure 9.3: formalization and decentralization. Rate your organization in terms of reliance on formalization and decentralization as mechanisms for coordination and control of work. Next, you can categorize the organization's governance approach as: family, machine, market, or clan/mosaic. To begin, answer the diagnostic questions below.[1]

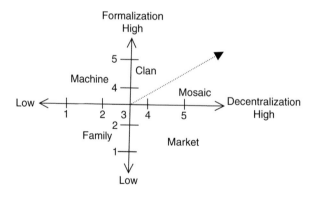

Figure 9.3 Locate your organization in the coordination and control space.

[1] As before, you can average your scores for the items within each question to create an overall score for each design dimension, or you can use the questions as a guide to assign an overall score for each design dimension.

2. Decentralization

To what extent does your organization govern work tasks, people, and processes using a decentralized approach: very little (1) or to a great extent (5)? To answer this question you may think about the following:

a. To what extent are subunit decisions and actions directed by corporate headquarters or another sole authority (1) versus managed independently by the subunits (5)?

b. To what degree does the top management leave control of operational decisions to managers or others in charge of those operations (1)–(5)?

c. How much discretion do subunit managers have in establishing their budgets (1)–(5)?

d. How much discretion do subunit managers have in determining how his or her unit will be evaluated (1)–(5)?

e. How much discretion do subunit managers have over how work exceptions are to be handled (1)–(5)?

3. Formalization

To what extent does your organization use formalized methods of coordination and control: very little (1) or to a great extent (5)? To answer this question you may think about the following:

a. To what extent does the organization rely on rules, codes, or policies to manage how work is done (1)–(5)?

b. Are there precise job descriptions to describe who does what and how (1)–(5)?

c. Are there well-known expectations about what is "correct," "acceptable," or "expected" of employees (1)–(5)?

d. Are there well-known penalties for violating rules or not meeting expectations of on-the-job behavior (1)–(5)?

e. To what extent are employee actions monitored, recorded, and/or provided as feedback to either the workers themselves or to managers (1)–(5)?

You can now locate your firm on Figure 9.3. What is its design model for coordination and control systems?

4. Next, examine the two dimensions in Figure 9.4: tacit nature of information and overall amount of information. Rate the organization in terms of these aspects of information processing. From there, you can

identify its information systems design model: event-driven, data-driven, people-driven, or relationship-driven. To begin, answer the diagnostic questions below.

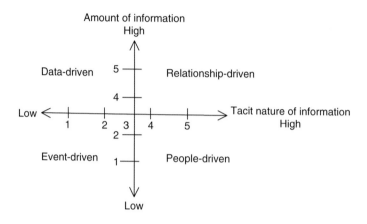

Figure 9.4 Locate your chosen organization in the information systems space.

5. Tacit nature of information

   Think about the kind of knowledge that is most critical to your organization's success in doing its everyday work. Rate your answer to each question using the scale from very little (1) or to a great extent (5).

   a. To what extent is the vital knowledge of the firm codifiable (1) or non-codifiable (5), in the sense that it does not lend itself to being explicitly captured, processed, and stored?

   b. Could most of the important information that is exchanged within the firm be readily recorded on paper or in a computer system (1 = yes, 5 = no)?

   c. Does the information exchanged within the organization require interpretation in order to be meaningful (1 = not much interpretation required, 5 = high interpretation required)?

   d. Is information relatively easy to understand and explain (1), or are there subtleties to understanding the information, requiring specialized experience or expertise to fully "make sense" of the information (5)?

6. Amount of information

   What is the overall volume of data that the organization must collect, process, and store on a regular basis, low or high? To answer this question you may think about the following, answering each question with a rating from very little (1) or to a great extent (5)?

   a. Are most of the organization's work tasks unique (1), or are the work tasks repeated in large volume (5)?

   b. Does execution of work tasks rely on having a relatively small (1) or large (5) amount of data available to the worker or decision maker responsible for the task?

   c. To what extent are there common types of data that can be captured and made useful for many transactions and tasks (1 = low extent, 5 = high extent)?

   You can now locate the organization in Figure 9.4. What is its model for information systems design?

 ## Fit and misfits

What models for coordination, control, and information systems should be used to design an organization's infrastructure? What is a good fit? In Table 9.1, we add the coordination, control, and information-systems models to the goals, strategy, structure, and process and people elements of organizational design. In each of the columns A, B, C, and D, the fit relations can be read vertically from top to bottom.

Table 9.1 shows how the infrastructure of coordination, control, and information systems for a firm should be designed so as to be in alignment with goals, strategy, structure, people and processes. In today's world, there is a tendency for managers to think that infrastructure, especially technology, should be up to date and similar in features and operations across all firms. The popularity of SAP, databases, video conferencing, and the like illustrates this trend. Although these technologies may be useful to any firm, our analysis emphasizes that a thoughtful approach to infrastructure design means taking time to map system priorities to those of the organization's overall design needs. A data-driven approach, for example, is not appropriate for all organizations. An event-driven, people-driven, or relationship approach may be more appropriate. It is useful to

Table 9.1 Fit and misfit to include coordination, control, and information systems

Corresponding quadrant in organizational design space	A	B	C	D	
Information systems	Event-driven	Data-driven	People-driven	Relationship-driven	
Coordination and control	Family	Machine	Market	Clan/Mosaic	
Climate	Group	Internal process	Developmental	Rational goal	
Leadership	Maestro	Manager	Leader	Producer	
People	Shop	Factory	Laboratory	Office	
Task design	Orderly	Complicated	Fragmented	Knotty	
Knowledge exchange	Ad hoc communications	Informated	Cellular	Network	
Geographic distribution	Global	International	Multi-domestic	Transnational	
Organizational complexity	Blob	Tall	Flat	Symmetric	
Configuration	Simple	Functional	Divisional	Matrix	
Environment	Calm	Varied	Locally stormy	Turbulent	
Strategy types	Reactor	Defender	Prospector	Analyzer with innovation	Analyzer without innovation
Organizational goals	Neither	Efficiency	Effectiveness	Efficiency and Effectiveness	

think in terms of first selecting among the coordination and control designs and next among the information systems designs, although these two go hand-in-hand as you design your firm's infrastructure.

If a firm is in column A in terms of goals, strategy, environment, and so on, then coordination and control systems should be designed with a family approach in mind. This means that there is great amount of informality, high centralization of authority and control, a shop-oriented approach to managing people, and a maestro leadership style. The configuration is simple and the business environment is calm, so elaborate coordination and control mechanisms, as well as high-tech information systems, are not necessary. In fact, the formality and high volume of information processing brought on by elaborate systems can distract a firm in column A from smoothly pursuing its goals. The mantra here for infrastructure development should be "keep it simple." The development of the more sophisticated infrastructure can wait until the strategy or the environment demand it. The family approach to coordination and control requires the executive to provide timely and detailed oversight of work and workers. Further, people must be ready to respond to announcements or directives as they are issued. Keeping people informed of what is expected on a regular basis is critical, since automated systems are not available to do this. The column A approach to infrastructure management will be very ineffective if the firm's goals, strategy, environment, configuration, or people and work processes lie in any other column. Misfits arise quickly in those cases. So, if a firm is currently using a family, event-driven approach to managing infrastructure, but its goals or other key design attributes lie in another column, then the firm should move to develop a more sophisticated infrastructure.

Moving to column B, we see that a machine-based model for coordination and control is consistent with a data-driven approach to information systems design, and these go along with a factory model of people management, a complicated task design, use of a manager style of leadership, and development of an internal process climate. The successful firm in column B values efficiency, is functional and tall in configuration, adopts a defender strategy, and manages knowledge exchange using an intelligent, informated approach. The information-processing capacity in column B is considerably higher than in column A, assuming the machine- and data-driven approaches to infrastructure development are implemented and all other design dimensions are in alignment (that is, they fall together within column B). The more complex data-driven approach to information systems design is necessary in order to support the high information-processing needs of the column B firm. Detailed job descriptions, policy statements, and methods for executing work tasks are critical, as are sophisticated monitoring and control systems. The commensurate climate has high tension with less trust and leadership credibility; but productivity and efficiency will tend to be high so long as new innovations are not needed on a regular basis.

If firm goals require greater innovation due to a locally stormy business environment and/or task designs are fragmented and the firm is arranged in a divisional or multi-domestic structure, then the organization's infrastructure cannot be as standardized as it is in column B. Instead, a column C approach is more appropriate. Firms in column C pursue innovation and foster autonomy of subunits, so variety in the infrastructure across subunits is needed along with people-based information systems that support high amounts of tacit knowledge sharing. Standardization of infrastructure is minimized in favor of more customized approaches to coordination, control, and information processing across subunits. This is a market-based model of coordination and control, and it is less efficient than the machine approach, but it is more likely to meet the firm's goals for continual innovation in the face of a locally stormy environment. As noted in earlier chapters, column C firms do best if top management adopts a leader style, a developmental climate, and a laboratory approach to managing people. The executive lets others make decisions and tolerates inconsistency in coordination and control infrastructure but accepts the entailed uncertainty and high coordination cost for the organization as a whole. The climate in column C has low tension and a high readiness for change. The downside, of course, is that the infrastructure within column C is not conducive to huge volumes of information processing. If both high volumes of information and high amounts of tacit information sharing are desired, then the firm should look to move to the column D approach to infrastructure design.

For column D, the firm has a leadership style that acts as a producer, a rational goal climate, a symmetric, matrix configuration, a turbulent environment, an analyzer strategy, and pursuit of the dual goals of efficiency and effectiveness. Infrastructure development for column D is undoubtedly the most difficult and requires continual updating and adjustment in order to be successful. Both people and data form the basis of information systems design, and the firm infrastructure combines high amounts of subunit autonomy with high amounts of formalization in control over people and work processes. The firm in column D is simultaneously disciplined and highly innovative. Consequently, design of coordination and control systems must be done with extreme care, and they must be continually improved and nurtured in order to remain supportive of the firm's information-processing needs. Flexibility is assured by either relying on developing a cooperative, clan mentality among employees, in which people tolerate high formalization while at the same time coordinating based on professional sharing of tacit knowledge, or developing multiple but compatible methods of coordination and control across subunits, with care taken to be sure that systems fit together across the firm into a meaningful mosaic. The clan and mosaic models allow the diverse subunits of the organization in column D to act in concert despite high volumes of information sharing and high decentralization of managerial control.

As we have observed before, the firm in column D relies on a producer leadership style in which top management delegates decision-making but also controls uncertainty, e.g., through a high degree of formalization. The climate has high tension but also has readiness for change. The organization in this column is performance-oriented, aiming to achieve both efficiency and effectiveness. It is a demanding place to work and operates with a high degree of professionalism and continual capture and sharing of tacit knowledge. Formalization of rules is dynamic, which means that rules are strong yet changeable as environmental conditions require the organization to respond to or anticipate changes. The relationship between formalization and decentralization in a turbulent environment is delicate. A turbulent environment may require that a low formalization is needed. In that case a high degree of centralization may be required (Jensen et al., 2010). If the turbulent environment turns into an environment that threatens the life of the organization, a highly centralized organization with full top management control is required until the environment is less threatening. Some organizations operate with different organization design for different organizational situations. Some military organizations have one design for operation during peace and another in combat situations.

If your chosen firm is located in different columns based upon your answers to the diagnostic questions in this chapter, then you should think about what you might do to bring your organization into fit in the column that meets your goals.

Summary

Coordination, control, and information systems collectively provide pathways for information sharing in the firm. Detailed design of these systems requires specification of how work is to be done, who is to do it, how monitoring and feedback will be managed, what information is to be captured, stored, and processed, how knowledge is to be shared, and so on. Job descriptions, inventory management systems, customer relationship systems, databases, meetings, rich media systems, Internet portals, and many other types of systems can be implemented as part of an organization's infrastructure for coordination, control, and information processing. This chapter has provided basic approaches, or models, for deciding design priorities and selecting among the many possible systems that might be implemented. We outlined two critical dimensions for the design of coordination and control systems and two critical dimensions for information systems design. Applying these dimensions to your firm, you should take steps to assure that the basic models that underlie the firm's infrastructure are in alignment with other aspects of its organizational design.

Glossary

Amount of information: overall volume of data that the organization must collect, process, and store on a regular basis.

Centralization: the degree to which coordination and control of the organization's work are managed by a core person or level of the organization, usually corporate headquarters.

Clan model: design of coordination and control systems that rely on high formalization, especially strong behavioral norms, and high decentralization; there is a greater tendency for homogeneity (rather than variety) of systems than in the mosaic model.

Control systems: methods for assuring quality and efficiency of information flow between the highest and lowest levels of the firm.

Coordination systems: methods for linking together the otherwise disparate elements of an organization's structure and supporting flexibility and adaptiveness within and across departmental or divisional boundaries.

Coordination and control systems: systems that integrate the various parts of the organization to support goal achievement and responsiveness to the environment or task demands.

Data-driven systems: an information-systems design approach that emphasizes capture, processing, and transfer of high volumes of data that is explicit in nature; an appropriate design model if the overall amount of information processing in the firm is high and the tacit nature of information is low.

Decentralization: the degree to which responsibility for coordination and control lies in the subunits of the firm and individual managers, rather than corporate headquarters or one specific level of the hierarchy.

Event-driven systems: an information systems design approach that emphasizes transfer of meaningful data associated with specific occasions or results as they occur; an appropriate design model if the overall amount of information processing in the firm is low and the tacit nature of information is low.

Family model: design of coordination and control systems that rely on informal and centralized means of control.

Formalization: the degree to which the organization specifies a set of rules or codes to govern how work is done.

Information system: methods for providing meaningful data to decision makers both vertically and horizontally in the organization; information systems may be computer-based, but this is not necessary.

Machine model: design of coordination and control systems that rely on formal and centralized means of control.

Market model: design of coordination and control systems that rely on informal and decentralized means of control.

Mosaic model: design of coordination and control systems that rely on high formalization and high decentralization; there is a greater tendency for heterogeneity (rather than similarity) of systems than in the clan model.

Organizational infrastructure: the collection of coordination, control, and information systems that provide pathways for information sharing in the firm.

People-driven systems: an information-systems design approach that emphasizes capture, processing, and transfer of data that is embedded in the minds and actions of people and so is difficult to codify in a routine way; an appropriate design model if the overall amount of information to be processed is low and the tacit nature of information is high.

Relationship-driven systems: an information-systems design approach that emphasizes capture, processing, and transfer of data that is embedded in the links, or relationships, between people and data; an appropriate design model if the overall amount of information to be processed is high and the tacit nature of information is high.

Tacit nature of information: the degree to which the critical information of the organization is causally ambiguous, difficult to codify, and so is difficult to transfer from one person or locale to another.

10 Incentives

Introduction

In the previous chapters, you began with goals and analyzed your chosen organization (unit of analysis) with respect to strategy, environment, configuration, task design, people, leadership, climate, coordination and control, and information systems. Now we add another vital component to the design of the firm: what incentives do you give to individuals and groups so that they make decisions and take actions that fit well with the other design characteristics and help to meet organizational goals? Incentives support the firm's infrastructure of coordination, control, and information systems, and thus help to assure that work tasks are executed and organizational goals can be achieved. Design of incentives goes hand-in-hand with all the other components of organizational design.

What do we mean by incentives? *Incentives* are means or instruments designed to encourage certain actions or behavior on the part of employees, or groups of employees (e.g., subunits of employees). Incentives are not just the objective set of rewards that the firm offers but also the way people interpret the rewards and act upon the rewards that the firm provides. Monetary rewards in the form of salaries, wages, and benefits are incentives, but they are not the only ones. People respond to praise, acceptance, belongingness, and recognition of self worth. A pat on the back as well as a paycheck can be an incentive. A promotion or title can be an incentive. In the end, the incentives must be internalized by people so that they accept the incentives, consider the incentives to be fair, and are motivated to do well. Roughly, an incentive will be viewed as fair if people think the reward is reasonable for the level of effort, and also if the reward is consistent with the rewards offered to other individuals or groups nearby.

The alignment of incentives with organizational goals can be problematic and many organizations get it wrong. In his famous paper entitled, "On the Folly of Rewarding A while Hoping for B," Kerr (1975) described many situations in which organizations misalign incentives, desired behavior, and outcomes. A common example is, as an executive, you reward what you can measure, not what you want to achieve. Executives do this when they hope for team work while rewarding individual performance. As another example, consider a company that is trying to be fair to its employees in a downturn and so devises a scheme whereby the employees get six months' pay if fired, but nothing if they leave voluntarily. In such a situation employees will begin to work in such a way so as to be fired. The intention to be very fair becomes an incentive for poor work and shirking.[1] These are unintended consequences of good intentions on the part of management. A heuristic you can use to help guard against the folly of rewarding B while hoping for A is to put yourself in the position of the employee and think about all of the things you might do in response to an incentive offered by the organization – make a list. For the situation described above, it seems reasonable to anticipate that some employees, though not all, would become poor performers in order to be fired. Being fired can be in the individual's self-interest, but it is not in the firm's best interest.

A traditional view of incentive design has taken a control perspective, that is, designing incentives so that they control either the behavior of employees or the results of what managers or employees do (i.e., how they make decisions or what actions they take). The distinction between controlling behavior and observing results is fundamental (Stinchcome, 1965). Controlling behavior involves monitoring the individual, i.e., how work is done. Controlling results involves monitoring the outcomes once work is completed. One reason for making the distinction between controlling behavior and controlling results is that it can be difficult, if not impossible, to see what the employees actually do from a

---

[1] For our executive MBA classes, we ask each student to describe an incentive situation where the firm is "Hoping for A, while rewarding B." The examples are easy to find. They can be categorized as: reward sales, when profit is the goal; reward what is easy to measure (in numbers), not what is important; reward what is measured when the real objectives are costly to measure; reward a false equity of treating everyone the same when differential results are desired and known; a false sense of fairness; executive fear of assigning differences. In the best situations, the incentive scheme supports the firm's goals; in the worst situation, it drives the individuals in the opposite direction of the desired behavior.

behavior or process perspective. In a virtual organization the employees may be far apart and it does not make sense to try to control the actual behavior. Further, it may not be possible to know what a person is doing by observation. For example, it is difficult to know if an individual is thinking deeply on a firm problem or loafing. For decades, it has been a norm to compensate the sales force on the road by awarding an individual bonus, as it is difficult to control their effort directly.

In other situations it may not be clear what the appropriate behavior is. The employee may have better information or better skills to make a decision or take an action, so he or she can judge better with regard to what to do. Here, to assure goal achievement, the control of the outcome is much better. The worker has better information and knowledge regarding behavior, so management bases rewards on outcomes instead.

You can influence the activities of the employees or subunits in an organization in basically three ways: you can tell them what to do; you can have a set of behavioral rules that specify what they should do in certain situations; and/or you can create an incentive system that indirectly influences your employees to do what you want them to do. These three ways of controlling the activities of the employees should be seen as a package. For example, there may be a rule that says what to do and an incentive system whereby the employees are rewarded if they follow the rule well. There may also be a central decision authority that tells the employees which set of rules to invoke in a particular situation. Or the employees can be given the freedom to make decisions about how to do their job, but their performance is evaluated on the basis of the outcome on which you are rewarded.

One further complication is that the employees may not determine the outcomes of their work. The uncontrolled environment could be a major factor in determining the outcome as well as the employee's decisions and actions. For an uncertain environment you have to sort out how much of the outcome is based on the employees' performance and how much is the result of uncontrollable events. Were the employees working hard or just lucky? Thus, an important issue is who bears the risk – the individual or the organization? Results-based incentives put the risk on the employee (or subunit) and thus may include elements outside the control of people in the organization. This is the basis for agency theory where the principal "gives" some of the risk to the agent, who has more, though imperfect, information (Kowtha, 1997). Agents are rewarded based on results, even though some of those results are outside of their control. Corporate shareholders who evaluate management based on stock value, or owners of sports teams who evaluate coaches based on their winning records (regardless of injuries or the intensity of competition) are examples.

For an incentive based on behavior (rather than outcome), employees bear no risk on the results, and thus the organization assumes the business risk. People are not responsible for bad decisions, bad luck, or unforeseen events in the environment that they cannot control. As an example, soldiers might be rewarded based on following military protocol and executing the orders of their superiors, regardless of whether their actions lead to winning one or another particular battle. Employees in a call center might be rewarded for the number of calls they process and the quality with which they treat customers, regardless of sales actually made. Of course, the illustration above is in a relative sense. If the organization fails for an extended period of time, it will disappear and the individual will lose employment, so the individual always bears some risk.

Why would an individual assume some of the risk? One reason could be that the amount of compensation is higher than it would otherwise be. Top managers are given large compensation packages in high-risk firms for this reason. Also, people vary in their risk preferences, and one's cultural background may affect willingness to take risks. So it may be appropriate to let some employees or business units assume more risk than others. For example, younger workers or entrepreneurs may prefer large risks, and research and product development departments may prefer large risks relative to other departments.

The level of employee education is an important element that can help to estimate whether an individual is willing to assume some risk (Kowtha, 1997). In general, the higher the skill level, the more risk the individual is likely to assume – perhaps due to greater understanding of the risk. If an individual is to assume some risk, he or she should have the necessary skills and knowledge to understand and adapt to the uncertainty. Also, the individual should be given authority to make the appropriate decisions in the course of carrying out his or her work tasks (Kowtha, 1997). This introduces the relationship between the degree of delegation and the design of the incentives. If decisions are delegated, the incentives should be aligned so that they support the organization's goals of efficiency and effectiveness.

There is little doubt that incentives affect employee behavior. This notion is supported by research in psychology and economics (Gibbons, 1998), as well as in everyday observations. The individual in the organization is affected by the particular incentives that the organization offers. The same is true for groups or other subunits. If people are provided incentives to work in concert with others, versus to work independently, behavior will be affected accordingly. Do we do it alone, or do we work in concert with other groups or subunits to achieve organizational goals? The answer depends on the design of the incentive system (Burton and Obel, 1988; Alonso et al., 2008).

In relation to organizational design, we examine incentives from a strategic organizational design point of view. This means that we look at the basic principles for designing specific incentive systems for the groups or individuals that make up the unit of analysis and the nature of their activities in the organization. We will not discuss the details of setting up a specific incentive contract or plan for a particular individual or subunit. The incentives may be related to monetary compensation or other types of rewards. Many issues have to be taken into account when the incentive system is designed.

From the above discussion we can see that a fundamental design choice is whether to base incentives on behavior or results. This design dimension is the *basis of evaluation* of the work. This way of looking at incentives goes back to the sixties. A survey of some of the theoretical issues related to this view can be found in Kowtha (1997). At one extreme, *behavioral* incentives focus on procedures: compliance with standards, rules, and routines. At the other extreme, *results* incentives focus on outcomes, i.e., the effectiveness of meeting the goals of the organization. An important issue is whether behavior (i.e., procedures) or results (i.e., outcomes) can be monitored and evaluated and whether the monitoring is possible on an individual or a group basis. Information is always costly, and the measurement of activities related to incentives – whether individual or group – is costly. The choice of controlling behavior versus results has also been analyzed from a transaction cost view. Hennart (1993) argues that the choice of controlling behavior or results is not a pure choice; the optimal form is a mixture of the two. A mixture of the two is often the norm.

A second fundamental design choice is the *target of incentives*, that is, whether to base incentives on individual or group work performance. Whether work incentives are individual or group-based depends on your unit of analysis. If your unit of analysis is a team, for example, then you can design incentives for the individual team members, or you can design incentives for the team as a whole. In the latter case, you could reward the team based on its collective behavior or results, rather than on the results or behavior of any one person. If your unit of analysis is a large organization with a collection of divisions or business units, then you could reward each division or subunit

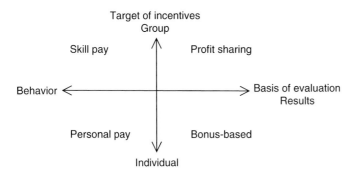

Figure 10.1 The incentive system design space.

based on its behavior or results (*individual*), or you could reward the divisions based on their collective (*group*) behavior or results. Individual and group represent two different targets in the design of incentive systems.

Using the two dimensions of incentive system design, basis of evaluation, and target of incentives, we can outline a typology of four distinct types of incentive systems as shown in Figure 10.1: *personal pay, skill pay, bonus-based*, and *profit-sharing*. This typology provides the overall principles on which the incentive system for an organization should be designed.

We will now discuss each of the four basic types of incentive systems: personal pay, skill pay, bonus-based, and profit-sharing.

Personal pay

Personal pay is particular to the individual people or subunits within the unit of analysis and their formal or psychological contract with the employer. A personal pay approach to incentive design is based on the behavior of the individual, as shown in the lower left quadrant of Figure 10.1. It is an agreement between the individual and the boss or organization.

The personal pay approach does not emphasize results or outcomes, but instead emphasizes individual compliance with rules or directives. There may be some evaluation based on performance (such as an occasional bonus), but this is not the dominant concern. Instead, rewards are designed with "doing work the right way" in mind. Usually, personal pay-based systems take the form of an incentive agreement or contract whereby employee behavior is measured in terms of people showing up at a particular time and then working for a number of hours. The measurement of the behavior is often done by "clocking in" and "clocking out." There may be job descriptions with particular rules that the individual has to follow. Within the rules given, the individual follows the directions of the boss and does things as requested. The actual pay is negotiated, and there can be significant differences between persons or groups doing the same job. There is a focus neither on efficiency nor on effectiveness, as the most important thing for employees is to follow rules or directives. The effectiveness and efficiency of such a reward system requires that the environment does not change too often and that the organization has chosen the right rules to follow. Further, to some degree this approach assumes that the people being evaluated have the kind of personality that can accept and function within such a reward system. Dynamic risk seekers will have a difficult time with such incentives. Further, the actual pay level will tend to be lower than that in other incentive systems as it is the organization or firm that assumes all the risk.

Skill pay

Skill-based pay is perhaps the most widely used type of incentive system in the modern world. It is the basis for pay in most organizations, whether private firms or governmental bureaucracies. Within this design approach, pay differentials are skill- or position-based rather than results-based. The salaries, or wages for a normal week, are determined by individual skills or particular position or job in the organization, that is, the group to which the individual belongs. In many organizations, particularly public ones, skill is measured in terms of formal education and seniority, which incorporates the ability to perform certain tasks. Thus, one can receive an increase in one's salary by getting more formal education, staying in the same organization for years, or moving up the ranks while becoming more skilled within the rules of the organization. Although rewards are related to the individual, the pay is based on belonging to a particular group described by seniority, rank, and education – the upper left quadrant of Figure 10.1.

This incentive system is based on the idea that people should utilize the requisite skills and follow job descriptions, rules, and the policies of the organization. The assumption is that it is possible to describe in some detail what the people should do in the course of their everyday work. In modern organizations, these details are often embedded in computer systems that provide information on how to execute tasks and, in turn, monitor the speed and accuracy of work performed. Further, it is assumed that people will accept direction from the organization's authority, usually the hierarchy, on how to do their work.

Bonus-based

We now move to the lower right quadrant in Figure 10.1. Here, contrary to the two categories above, a bonus-based incentive system changes the focus from the behavior to the results – i.e., from process to outcomes. The organizational results can be mapped back to the accountable party, who then is given the bonus. Usually, the bonus is "in addition to" the normal pay as skill-based. However, there are some employees such as salespersons who receive the totality of their compensation based upon the resulting sales. We consider both of these as bonus-based. The bonus-based view of incentive system design is rooted in a management-by-objectives philosophy. Goals are set for employees (which are derived from the organizational goals), and rewards (e.g., pay, promotions, travel, stock options, etc.) are distributed based on performance which is compared to pre-established targets or goals. It could be a sales or production target, but it could also be the outcome of an organizational unit (e.g., business unit profit). The use of results-based incentives is appropriate if the organization has the ability to clearly link the performance and outcome to behavior. Some uncertainty in this link is acceptable, so long as people generally view the behavior–outcome link to be fair and largely under their control.

An example of such bonus-based incentive scheme is when a top manager's salary is dependent on the profit of the organization or, if it is a public traded company, on the stock-value. The idea here is to align the incentives of the top manager with the owners, such that decisions are taken to increase the value of the company. Such an incentive approach has been highly recommended by many stock analysts, but there are also many unwanted side effects of these schemes. They may trigger unethical or even illegal behavior on the part of executives anxious to get the expected results when results do not come out as desired. There can also be a tendency to withhold information – hiding bad news – from superiors providing rewards. Thus, when you design an incentive scheme for an organization, it is important to not only consider the results you want from employees but also to anticipate negative side effects that might occur if the scheme is implemented (Hennart, 1993).

Bonus-based incentives can also be used in informal and short-term relation-ships, such as day work for unskilled labor or compensation of skilled individuals engaged in specialized tasks (e.g., project consulting or repairing high technology equipment). For the unskilled individual, the boss may give very detailed directions. But for high-skilled workers, the request may be as simple as "It does not work, fix it," and the employees are compensated if fixes are made. Contract lawyers might be paid based on winning litigation. Real estate agents or brokers might be paid on closing important sales deals. In the consulting business there are "no cure – no pay" contracts. In either situation, the relationship is individualized and customized to meet the needs of the organization. Relationships may be long-term, as in long-term IT outsourcing contracts in which service-level agreements determine compensation level, but bonus-based systems more often are short-term focused and linked to a particular task.

The advantage of a bonus-based incentive system is its flexibility for the organization. First, the organization can ask the individual to do whatever is needed to be done. Further, bonus-based requests can be created by the organization on an ongoing basis and little planning is required. Second, the bonus aspect of the contract normally does not have a long-term commitment by the organization. Thus, the organization can change its requests on short notice, terminate the relationship, or renegotiate the bonus aspect of the contract. Such relationships were common in the old days for manual work. In Denmark today, it only exists for the people who work in the harbors loading and unloading ships. However, it is coming back for a number of freelance workers, e.g., workers in virtual networks without long-term contracts, call-center workers, and some factory workers. For the individual, the relationship provides some freedom but is less desirable in the sense that there is little security in the relationship and the organization can be quite arbitrary in creating and terminating incentives. Cisco, the maker of network routers, has used bonus-based pay to increase productivity of router assembly groups during periods of peak demand. The incentives then are removed during periods of low customer demand (with skill-based pay remaining as the base pay for the unit). Jack Welch, CEO of GE for many years, told his business units that they had to be top-performing in their respective business, or he would sell them off. Incentives were tied to results, along with the threat of breaking off the relationship if results did not meet expectations.

To summarize, bonus-based incentives are related to contractual relationships between the individual and the firm, and they can take many different forms in today's modern organization.

Profit-sharing

The fourth category in the upper right quadrant of Figure 10.1 is profit-sharing, which is group-based, either among a group of individuals or a collection of subunits. The basic idea is similar to bonus-based incentives that tie compensation to results rather than behavior. People are rewarded on the basis of effective collaboration with others to yield high performance on the part of the group. Profit-sharing is not only giving a fixed bonus to the unit of analysis, but also a share in the profits (revenue less costs) to all members of the unit. As such it is more group-based than individual-based. The group could be a team, a division, department, or other subunit; it could also be the total organization – the firm. The idea behind a profit-sharing incentive system is that it should enhance group performance in a developmental mode where it is not possible to anticipate or control the actual outcome by controlling behavior. For the profit-sharing scheme to work, people should feel that individual performance can make a difference for the group outcome. The task itself must depend upon the joint efforts of everyone in the target group. The profit-sharing incentive system is appropriate when results are based on different individuals coordinating their skills and knowledge, and where excellent individual performance is not sufficient to yield high group performance. In other words, this incentive system presumes interdependency among the work of the individuals who make up the group that is the target.

Team-based sports illustrate how this type of incentive system can be beneficial. Successful teams require not only highly talented players but also effective collaboration among teammates to yield high performance on the part of the group. Michael Jordan may have been the best National Basketball Association player in his time, but that was not enough to ensure top performance by the Washington Warriors. In a similar way, teams, departments, or other subunits within your firm may depend on not only excellent human resource talent but also high group performance for maximum effectiveness. Whole Foods, a large US gourmet grocery chain, divides its stores and the departments within them (meats, fish, dairy, prepared foods, etc.) into profit centers that receive rewards on a regular basis for P/L performance at both the store and departmental levels.

The smaller the target group the more likely the profit-sharing scheme will have the anticipated effect. If the firm is large then profit-sharing based on the total outcome of the organization is less likely to be effective, since individuals cannot see the effect of their efforts on the organizational performance. A so-called free rider problem can result, with some people relying on the skills and success of others to carry the group to success. On the other hand, the profit-sharing approach can be very effective if people believe their contributions to group efforts "matter," so they are committed to working together with colleagues, and they view the incentive scheme to be fair.

Diagnostic questions

The above four categories are prototype incentive schemes. Often, firms design incentive systems with a combination of approaches, such as a behavior-based incentive program that is augmented somewhat with results-based incentives. This yields a lower risk for the individual, but the basic philosophy is the focus on results. So the important issue from an organization design perspective is to establish the driving philosophy. From there you can determine the specifics of the incentive scheme for your organization.

Now it is time to look at your unit of analysis and determine where your chosen organization is located in Figure 10.2 and where you would like it to be located.

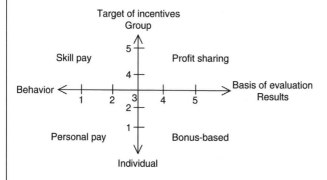

Figure 10.2 Locate your organization in the incentive scheme design space.

1. What is your unit of analysis that you chose in Chapter 1 and have used throughout our step-by-step process? Use this unit of analysis as the organization when answering the questions below.

   The questions below will help you locate your organization on the behavior–results and individual–group dimensions. For each question use a 1 to 5 rating scale to score the organization as follows:

1	2	3	4	5
very low		moderate		very high

2. To what degree are results-based incentives used in your organization (1)–(5)? To help you answer this question you may consider the following:

   a. Are people rewarded using a fixed salary or hourly/daily wage (1), or are they rewarded based solely on the quality/quantity of their work output (5)?

   b. To what degree are salaries or other rewards based on the skills, experiences, on-the-job efforts, or cooperativeness of the employee (1), versus the quantity or quality of their work results (5)?

   c. In evaluating people for promotions, benefits, or other rewards, whether tangible or intangible, does management emphasize how work is done (1) or the results of the work (5)?

3. To what degree are group-based incentives used in the organization (1)–(5)?

   To help you answer this question you may consider the following:

   a. Do the activities in your organization require collaboration by individuals (1) or can they be done by a group (5)?

   b. To what extent are teams compensated based only on individual performance (1) versus performance as an organization (5)?

   c. In evaluating people for promotions, benefits, or other rewards, whether tangible or intangible, does management emphasize the individual's work (1) or the total organization's (unit of analysis) work (5)?

4. Now with the values of behavior–results and individual–group dimensions, locate your chosen organization on the graph. What is its incentive scheme?

Fit and misfits

Table 10.1 shows the fit and misfit relations for incentive scheme design relative to the other aspects of organizational design that we have considered in our step-by-step approach. Again the columns represent fit with the design dimensions. Misfits occur if the organizational design elements do not all fall within the same column. The four columns correspond to the four main quadrants of the organizational design space.

The personal pay approach in column A fits well with the simple configuration where the boss can change tasks quickly. Employees are paid basically for being there and doing what they are instructed to do. This incentive scheme works well if there are not a lot of information-processing demands for the organization, such as in a calm environment or for a reactor strategy. The personal pay approach is focused neither on efficiency nor effectiveness. It will not work well in situations with few rules and a high degree of decentralization, which will be required in non-static environments with a prospector strategy.

The skill-based incentive system in column B fits well with a bureaucracy or machine type of organization with a high degree of specialization that can form the basis for group-based incentives. With a focus on skills, the desire is to obtain efficiency to defend the organization's position. This incentive approach works well in stable environments and can handle a great deal of complexity both in the environment and in the organization. "What to do" is based on a set of rules and standardized behavior. The skills are often associated with a high degree of specialization that comes with training and experience. This fits with situations with long periods of stability, job specialization, and a high degree of formalization. Thus, this incentive structure fits an organization with a relatively stable environment, a defender strategy, and a high degree of specialization in functional configuration. A machine approach to coordination and control, complemented with a data-driven approach to information-systems design, will serve to reinforce the success of the skill-based incentive system. Such an incentive system is an integral part of a bureaucracy. Here the individual runs no risk *vis-à-vis* the actual outcome of the organization. This could also be the reason why such a system is often the preferred incentive structure in organizations where it may be difficult to specify what the outcome is (as is the case in many public organizations).

The skill-based incentive approach is a misfit with a prospector strategy in stormy environments with a focus on product innovation and a quick reaction

Table 10.1 Fit and misfit table for incentive alignments

Corresponding quadrant in organizational design space	A	B	C	D	
Incentives	Personal pay	Skill pay	Bonus-based	Profit-sharing	
Information systems	Event-driven	Data-driven	People-driven	Relationship-driven	
Coordination and control	Family	Machine	Market	Clan/Mosaic	
Organizational climate	Group	Internal process	Develop-mental	Rational goal	
Leadership	Maestro	Manager	Leader	Producer	
People	Shop	Factory	Laboratory	Office	
Task design	Orderly	Complicated	Fragmented	Knotty	
Knowledge exchange	Ad hoc communi-cations	Informated	Cellular	Network	
Geographic distribution	Global	International	Multi-domestic	Transnational	
Organizational complexity	Blob	Tall	Flat	Symmetric	
Configuration	Simple	Functional	Divisional	Matrix	
Environment	Calm	Varied	Locally stormy	Turbulent	
Strategy types	Reactor	Defender	Prospector	Analyzer with innovation	Analyzer without innovation
Dimensions of strategy	Neither	Exploit	Explore	Exploit	Explore
Organizational goals	Neither	Efficiency	Effectiveness	Efficiency and Effectiveness	

to changes in, for example, customer requirements. In such situations a results-based incentive is preferable. The skill-based incentive system is often one part of an incentive structure that is then topped off with a results-based part (such as bonuses).

The bonus incentive system in column C requires that people are willing to assume the risk where the reward will depend on some issues beyond their control. Usually such people like to understand the risk they are taking. Depending on the situation, this may mean that the skill level of people involved in this incentive system is relatively high and/or the personality or cultural expectations of people are such that they accept risk taking. The bonus incentive system fits well with a developmental climate that has low tension and a low resistance to change. The market style of coordination and control, along with people-based information systems, serves to reinforce the success of the bonus system. A locally stormy environment calls for fast response to novel solutions; in that case you may not have the appropriate information at the top level. Thus you need to delegate. Once you delegate, more incentives have to be based on results rather than behavior (Nagar, 2002). In this way, the bonus-based incentive system fits well with a prospector strategy in a divisional or cellular configuration with a high degree of decentralization for the locally stormy environment.

The profit-sharing incentive scheme in column D works well in a matrix or transnational organization where there is an emphasis on coordination among the people in the organization to achieve successful projects with limited resources. It is also a good fit with an analyzer strategy in a turbulent environment as well as a rational goal climate which strives for change with a cooperative spirit and high tension. Along with the clan or mosaic approach to coordination and control, a leadership style with controlled delegation, and relationship-based information systems, the profit-sharing incentive approach is part of the cultural glue that holds the organization together, integrating disparate subunits that confront a turbulent environment.

Some firm outcomes are more sensitive to incentive schemes than others, and thus the design of incentive schemes is more important for the former. For example, the divisional configuration is rather insensitive to a behavior- versus a results-based incentive system. On the other hand, a functional configuration is very sensitive to choice of incentive system. To introduce a results-based incentive system for a departmental outcome in a functional structure will introduce a negative competition that most likely will destroy the required cooperation between the departments (Burton and Obel, 1988). It may seem like a good idea to put the department on a profit scheme, but it can lead to conflict and poor firm performance if not managed such that the other organizational design components fit with such an approach.

To get an incentive system to provide the behavior you want, the individual must accept it. People must perceive it as motivating. Further, it must be related to dimensions that you want the incentives to affect. Here you must remember that incentives affect the other organization dimensions that are not a part of the incentive system. If the pay is based on volume but not on quality, then you get volume, but not necessarily quality. Thus, there are often undesired consequences of an incentive scheme. As a heuristic, it is a good test to ask the question: what might I do in this situation? Some possibilities are likely to be desired, whereas others are not. Hoping for A while rewarding B is a frequent mistake.

In the long run the various dimensions in the step-by-step model may influence each other. The equity question is very important as an incentive scheme that is seen by people as being unfair will affect the climate and may weaken the coordination and control infrastructure. From the theory of motivation we have a simple model which says employees compare their compensation to a peer group and that the comparison has to be viewed as fair. If not, it will very likely create dissatisfaction and thus influence the climate. Perceptions of non-equity may not lower organizational performance (Bartol and Locke, 2000), but they can indirectly lead to misfits in the climate, leadership, and coordination and control aspects of organizational design. In the long run, misfits will tend to reduce organizational efficiency and effectiveness.

Summary

In this chapter we have described the basic incentive dimensions and categories from a strategic organizational diagnosis and design point of view. The focus has been on whether the incentives system has a primary focus on individual versus group and whether the incentives are based on affecting behavior or results. There are numerous examples where the chosen incentive system does not support the firm's goals. We concluded by relating the four basic incentive categories: personal pay, skill pay, bonus-based, and profit-sharing, to the design dimensions presented in the previous chapters. A firm that designs its incentive system so as to align with other aspects of organizational design is more likely to achieve its effectiveness and/or efficiency goals.

Glossary

Basis of evaluation: a fundamental design choice of whether to base incentives on behavior or results.

Behavior evaluation: measure of the adherence to work orders, standards, and/or rules; contrasts with results evaluation.

Bonus-based pay: an incentive system where the rewards are based on results evaluation as executed by an individual.

Group rewards: pay or other rewards which are given to the individual based upon a group's behavior or results.

Incentives: means or instruments designed to encourage certain actions or behavior on the part of employees, or groups of employees.

Individual rewards: pay or other rewards which are given based upon the individual's behavior or results.

Personal pay: an incentive system where the rewards are based on behavior evaluation as executed by an individual.

Profit-sharing: an incentive system where the rewards are based on results evaluation as executed by the group of people within the unit of analysis.

Results evaluation: measure of the outcomes of work or performance; contrasts with a behavior evaluation.

Skill pay: an incentive system where the rewards are based on behavior evaluation as executed by the particular group of people within the unit of analysis.

Target of incentives: a fundamental design choice of whether to base incentives on individual or group work.

Where are you in the step-by-step approach?

STEP 1   GETTING STARTED

(1) Goals

STEP 2   STRATEGY

(2) Strategy
(3) Environment

STEP 3   STRUCTURE

(4) Configuration complexity
(5) Geographic distribution knowledge exchange

STEP 4   PROCESS AND PEOPLE

(6) Task design
(7) People
(8) Leadership and organizational climate

STEP 5   COORDINATION AND CONTROL

(9) Coordination, control, and information systems
(10) Incentives

You have now completed the step-by-step approach to organizational design. By completing all steps, you have taken a holistic approach, rather than a piecemeal approach, to assessing and planning for change in your organization. The holistic approach is more complete and will help the organization confront the change and move toward its goals. In this last step, Step 5, you assessed and planned for change in the firm's coordination and control systems, information systems and incentives. These systems are just as critical as the design components considered in the earlier steps, and it is important that you have completed Step 5 with care to help your firm realize its goals. As previously, these coordination, control, information systems, and incentives should fit with the strategy, structure, processes, and people in the firm. If there are misfits, they should be addressed. Think about and plan for changes that will need to be made to reduce misfits and bring all components of the organizational design into alignment. First, consider alignment within the coordination, control, information systems and incentives, and then alignment among all the design components of the previous steps for a holistic approach. In the next chapter on design dynamics we consider the process of organizational change in more detail.

Applying the step-by-step approach in a dynamic world

11 Design dynamics: managing change

Introduction

In this book, we have developed a step-by-step approach to organizational design, focusing on analysis of an existing organization and identification of misfits among organizational design components. We have outlined a way to diagnose whether a firm has strategic organizational design misfits and considered what you might change to align the basic design components so as to fix misfits and meet organizational goals. In this chapter we address what to change and why. It is a summary of the design process with special attention to the question, what aspects of your organization should be changed? First, we will briefly restate the step-by-step approach and then we will examine the change process in more detail.

Where are you in the step-by-step approach?

If you have systematically followed the steps outlined in Chapters 1 through 10, then you have completed the step-by-step approach for your chosen firm. You have followed each step below by, first, assessing your firm's current organizational design; second, identifying misfits (i.e., detecting components that are not well aligned to meet organizational goals); and, third, deciding what you might do to either bring the design components into the same quadrant of the organizational design space or tolerate the misfits. To summarize, the step-by-step approach is:

Step 1: GETTING STARTED: Define the scope of the organization and assess its goals.

Chapter 1

Step 2: STRATEGY: Review the organization's strategy, and assess the environment in which the organization operates.

Chapters 2 and 3

Step 3: STRUCTURE: Review how the organization is configured in terms of its reporting relationships. Assess how a configuration operates across time and space boundaries.

Chapters 4 and 5

Step 4: PROCESS AND PEOPLE: Review the organization's work and how it executes its tasks. Assess the organization's tasks, people, leadership, and climate.

Chapters 6, 7, and 8

Step 5: COORDINATION AND CONTROL: Assess the range of devices that make up the organization's infrastructure, including coordination, control, and information systems, as well as design of incentive systems.

Chapters 9 and 10

The approach is a holistic one where you consider all fourteen design components in a step-by-step manner. Research has shown that serious performance losses are quite likely if a non-holistic approach is taken, that is, if some design components are changed but not others such that the organization is not in alignment (Burton et al., 2002).

Beginning with goals and strategy, environment, configuration, etc., and proceeding through to the design of incentives in Chapter 10, we developed a complete set of typologies for organizational design components, as well as fit and misfit statements, which were summarized in Table 10.1. In Table 10.1 there is fit within a column and misfit between columns.

In Figure 11.1, we summarize these fit and misfit relations. There is fit within each quadrant and misfit between the quadrants. This is an equivalent statement to Table 10.1. Note that there is a legend to the left of quadrant A indicating the fourteen major design components in this book.

To review quickly, there is fit within each quadrant A, B, C, and D. In quadrant C, for example, there is fit for a prospector strategy in a locally stormy environment with a divisional configuration, and a flat type of organizational complexity with a bonus-based incentive structure. A similar matching of components exists within each of quadrants A, B, and D. Each

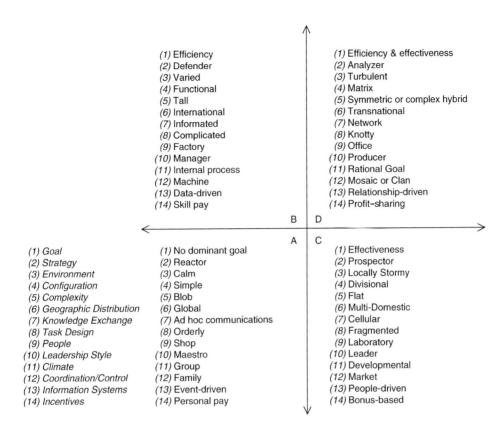

Figure 11.1 The complete set of component types within the 2 × 2 organizational design space.

quadrant has its specific characteristics. Table 10.1 summarized the character-istics for each quadrant, where quadrant D is the most complex one. Many companies are driven towards quadrant D due to changes in the environment (Huber, 2003).

There is a misfit for the firm when one or more organizational design component falls in different quadrants. For example, a prospector strategy in C is a misfit with calm environment in A. Because there are so many design components, a very large number of misfits is possible. One way to quickly assess the extent of misfits for your chosen firm is to circle the design type you identified as you answered the diagnostic questions at the end of each of the ten chapters. If all, or nearly all, of the firm's design components fall within the typologies of the same quadrant, then there are no or few misfits, and change may not be necessary at this time (unless you anticipate changes in the near future). On the other hand, if your firm has components that fall across all four quadrants, then there is a very large number of misfits, and you must give some serious thought as to how to redesign the organization so as to reduce misfits and bring the design components into alignment.

The design and change process is a holistic consideration involving many possible changes. In the step-by-step approach we have developed an orderly and systematic way to take on this complex managerial problem.

What should you change first? Make changes within each step

Beginning with step 1, choose goals of efficiency and/or effectiveness that match what you, as the executive, want for the firm. Then, in step 2, be sure that the strategy and environment fit the goal(s) selected in step 1. Next, in step 3, the organizational configuration should match the strategy. In step 4, the task design, the people, the leadership style, and climate should fit together so as to facilitate the success of the strategy and structure. And finally, the control, coordination, information, and incentive systems should be designed so as to be compatible with the design of people and process systems.

To summarize, the ideal approach is to fix any misfits within a step before proceeding to the next step. At the end of each step check the consistency with each of the previous steps. It may be necessary to make a number of backward iterations to obtain a holistic solution. The step-by-step approach is an analytical solution approach and not necessarily the best sequence for implementation of a new design. Nonetheless, the step-by-step order provides an approach to develop a managerial action plan.

Opportunity losses for misfits within a step can be quite large; and further, changes within steps are relatively less difficult to make than between-step changes. Within step 2, for example, a misfit between the strategy and environment can be devastating for your chosen firm. Consider the prospector strategy, which, if used in a calm environment, incurs two losses. First, the prospector will develop new products and services which are not needed; and second, the prospector costs will be high. Within step 3, consider a functional configuration in a multi-domestic firm. Conflict is very likely between the functions and the country/regional locales, which will lead to gross inefficiencies and lack of responsiveness to the local conditions – potentially bringing significant losses for the firm. Within step 4, consider a leadership style of a manager who operates in a developmental climate. The manager may well impose restrictions that will destroy the benefits of the developmental climate

(Burton et al., 2004). Within step 5, a bonus-based incentive system within a clan type of governance may encourage costly, non-clan behavior. These are only a very few of the large number of possible costly misfits that can occur within a step.

What should you change second? Make changes between steps

Now, turn to changes between steps. If your goals in step 1 are a misfit with your strategy in step 2, the goals will most likely not be realized. For example, adopting a defender strategy will not allow the organization to meet its effectiveness goals. For step 2 and 3, if the strategy does not fit with the structure, then the structure will dominate and the desired strategy will not be realized. This situation is the complement proposition to Chandler's (1962) famous dictum, "structure follows strategy." A functional configuration does not support a prospector strategy. For example, consider step 2 and 4: if you have a defender strategy and adopt a leader-oriented leadership style, the result may lead to conflict and losses as the leader will tend to let subunits move away from executing current activities with machine-like discipline in favor of spurring innovation. If you are able to fix misfits within a step and between steps, then you can yield a comprehensive solution for the organizational design of your firm.

Why change? Should we live with some misfits?

We know that any misfit has an opportunity loss in that performance suffers (Burton et al., 2002). So at first glance it seems that all misfits should be changed – immediately. If the misfits could be fixed without any cost of change, then it would make sense to fix all misfits as quickly as possible. But there are difficulties to changing organizational design components. The fixing of misfits is not free and can involve considerable cost. Should we live with some misfits? Yes, we can live with some misfits, and it is helpful to weigh the benefits of fixing misfits against the costs and difficulties of undertaking the change process. For example, suppose the leadership style is a misfit with other components of organizational design, but to fire existing senior management and recruit new executives will take time and yield short-term morale problems that must be managed. An alternative approach may be to live with the misfit for a while; work with senior managers to create awareness of the leadership style problem. Work with them to adjust their style to reduce the impact of the misfit. Replacing senior management may be expensive and time-consuming, thus outweighing the potential benefits.

Next, we want to examine the balance between the benefits and difficulties of change.

What are the benefits of change?

The benefits of changing organizational design components to reduce or eliminate misfits will help improve your firm's performance and help you to realize goals of efficiency and effectiveness. Misfits decrease a firm's performance. This is clear (Burton and Obel, 2004). There is a long tradition of research demonstrating the opportunity losses from misfits (Gresov, 1989; Miller, 1992; Naman and Slevin, 1993; Donaldson, 2001).

What is less clear is the exact nature of the opportunity-loss function, i.e., whether more misfits significantly decrease performance or not. In a study of 222 Danish medium-sized firms, Burton et al. (2002) found that any deviation from total fit, i.e., even a single misfit, diminished performance, but that additional misfits did not further diminish the loss significantly. The implication is that all misfits should be fixed, if any are to be fixed. In contrast, Håkonsson et al. (2005) focused on climate and leadership, where they found that additional misfits, beyond one misfit, diminished performance significantly. Donaldson (2001) argues that it is the degree of deviation from the fit line that determines the effect on performance. The implication here is that it makes good sense to fix some misfits, even if you cannot fix them all.

A further consideration is that some misfits are more problematic than others. We know that, if a firm is in a turbulent environment, misfits have a more significant effect on performance than in a calm environment (Obel, 1993; Håkonsson et al., 2005; Siggelkow and Rivkin, 2005). This suggests that if you are in a turbulent environment it is more important that you take a holistic approach (i.e., attend to as many of the 14 design components as possible, rather than just a few) to fixing misfits than if you are located in a calm environment. In a calm environment you can live with more misfits than in a volatile situation.

What are the difficulties of change?

There are two difficulties in making changes and fixing misfits. First, some misfits are easier to fix than others – the ease of change. Second, fixing misfits is not a simple linear procedure; namely, when you fix one misfit you may create another one. We want to consider these two issues in turn.

Which misfit is the easiest to change? We asked our executive MBA students who are practicing managers. Figure 11.2 summarizes their results. Formalization of the organization is the easiest to change; and the environment is the most difficult. Formalization reflects the firm's rules; it is relatively easy to add more rules or change a rule. The next thing is to get compliance with the rules, which may be more difficult and is related to the design of the incentives. The environment is the most difficult to change; in practical terms, it means new markets, products, or services with different levels of uncertainty and environmental complexity. Your firm might have to be very different in its strategy and structure and perhaps its people to move to a new environment. This is likely a very difficult change process. These difficulties are consistent with the step-by-step approach. The environment is difficult to change, so for step 2, the strategy can be adjusted to it. Then in step 3, the complexity, geographic distribution, and knowledge sharing can be changed and matched with the strategy. The

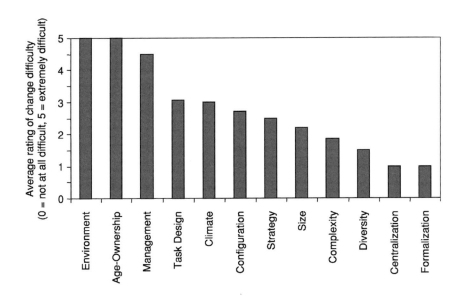

Figure 11.2 The difficulty of change.

Table 11.1 My firm's difficulty of change

Design component	Difficulty of change for your firm (1=low, 5=high)
Goals	
Strategy	
Environment	
Configuration	
Organizational complexity	
Geographic distribution	
Knowledge exchange	
Task design	
People	
Leadership style	
Organizational climate	
Coordination and control systems	
Information systems	
Incentives	

components of step 4, task design, people, leadership, and climate tend to be very difficult to change and can be addressed following the other changes.

The ratings of difficulty of change shown in Figure 11.2 are suggestive for your firm, but not definitive. You must develop a similar chart for your own firm. Your chart depends upon your particular situation and its challenges. For example, there may be insurmountable political barriers to your changing the strategy or task design in your firm. If the top management owns the firm, changing the leadership style may not be an option at all. For your firm, fill in numbers from 1 to 5 for each design component listed in Table 11.1. For each component use a 1 to 5 rating scale to score your organization as follows:

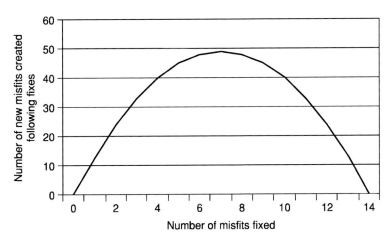

Figure 11.3 The misfit possibilities curve.

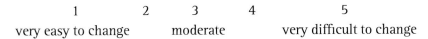

1	2	3	4	5
very easy to change		moderate		very difficult to change

For each component, you can then indicate more specifically what your firm would have to do to make desired changes.

Knowing what misfits your firm has, you can now balance them against the difficulty of making any changes, and what to do using the step-by-step approach as a guide.

Unfortunately, change is not a simple process whereby fixing one misfit reduces the total number of misfits. A fixed misfit may create other misfits. Examine Figure 11.1 on page 213. Let us assume you have a total fit in quadrant B. Now, let us assume a new senior executive is put in place who adopts a leader style rather than a manager style. With this one change in leadership style, you now have even more misfits as there is a misfit with all of the other characteristics, i.e., leadership is now in quadrant C and everything else is in quadrant B. Then assume the strategy is changed to a prospector to fit the new leader; now you have those two in fit, but each of those two is in misfit with everything else, resulting in more total misfits.

In Figure 11.3, we map out the implications where we begin with total fit of design components on the left side and work through the possible number of misfits as they are fixed one by one. First, there are more misfits, as suggested above, then eventually the number decreases as the firm is brought back into total fit.

The implications of this discussion for managing change are enormous. First, just fixing one misfit may not make the situation notably better. It probably requires fixing at least a few so that you stay near the bottom of the curve in Figure 11.3. Otherwise, if you only fix one, you may well make things worse. Second, if you are thinking of fixing one misfit, you should map out a total plan of a sequence of fixes – a holistic approach. You may find yourself in a rather unplanned drift of fix and indication of new misfits which require fixing. A myopic fix approach will not work well. As suggested earlier, fixing the misfits within a step is not sufficient; the fixing of misfits between steps is also needed.

It is a difficult balance of identifying misfits, choosing which ones to fix, and in what order, and balancing the benefits of fewer misfits with the difficulties of changing design components. Taking a holistic and systematic approach to organizational design is vital.

Managing misfits over time

Misfits arise from three sources: external to the organization, internally from managerial action, and jointly from a combination of external and internal sources. Table 11.2 provides illustrations of these types of misfits. Internal sources of misfits are on the left, external ones on the right, and joint ones in the middle. Generally, the environment evolves on its own with very little effect from managerial action. The competition can introduce new products and services. The government can impose new regulations or form new trade agreements. The economy can spur business activity or stifle it. Political conditions can create turbulence or promote calm. On the other hand, internal changes are largely under managerial control. You can develop a new strategy – step 2. You can change senior management to fit a desired leadership style and you can redesign how tasks are done – step 4, but this may be more difficult. You can adopt a new IT system or a new incentive system, and so on – step 5. In the mid-range are alternatives that are partially under managerial control but not fully. For example, the organizational climate may evolve without your intention, although management certainly can influence it – step 4. You can change the structure of incentives, but how employees view them may not be something you can fully anticipate – step 5. You can specify an approach for knowledge exchange – step 3, but things may shift over time if information that once was tacit should become more explicit (e.g., subtle knowledge about customers may become more explicit if it is documented and tracked, moving out of the heads of a few and into an accessible format for many to use), possibly moving your organization's knowledge system from one type to another.

Table 11.2 Examples of internal, external, and combined sources of organizational design misfits (modified from Burton and Obel, 2004, p. 395)

Internal: Misfits created through managerial action	Combined Internal & External	External: Misfits created from environment sources
• A change in organizational strategy	• Management tries to improve the organizational climate, but despite efforts to increase trust and morale, tension remains high due to uncertainty in the industry	• Competitors introduce new, unanticipated products or services, so that the environment is no longer calm
• A divisional structure is consolidated into a matrix structure	• The incentive system in an international locale is changed to bonus-based, but employees perceive the new system to be unfair given the nature of their local culture	• The government imposes new regulations requiring more stringent control systems
• Separate multi-domestic units are consolidated into an international design	• Knowledge exchange systems designed on a people-driven model become obsolete as customers presume systems are relationship-based	• The government forms new trade agreements that open up new market opportunities
• Promotion or hiring brings about a new leadership style		• Political conditions become highly turbulent and unusually difficult to forecast
• A large number of employees are laid off, changing the people dimension		• Terrorist activities create an environment turbulence for which there are few or no plans
• Employees neglect continued skill development, thus decreasing their professionalization over time		• Public pressure creates a strong focus on safety for employees and for the environment

Table 11.2 *(cont.)*

Internal: Misfits created through managerial action	Combined Internal & External	External: Misfits created from environment sources
• Formalization is increased to move from a family governance approach to a more disciplined machine approach		• Corporate social responsibility becomes a constraint, but can open up new opportunities for efficiency
		• The 2008 financial crisis leads to new regulatory restrictions
• The organization merges with a firm that is quite different in structure, process, and people		• All of the above change the risk profile of your firm

Since managers have more control over managing misfits that arise from internal sources, let us examine these in more detail. You have the best possibility for managing organizational design changes with success when you attend to those components that are under your control.

You have many ways to potentially change your organization and thus to create or fix misfits. If your firm is in reasonably good alignment but yet not achieving its long-term potential and anticipates that it will not perform well in the future with its current fit, then you can and should create short-term misfits for a better long-term performance. You are anticipating that the current, good situation will create opportunity losses in the future, even if you have a current fit. Thus, you should act now to create misfits. You have a choice which will create a misfit today, but it may make good sense for the longer run. Examples of changes that you might make in organizational design components include the following within the step-by-step approach:

- a new strategy for the firm;
- a new product or new product line;

- a new way of designing work tasks to satisfy new customer needs;
- a new information system;
- a different approach to people management and incentive system design;
- hiring or promoting a new top management team with a different leadership style;
- a new approach to optimal sourcing;
- a greater reliance on virtualization for knowledge exchange;
- a major expansion or growth;
- a merger with another firm;
- a strategic alliance or partnership with another firm; and
- generally, the introduction of continuing change.

Any one of the above may create a misfit now. Once it has been created, then you should work to bring the organization back into fit as we have discussed throughout this book. If the misfit persists, then there are significant opportunity losses to incur. Most of the situations listed above we have discussed earlier in the book. In the next section, we will analyze some situations that companies faced e.g. during the financial crisis in 2008–10 and how the step-by-step approach can be used to suggest and analyze potential solutions.

Can you do anything to manage external sources of misfits? External shocks can be gradual, evolving, and predictable. You may have time to anticipate and adjust, and fix the misfits in a timely manner. But, external shocks can be large, sudden, and unpredicted. The latter situation has been called a *punctuated equilibrium* by some scholars (Tushman and Romanelli, 1985). A period of environmental predictability is suddenly disrupted in a way that managers could not detect in advance; or, even if the shock is detected, the organization is not able to react in sufficient time. In such a setting, the environment optimizes – not the firm, and even analyzer firms may find themselves in defender mode. So what can you do when the environment changes very suddenly and rapidly? One approach is *time-paced innovative action* (Eisenhardt and Brown, 1998). It is a strategy of period-based innovation or change. The organization engages in redesign on a continual (time-determined) schedule, so that it becomes nimble and adept at reorganizing (experiencing misfits and adjusting for them). Intel builds new factories in a clockwork fashion even before they know what will be housed there. Gillette introduces a new razor regularly. Some public European companies replace their executive leaders as a function of their age, not their performance (i.e., forced retirement); the organization wants to move on and try a fresh leadership style, even if things may be proceeding smoothly. Carlsberg has a new Christmas beer each year. Some high-tech start-ups reorganize every six months to keep workers skill adept and ready for change. Even universities begin classes each year according to a fixed calendar. In brief, you are in command of what you do without waiting for events to dictate your actions. You create your own environment and situation (to some extent) rather than waiting. Using time-paced innovation, there is the risk that you can become very disconnected with the environment, leaving it behind while the organization changes, which can lead to poor performance. On the other hand, you are more likely to maintain internal fit for your firm despite occasional disruptions, which has certain advantages.

The financial crisis 2008–10

For many companies the financial and economic crises in 2008–10 represented a punctuation of an equilibrium situation. The previous decade was one of many changes: the focus on optimal sourcing, decreasing the cost of transportation, rapid developments in communication technology, global trends in deregulation in the transportation and the financial industries, the quest for thinking globally, and industry reorganizations including mergers, the hype on innovation and rapid investments, among others. These changes had driven many companies from a locally stormy or varied environment to a turbulent environment that is both complex and uncertain. The simultaneous exploitation and exploration strategy required equally complex structures: producer-style leadership, a matrix configuration, people who want to move forward in a controlled fashion. These are fit characteristics in quadrant D of Table 10.1 or Figure 11.1. In our model, many companies have been pushed from quadrants B and C towards quadrant D. This move was an appropriate reaction to misfits created by a change in the environmental condition, which both created threats and numerous opportunities. Further public listed companies in this period of rapid growth were pushed by stockholders to report constant quarterly growth figures. Such pressures create a burning platform for change.

The financial crisis of 2008–10 created a punctuated stop in rapid growth. The financial crisis hit the banks first, then had an effect on the economic system, and finally on firms. In short, the financial crisis had an effect on cash flow, stopping company investments, and an increase in unemployment with the slowdown in consumer spending. Truly a vicious circle! How did many companies in quadrant D respond? Some firms made modifications in each step as suggested above. They cut cost, reduced debt, introduced high focus on productivity, reduced product lines and services to have a more narrow focus, and slowed down innovation. But others also adapted between step changes, including closing down the R&D department to further reduce cost and cash flow. Thus, many companies' response to the environmental change was to try to make a quick jump from quadrant D to quadrant B. Was this change an appropriate response?

To be appropriate, the environment had to change from a turbulent or complex and unpredictable environment to a varied or complex and more predictable environment. This was the changed situation for some companies – not for others. Those companies in quadrant D with a strong basis on products and services with long tenure and in industries that were not hurt significantly by the downturn were probably correct in their assessment of the environment. They had the luxury to be able to exit the highly unpredictable part of the environment and thus reduce their investments in risky new developments. Further, by reducing cash requirement and external financing, they were moving towards quadrant B from an environment perspective.

One example is the Danish-Swedish dairy company ARLA. Despite a normal volume of sales, they had a decreased profit in 2008. In 2009, profits recovered slightly, even with a smaller volume. How did they obtain these improved results for the short run? Arla concentrated on their existing and traditional dairy products in Europe, the Arabic countries as well as China. They cut cost significantly – including closing down their R&D department; consolidated their many brands into three major brands; reconfigured their organization into four departments: global categories and operations, consumer international (including Arabic countries and China), consumer Nordic, and consumer UK. The effect was significant across all fourteen dimensions in our model. It required not only a change in strategy and organization; it also put new requirements on the management team as well as on the employees. It was a quick fix approach to change and redesign. There is the risk that the change in the environment may be short-term and the adaptation to a temporary new environment will be costly in the long run because of missed opportunities when the environment changes again – and further a significant cost of organizational re-adaptation if the environment returns to its previous or perhaps normal situation. Once an organization is set in the B column or quadrant, it is difficult and costly to move to C or D where innovation is the norm. Many companies which significantly reduced their innovation focus in the crisis will find it difficult to rekindle the fires of innovation.

With a change such as the one initiated by the financial crisis it is very likely that neither environmental complexity nor the predictability of the environment will decrease. The change required may therefore be from an analyzer with innovation strategy in D, to a prospector in quadrant C. Thus the focus is not only to reduce activities, cutting cost and improving cash flow, but also to find new areas where development is required in this new situation. Here you have to look into the future and try to estimate what the future may bring. Parallel to the financial crisis, numerous other crises were highlighted, such the scarcity of natural resources, poverty, pollution, etc. That brought about issues of sustainable business, CSR (corporate social responsibility), and ethical leadership. As we discussed above, you ought to be cautious when making changes due to the financial crisis, as you may introduce more misfits than you fix. In any case, the changes should be taken within a holistic approach, beginning with changes within a step first and then moving on to the changes between steps.

The issue discussed above is when you look at change, the future set of stages has to be taken into account. For example, in the financial crisis situation you had to survive in the short run and still be prepared to take advantage of new possibilities in the long run. You have to create a dynamic fit situation.

Dynamic fit and time

Dynamic fit goes beyond the organizational misfit model discussed above, which is the application of a control logic and a comparative statics approach; that is, observe the characteristics of the organization and if there is a misfit, then correct it by changing the observed situation to a fit state. In misfit analysis, time is implicit as you want to restore the organization to fit. In dynamic fit, time is the central element; the time to fix a misfit is explicit in *dynamic stability* by analyzing opportunity losses during the time in misfit. Change takes time and requires resources. In Figure 11.2 the difficulty of changing a dimension is very much related to the time it takes to make the change. Applying a systems dynamics change model, Sastry (1997) found that the change period is both costly and detrimental to performance. In Table 11.2, dynamic stability is the time required to adjust to an external shock and the opportunity loss is the magnitude of the loss for the time in misfit. Your organization has greater dynamic stability if the opportunity loss is smaller for a given external shock. Time is also central to organizational *maneuverability* as you are concerned with the time it takes your organization to adjust or change to a new strategy. In Table 11.2, your organization is more maneuverable if the opportunity loss from an internal shock is small (Nissen and Burton, 2010). The old adage that "time is money" is especially true for organizations. Being in misfit is costly; being longer in misfit is more costly. This is the essence of dynamic stability and maneuverability for your organization. Therefore you want to consider time as a scarce resource, look into dynamic fit and relate it to the organizational concepts developed earlier.

From your own experience, you know that time is a scarce resource – perhaps your most limited resource. Ocasio (1997) extends the information-processing concepts to introduce managerial attention as a scarce resource. The four leadership styles utilize time differently. The maestro, quadrant A, is involved in making most decisions and controlling operation – focusing on the "here and now." The manager, quadrant B, avoids uncertainty and is deeply involved in controlling operations. For both the maestro and manager, their time is allocated to the details of current operations. The leader, quadrant C, delegates and is less involved in the daily operations, but rather spending his time on strategic considerations and creating structure, processes and climate for the organization. The producer, quadrant D, is more aware of the details of operations, but still spends a good deal of time on strategic considerations. The four leadership requirements of the organization demand that the leader spend his time on different tasks and thus allocate his time accordingly. Time prioritization follows the leadership demands. If the leader does not change his time allocation to fit a new strategy, a misfit is created which can lead to significant losses. Some individuals may find this adjustment difficult. Your time utilization is set by the organization as well as your own preferences. But your organization can help you in the efficient utilization of your time if there is a good fit with the other characteristics of the organization as discussed in our five steps.

In step 1, you determined the organizational goals in terms of efficiency and effectiveness. Effectiveness is a focus on the organizational products and services; efficiency is resource-focused with a goal to use less to accomplish the same results. With time – both the leader's time and the organization's time – as a scarce resource, organizational efficiency must include the efficient utilization of time. That is, the organization desires to use time well to make decisions and implement them. At first reflection, we might think that quickness in decision-making might lead to poor decisions. Eisenhardt and Brown (1998) found the opposite to be true in a high-velocity environment where time for action is extremely limited; namely, the more limited the time, the more extensive the examination of alternatives, and the better the resulting decisions. Burton and Obel (1984) in a simulation study also found that a small number of planning iterations yields good decisions. Thus, time limitations can yield effective decisions efficiently. In step 1, the setting of goals is extremely important and sets the basis for the design of the organization; it does not imply that the goals or the re-examination of goals require a long time to develop.

The organizational configuration sets time allocation priorities. In step 3, you examined four configurations: simple, functional, divisional, and matrix. As for the leader, each configuration requires its own attention to decisions and communications. The simple configuration, quadrant A, can be quick in its response to environmental shifts in column 3 of Figure 11.2 and it can be quick to respond to changes in the maestro's own desires in column 1 of Figure 11.2, which suggests a high level of maneuverability to adapt to new goals without incurring opportunity losses. A simple configuration requires a fast clock, but it also can lead to information overload and non-adaptiveness. Due to the time limitations, the simple configuration has a high risk of misfit. The functional configuration, quadrant B, has its own clock which is driven by the need to coordinate operations among the functional units, as depicted in Figure 4.3. The priority of time utilization is to make the functional activities fit and work together. The risk is that more strategic issues are overlooked. The divisional configuration, quadrant C, requires a less precise clock for activities. Once each division has its goals and resources, the headquarters unit need not be involved in operational details. Each division can proceed on its own clock. The headquarters unit can establish annual divisional budgets, and longer-term goals and strategies. For the matrix configuration, quadrant D, time has dual aspects of short-term operational coordination as well as longer-term focus on goals and strategy. When it works well, the organization is a finely tuned clock; when it works poorly, too much time is spent in coming to decisions that impact across the two or more dimensions. For each configuration, the clock and the time priorities of the organization are specific and different.

In step 5, you examined the coordination and control systems using the dimensions of decentralization and formalization. A family coordination and control, quadrant A, is informal, but centralized; the maestro sets the clock and time focus. The machine, quadrant B, relies upon high formalization and centralization, which provide the pace for decisions and coordination among the several functional units requiring a precise use of time. The market, quadrant C, is low on formalization and high on decentralization. Coordination among the divisions is minimal and time is not managed precisely. The clan/mosaic, quadrant D, demands a precise clock for operational coordination across two or more organizational dimensions. Each coordination and control mechanism has its own clock and precision in the use of time.

Also in step 5, you examined four information types: event-driven, data-driven, people-driven and relationship-driven along two dimensions: amount of information and the tacit nature of the information. The event-driven information system, quadrant A, involves sparse, but exact information, e.g., your competitor increased his price 10 per cent; there is one element of information with an exact value. The organizational clock is driven by important, but not regularly set events. The allocation of organizational time is a reaction to these events. The data-driven information system, quadrant B, contains lots of exact information which is gathered in clock-precise fashion, e.g., the data-driven information system monitors the daily prices for twenty-five competitors. The time pace demands are matched well with large trans-actional data bases. The people-driven information system requires small amounts of tacit, imprecise information, demanding a broadband for inter-active communications. The time pace is emergent as the time required for decisions and activities is not known and is subject to the back and forth of information-sharing and negotiation. Broadband and less formatted information such as email, telephone, and face-to-face are required with time utilization emergent. The relationship-driven information system, quadrant D, requires lots of information which is tacit and ambiguous – demanding multidimensional broadband communications. The time pace of the organization is hectic, with many agendas active at the same moment. Each information system has its own clock or pace of activity as well as the quantity and tacit nature of the information.

Time can also be considered in the short run and long run, with implications for change and opportunity losses. In Chapter 8, we examined the relationship between the leadership style and the organization's climate – both in the short run and in the long run. In the short run, the leader should understand and make accommodation to the climate as the climate has high inertia and is difficult to change. In order to avoid opportunity losses in the short run, the leader should adjust to the climate. For the longer run, the leader may want to change the climate to be more compatible with his own leadership style. This requires a consistency of emotion and affective events which are incorporated into the psychological climate of the organizational members.

The short run, long run dilemma can obtain in other misfit situations. For example, assume there is a misfit between the environment and the strategy; which one should be changed? In the short run, the environment is difficult to change (see Figure 11.2 above); the strategy is easier, but still difficult. To minimize the opportunity losses (magnitude and duration), the misfit is most often fixed by changing the strategy. That is, in the short run, you want to take the easier path; however, you do not want to create situations which make the subsequent long-run changes even more difficult. If the new strategy calls for increased efficiency which reduces the R&D, it will probably reduce the capability to make the needed changes in the long run if the organization wants to choose a new environment with new products, processes, and customers. The short-run changes create the context for long-run changes. The highly maneuverable organization can make these changes quickly and minimize the opportunity losses.

There are many examples of short-run, long-run changes. Using the logic above, you can develop the short-run, long-run dilemmas for strategy and structure, where in the short run the strategy can be changed quickly, but a changed structure to minimize opportunity losses may take much longer; a traditional misfit is the coordination and systems with the information systems where it takes much longer to develop new information systems which fit the organization than is usually assumed. It is not unusual for two merged companies to be operating on different information systems some years after the merger, and incurring continuing opportunity losses – including irritated customers. The Maersk–P&O Nedlloyd merger is one such example. There are also examples from banking, pharmaceuticals, and airlines, among others.

For your organization, look for two design elements which are in misfit; examine which one is easier to change in the short run; develop both a short-run plan and a long-run plan which will minimize the opportunity losses for the organization.

The organizational life cycle

The organizational life cycle is an explicit consideration of time as it affects the organization development and its characteristics. The usual life cycle is the entrepreneurial startup, moving to a larger functional configuration and perhaps to an even larger divisional configuration. Many organizations or firms progress from simple configuration in quadrant A, then to the functional configuration in quadrant B, and then on to the divisional configuration in quadrant C. The matrix configuration in quadrant D may follow the functional configuration, or it may follow the divisional configuration. That is, there are different paths in the life cycle of an organization. Yet, ignoring the matrix configuration, the usual growth path is startup to functional to divisional. Reversing the cycle is also possible, e.g., moving from a divisional configuration to a functional configuration. In today's complex world, many organizations end up in quadrant D with an equally complex organization.

You might take your own company's development and try to map it into the four quadrants. If your own company is still in its early stages then try to think of how you see your company progress in the future. Now look at the development of misfit creation and misfit resolution. This is looking at the change from a dynamic fit perspective. Moving from one quadrant to the next causes, as we have described, numerous misfits that have to be dealt with in the process of change. Many companies make the move in an evolutionary way, while others make the steps in quantum leaps. Such quantum leaps may involve takeovers and mergers. We will discuss that particular situation in Chapter 12.

In moving from quadrant A to B, you can compare the A and B columns in Table 10.1 or the A and B quadrants in Figure 11.1 to compare the requisite changes. For each step and in each chapter, we have discussed what is required to move from one quadrant to another. Starting at the bottom of Table 11.1, there is a new focus on efficiency, a defender strategy with exploitation, a functional configuration, individuals with greater specialization, a manager style of leadership, a machine approach to coordination and control, an information system with much more detailed data, among other changes. As we have discussed above, these changes are not easy; some succeed, many fail to make the transition in the life cycle.

Moving on to quadrant C moves the focus from efficiency to effectiveness. Again, refer to Table 10.1 and Figure 11.1. When current markets are exhausted a defender strategy is sufficient, or when innovation and exploration are needed, there is a basis for continued growth and movement to quadrant C.

As we suggested above, the movement to matrix, quadrant D, is more complicated. The firm can move to quadrant D from either quadrant B or quadrant C in Figure 11.1. This is same change from columns B or C to D in Table 10.1. It is important to note that the changes to matrix, D is quite different for a firm in functional, B or a divisional, C.

Further, there are examples of moving from matrix back to functional, or the divisional. ABB adopted a matrix organization in its early years, but then moved back to a divisional. LEGO has recently moved back to a functional, from its earlier matrix. The life cycle is not unique, with many paths possible and observed among successful firms.

Summary

In this chapter, we have reviewed the step-by-step approach and then extended it in terms of the difficulty of change for your organization. Examining and fixing the misfits within a step and then moving on to the misfits between steps is the recommended approach to achieving a holistic organizational design. The step-by-step approach brings a disciplined and comprehensive approach to the complex process of organizational design. We showed how you can think through the costs and benefits of implementing design changes in your organization.

We have extended the misfit concept to dynamic fit and the explicit examination of organizational time. Misfits are not easy to fix; fixing misfits may introduce more misfits; the opportunity losses of misfits indicates the value of adjusting to external shocks as well as maneuverability for new goals and strategies.

Now you have completed the step-by-step approach for an organizational diagnosis and design. You have completed a guided tour of your own organization and achieved a better understanding of the design challenges for better goal attainment.

Glossary

Dynamic fit: quickness of the organization to adjust to an external shock.

Dynamic stability: the time to return to initial profit level following a deviation from a change in consumer preferences.

Maneuverability: the time it takes your organization to adjust or change to a direction, new goals and strategy. A highly maneuverable organization incurs low opportunity losses due to internal shocks by management.

Opportunity loss: the magnitude of the loss for the time in misfit, i.e., the opportunity loss is the magnitude of the loss due to misfit for the duration or time that the organization is in misfit.

Punctuated equilibrium: an unpredicted, extreme external shock to the organization.

Time-paced innovative action: an organization engages in redesign on a continual (time-determined) schedule.

12 New forms and multi-unit organizations: building on the fundamentals

Introduction

In this chapter, we discuss new and more complex design situations, that is, multi-organizations, including joint ventures, mergers, and strategic alliances/partnerships, including outsourcing. Major design challenges arise in situations where multiple units have to be consolidated into one operating unit. The name for such combined units may from a legal point of view be merger, joint venture, or strategic alliance, but the challenge for these new forms still follows the fundamentals that we have laid out.

How do you combine and create a new organizational unit based on new or existing units? We could call it the LEGO approach where put the bricks together to form a new design. To do so we need to know what the design should look like, and the characteristics of the bricks at hand. The financial crisis has not notably diminished the number of mergers and acquisitions. In 2010 SAP acquired Sybase and HP acquired PALM, to mention two in the technology based industry. Many more mergers have appeared on the front pages of business journals. The number of banks has decreased significantly worldwide, mainly due to troubled banks having been taken over by more healthy banks. The Database on Mergers in Europe (DOME), compiled at the Kiel Institute of World Economics, is the most recent list of mergers which has been under the examination of the European Commission. The database lists 1,515 merger cases for the period 1990 to 2000, with an increase from 1999 to 2000 of 492 cases (Kiel Institute for World Economics, 2004). Thus organizational designs of multi-unit organizations have become even more important than earlier.

So far, we have considered a single unit of analysis: a firm, a division, a department, or a team. Now, we examine multiple units of analysis, such as the joint venture, the merger, and the strategic alliance or partnership – putting the LEGO bricks together.

Multi-organization: multiple units of analysis

Multi-unit organizational designs have come to the forefront of interest today as firms are continually involved in forming relationships with other firms. At first glance, we might expect that there is something new or different about how these multi-organizations should be designed when compared to their simpler single organization counterparts. But this is not the case. The basics of organizational design still hold and should be applied when managing multi-organizations. Why? First, multi-organizations are not a new phenomenon. Firms have been engaged in these activities for many years. We know from experience that the majority of multi-organizational initiatives fail; yet, the firms that are able to manage the change process associated with joint ventures, mergers, and alliances to build an integrated, aligned organization are more likely to be successful (compared to those that fail to integrate and align a newly formed multi-organization) (Carey et al., 2004). During the twentieth century, General Motors, IBM, and Cisco grew, in part, as the result of their success in integrating acquired firms into their companies. Many firms have been badly hurt by their inability to integrate acquisitions or to work in alignment with partners. HP's failure to integrate Compaq into its larger enterprise provides a recent example of a troublesome multi-organization experience.

Second and perhaps more importantly, these multi-organizations are organizations in their own right, where each has its own strategy, environment, configuration, distributed organization, people, leadership, climate, coordination, control, information systems, and incentives. That is, the fundamentals that we have developed throughout this book apply here as well. The unit of analysis is different, but the step-by-step approach applies. You can analyze a joint venture, merger, or alliance in the same way as you do a single organization. You can also examine misfits and plan to change the organization. The tools are the same. The complication is that you must consider more than one unit of analysis when designing these ventures.

The joint venture, the merger, the strategic alliance or partnership – each one is its own unit of analysis, but each is closely related to its parent organizations

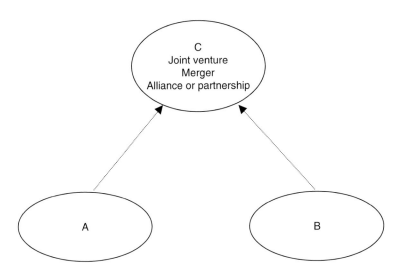

Figure 12.1 The multi-organization.

in ways that are not present in stand-alone organizations. Here, we have three organizations (units of analysis) to consider in concert: the organization itself and its two parents. In Figure 12.1 we show the three organizations. The two parents, A and B come together to form C, the focal organization, which may take the form of a joint venture, merger, alliance, or partnership. When considering a new organization of this type, you want to examine all three organizations, and the relationships of the parents to the new organization, C.

Sometimes A and B form C to be similar in design to the two parents – similar in goals, strategy, people, leadership, and so on. But many times A and B form C to create something quite different from themselves. A and B may think of themselves as having *complementarities*, or different (yet compatible) design components, rather than similarities in design components. For example, A may have market access to a new region but not the required product know-how, which B holds, that is needed to produce the product for the region. A and B thus bring complementary capabilities to the formation of the C organization. Complementarities may make great strategic sense as a reason for creating C, but these also may reflect design differences that yield misfits. If so, then the misfits must be identified and managed. Many misfits put the success of C at risk. Indeed, many multi-organizations fail precisely because strategists have embraced complementarities between A and B but overlooked the downsides of organizational design misfits that carried into the C organization.

Let us develop the step-by-step approach for the multi-organization, building directly upon the step-by-step approach for the single organization. Then we will apply this approach to each of the multi-organizational types: the joint venture, the merger, and the alliance/partnership. We analyze C as an organization even if it is not a separate legal entity, which is the case in some alliances and partnerships. Even if C is not a separate, independent organization, the strategic alliance or partnership has goals, strategies, structure, people responsible for leading it, systems for coordination and control, and incentives. It should be created with organizational design components in mind so that it can be managed to meet its goals. So think of C as an organization in its own right, no matter how big or small, or how independent or intertwined it may be with its parents.

To begin, you want to first examine the focal organization, C. Next, examine the parents, A and B. (If there are more than two parent organizations, then examine all of them, especially those that are most influential in shaping the design of the new, focal organization.) Finally, examine the relationship between C and its parent organizations, A and B. Our thesis is that C is better understood when we examine it together with A and B.

The multi-organization step-by-step approach

To analyze a multi-organization, here are the steps you should follow:

1. Analyze C as a separate organization applying our single organization step-by-step approach. Remember that C is an organization with its own goals, strategies, environment, and so on (which includes A and B in the environment; this is very important). Here, you want to examine the misfits and possible changes for bringing C's design components into alignment.
2. Analyze A separately using our step-by-step approach. Again, the emphasis is on the misfits within A and possible changes.
3. Analyze B separately using our step-by-step approach. Again, the emphasis is on the misfits within B and possible changes.

In the above, it is important to examine A, B, and C as separate organizations, even if they share some personnel, goals, coordination and control systems, or other design components. For purposes of analysis and design, each one is its own unit of analysis and has its own organizational boundary. Analyzing each as a separate unit of analysis will allow you to see points of fit and misfit and identify possibilities for change in organizational design, especially for C.

The next step is to examine the relationships between A and C, and then B and C.

1. Examine the relations between A and C. Here, you want to analyze and understand:
   a. What goals does A have for C? What goals does C have for A?
   b. What results, outcomes, and outputs does A expect from C?
   c. What resources – leadership, personnel, and financing – does A give to C?
   d. What policies and limitations does A place upon C?
   e. What agreements and contracts does C have with A?
2. Repeat step 1 to examine the relations between B and C as above.
3. The next steps are to do a higher level of misfit analysis and possible changes.
   a. Take the analyses above for A and C. Make two lists side by side – one for A and one for C. Then compare A and C on each of the dimensions from your analysis: goals, strategy, environment, etc. Many of these entries will be different, perhaps almost all. But focus on the different ones that will impede C in realizing its goals; these are significant misfits.
   b. Develop a list of changes in the relationship between A and C that will ameliorate these misfits and facilitate C in the accomplishment of its goals.
   c. Repeat these steps for B and C.
4. Do a comparison of A and C with B and C. If these relationships are quite different, then there is likely to be conflict between A and B, which will make it difficult for C as it pursues its work. C then needs to address these issues and make a determination of whether to live with them or work with A and B for a solution.

Next we want to review how the step-by-step approach just described can be applied to three types of multi-organizations: the joint venture, the merger, and the alliance/partnership.

Joint venture

The *joint venture* C is an organization that is given resources and supported by its parents, A and B, but C is largely independent of A and B. Joint ventures may take different forms both practically as well as legally. In some cases the legal structure may be rather loose, while in others the joint venture is set up as a separate legal entity with the parents as stockholders.

Applying the approach above, the first step in analyzing a joint venture is to do separate analyses of A, B, and C; and then turn to their relations.

As an example, consider a bio-tech startup that is a joint venture of two larger pharmaceutical companies. You should begin with a single organization step-by-step approach for the joint venture C; then do the same for the parents, A and B. Next, analyze the relationship between C and its parent organizations. Suppose the goal for C is to develop new drug-assessment algorithms which are to be used by both of its parents, A and B, but in different ways. Suppose that A has assigned six professional algorithm developers to the joint venture and also the CEO. In addition, A has made available substantial funding. In return, it wants access to any of the assessment algorithms developed by C for its application in its entity drug development. This agreement is formalized in a very detailed contract, particularly the intellectual property (IP) rights. Suppose B, on the other hand, has its own goal and different relationship with C. B has supplied a large number of highly trained but less experienced scientists, and it has provided the space, equipment, and support personnel for the joint venture. B hopes to learn how to develop assessment algorithms for its own entities but will not use the specific algorithms developed by C. That is, it does not have IP rights in the joint venture. In sum, A and B have differing relationships with C, and these are formalized in a detailed contract at the time of creation of the venture.

This is a quick sketch of the relations between the joint venture C and its parents, A and B. The joint venture C should plan its organizational design and assess its misfits as the venture evolves. C should be assessed as an independent unit of analysis. Then it should look at the goals that A and B have for the joint venture and the resources they are supplying. Can C realize its goals? Are there sufficient resources? If there are misfits here, then C, the new development laboratory, must decide to live with them, or approach the parents to obtain a resolution.

Usually when a joint venture is formed, the goals and the strategy are spelled out. When you access the environment you have to take into account the parents as being part of the environment. They may add restrictions, uncertainty, and complexity to the environment.

Sony Ericsson is a joint venture of its two parents, set up to develop and market mobile phones. Both Sony and Ericsson have other significant businesses which do not involve each other.

Merger

The merger is the result of A and B becoming a new organization, C. At first glance, you might think that A and B will go away as C is formed and can be ignored. But the shadows of A and B can be long. C cannot be understood (alone) without an assessment of where it came from. The people, climate, coordination, and control systems, and many other organizational design components of A and B will be imported into C and will influence C's organizational design in significant ways. For this reason, an analysis of the C organization prior to its formation, and an assessment of the parents' influence on C, can be very helpful.

GlaxoSmithKline (GSK) is a recent merger of Glaxo Wellcome and Smith-Kline Beecham. The new GSK is made up of people, facilities, drugs, brands, etc., from the parents. In the step-by-step approach, you would examine GSK – the C organization. You also would assess Glaxo Wellcome (GW) and SmithKline Beecham (SKB) – the parent organizations. As the merger occurs, the parent organizations are shadow or legacy organizations, but they greatly affect the new GSK.

To assess the design of the new, merged organization, you should first do separate step-by-step analyses of each of the three organizations, revealing possible misfits and ways to change them (SmithKline Beecham and Glaxo Wellcome were themselves the results of previous mergers). Then turn to differences that create misfits after the merger. Our suggested approach is as follows:

1. Make two lists side by side – one for SKB and one for GW. Then compare SKB and GW on each of the organizational design components: goals, strategy, environment, etc. Some of these entries will be similar, and some will be different.
2. Focus on the differences, as these will create variation in the particular dimension for the merged organization. Assess if these differences are important and how they should be handled. Develop a list of changes in the relationship between SKB and GW that will facilitate reduction of misfits, thus enhancing alignment in the new GSK organization.
3. Look at the misfits for the new potential organization. Consider how they should be addressed. Here you should consider how to realize the "best" of the two parent organizations.

Now let us be a little more precise with respect to where the two companies may be located in our design space. Look at which quadrant the two companies are located in in Table 10.1 or Figure 11.1. If the two units are in the same quadrant and both are well aligned with no misfits, a "simple" merger is possible. Then the action depends on which quadrant the two units are located in.

To begin, let us now assume that the two companies are located in quadrant A. The merger is probably necessary because neither of the two companies could make it alone. Each company has a reactor strategy. This strategy is not viable in the long run. So each company will die, merge or move to another quadrant, as described in the organizational life cycle discussion in Chapter 11. Here, we consider a merger which will increase the size of the new company in a different quadrant, say B. A major redesign is required. The new strategy and structure will be relatively easy. The people and processes will be much more difficult. It is very likely that a new CEO and management team will be required. Further, the climate in both organizations has a high resistance to change. Even with the initial similarities of the original companies, the new merged company is not an easy transition.

If the two units are located in quadrant B they both have a configuration based on the functional form. The first step will then be to look into a merger of similar functional departments. That will normally include a reduction of staff, and cost-cutting. The focus will be on obtaining further efficiencies by choosing best practice. That includes going through the various dimensions in the model. Second, personnel issues are critical. You have to choose new department heads. That could be done by selecting one of the existing ones, or by hiring someone from outside. Third, and even more critical, you have to diagnose climate issues. In quadrant B, both units have an internal process climate which includes high tension and high resistance to change. This analysis assumes that we have a merger of two relatively similar organizations, e.g. two banks. If that is not the case, fewer similar departments can be merged. Then, a more thorough analysis is required; begin with the new organization's combined environment and then go through the remaining steps.

If the two organizations to be merged are located in quadrant C we are looking at two divisionally organized firms. First, examine how similar the divisions from the two original organizations are. If there are few similarities, leave the divisions as they are and cost reduction can be obtained at the central or corporate level. Second, if there are similar divisions, you can use the process described from quadrant B. The main difference here is that there is less resistance to change and less tension in the two organizations' climates.

Further, you need to assess the effect of a potential increase in complexity and the change in the demand for and supply of information. That will include an assessment of the choice of IT systems, new procedures, incentive systems, etc. A new combined environment may require a complete reassessment of the strategy, triggering the cascade effect to go through the step-by-step approach from the beginning to the end.

Finally, consider two companies located in quadrant D. Both companies have high exploration and exploitation and a relatively complex score on the situational factors as well as on the organizational factors. Economies of scale and rationalization should be analyzed. An analysis such as the one described for quadrant B should be carried out. Careful attention should be given to the effect of the organizational climate, which has both high tension and low resistance to change. It will allow for a smooth transition but also have potential conflict embedded in the climate.

Now, let us turn to the more difficult situations, the merger of two dissimilar organizations, i.e., two organizations that are not in the same quadrant. Basically the three steps analyzing the parents and the new organization presented above should be carried out. Since the two companies are not located in the same quadrant, there is an issue of where the merged company should be located. For a takeover, the smaller organization will have to adapt. For more equal organizations, use the goal, environment, and strategy analyses in step 1 to determine which quadrant to go to. That will also be the case when one or both companies have misfits.

The above merger analyses are not easy to do, and frequently are not taken beyond the selection of a new CEO. The more normal financial approach to a merger analysis is to anticipate the benefits of a merged company, which has inferred synergies or cost savings. But organizational misfits between the parent organizations in a merger are very likely to create higher-level misfits in the new, merged organization, C, which can linger for some time, and not yield the hoped-for results. Failed mergers which do not realize the promised synergies are usually those which spawn misfits when incompatible organizations, A and B, become merged organizations without full organization analysis, identification of misfits, and managerial steps to fix misfits. Any one of the factors of strategy, structure, climate, leadership style, technology, incentives, and IT systems will be sufficient to derail the benefits of a merger. There are many ways to fail, and few holistic designs for success in a merger.

The pace of merger is an important concern. Should you merge quickly, or take a longer time? Two Danish banks took quite different approaches. Den Danske Bank is the outcome of the merger of three banks of almost equal size. This merger was realized in quick time. Over a weekend, a common name, a common facade, a common letterhead, among other symbolic elements were realized. Since all three banks had a common IT platform, a common IT system of accounts for all customers was adopted very quickly, from the customer point of view. For many bank operations, the misfits were eliminated, demonstrating maneuverability with less opportunity loss. For Den Danske Bank, the strategy, the structure, and people policies soon followed, including information about those people who would be laid off.

At the same time, a similar merger took place of three other Danish banks to form Unibank, which now is part of the Scandinavian bank Nordea. In contrast, this merger took a much longer time to realize. The three banks continued to operate under their original names, and to the customer there was little apparent change for some time. The three original banks used different IT platforms, which seriously impeded the integration of customer accounts. More generally, each original bank continued to operate much as it had before the merger. Over a longer time, unity was accomplished with a new strategy, structure, people, and finally a common customer IT system.

Den Danske Bank eliminated its misfits quickly, demonstrating high maneuverability. Unibank fixed its misfits over a longer time in a sequence of changes. Which is the better approach? In comparison, Den Danske Bank's stock price did better than Unibank's. In our analysis, we suggest that Den Danske Bank's greater maneuverability and lower opportunity losses from the change of merger were correctly recognized by the stock market. In the discussion above, we focused on the IT system of the two mergers. In banks, the IT system is the operations of a bank; some would argue that the bank *is* an IT system and one of the pure information-processing organizations.

In making the choice of reducing the misfit in a merger in either a quick parallel process or a sequential process, you have to assess whether or not the misfits are easy to change. Further, you have to assess the degree of misfit between the units that have to be merged compared to the misfits in the external context. Generally, a merger should be done as quickly as possible to eliminate opportunity loss, i.e., high maneuverability. Further, a long merger process may be an affective event that will evoke negative inactive emotions that will increase the resistance to change, which may make the merger process even more difficult and extend the time it takes to finalize the merger.

Strategic alliance or partnership

A strategic alliance, or partnership, is planned collaboration among multiple firms for conducting business activity together for purposes of mutual benefit. Alliances are contract-driven and arise in many different forms: suppliers with manufacturers, sharing of IP in research and development, joint product development, and integrated marketing efforts, among others. Although the C organization formed by A and B is typically not a stand-alone organization, a strategic alliance, once formed, can be considered as an organization in its own right in that it has its own goals, strategies, leadership style, etc. Usually, the goals for C are spelled out in the contract agreements between the parents. Many have a joint oversight and policy committee made up of members of the parent organizations. In addition, the leadership (e.g., top management team) of the alliance is typically shared by representatives from each parent company. C is, in a sense, an implicit or fathom organization with very few resources of its own and little autonomy from A and B. The assignment of people, leaders, infrastructure, and other organizational components of C are drawn from the parent organizations and typically remain there as the partnership operates. In this sense, an alliance is the opposite of a joint venture or a merger.

Nonetheless, planning for the organizational design of an alliance is vital. In addition to stating the goals in the formal alliance agreement, the parent organizations, A and B, should also plan on defining the environment, strategy, configuration, and all other components of organizational design. A complete design is important to alliance success. One way to do this is to follow our step-by-step approach, identifying the organizational design components for C and their relationship to the parent organizations. If you are creating an alliance, you need to have a very good understanding of the strategic alliance from an information-processing view: who does what, how, and based upon what information? A close coordination of the organizational design of the strategic alliance as well as the parent organizations is fundamental for such an endeavor to be successful.

As an example, consider a strategic alliance between an automobile manufacturer and one of its suppliers. Saab and others have many such alliances. Each begins with a reasonably well-understood agreement and/or formal contract between the two parents. The goal of the strategic alliance as its own organization is to develop and manufacture parts, modules, or subassemblies which perform the automotive function, but more importantly are integral to the automobile. GKN, a British conglomerate, is another example of such an alliance. GKN makes drive shafts for many companies, and each one must be engineered for that specific application. The strategic alliance is the development process in which the drive shaft is adapted to the automobile, but the automobile including modules from other suppliers will adapt to the drive shaft – all of which are yet to be built. The information-processing demands are very high with many reciprocal adjustments where decisions are made jointly by the parent organizations.

In the airline industry, oneworld and StarAlliance are examples of strategic alliances. Here the strategic alliance also has reciprocal effects on the parent organizations. Arrival and departure schedules have to be coordinated. There are joint and/or separate marketing efforts as well. A well coordinated IT infrastructure has to be set up, e.g. to facilitate joint boarding cards, use of frequent flyer miles and much more. On the cost side, the system of code-sharing reduces the number of flights and also helps fill up planes; it becomes an opportunity similar to the one described in the previous chapter with respect to the financial crisis.

When forming a strategic alliance, we suggest that you begin with an analysis of the anticipated C organization, following the step-by-step approach as outlined in this book. Next do the same for A and B, and any other parents that are a part of the alliance. Then, move on to the higher-level misfits between the strategic alliance and the parent organizations. The analysis and resolution of the higher-level misfits must be addressed for a successful strategic alliance or partnership.

Robinson (2008) suggests that long-shot projects should be organized through alliances, while relatively safer projects should be organized within the firm. Now assume that the strategy and the environment require that relatively risky projects have to be initiated. If the CEO of the firm is risk-averse, then creating a strategic alliance may be the solution. A strategic alliance could in this respect also be a way for an organization that does not have a high degree of exploration, e.g. being located in quadrant B, to start exploration as a first step on its way to quadrant D. A strategic alliance may also be used to reduce misfits.

Summary

We have examined three kinds of multi-organizations: the joint venture, the merger, and the strategic alliance/partnership. Each involves at least three organizations: two or more parent organizations and the focal organization. The joint venture, the merger, and the alliance can be quite different from each other in their legal and contractual natures; however, from an organizational design perspective, their components are the same as any other organization. Thus, they should be analyzed using a single organization step-by-step approach, following the approach outlined in Chapters 1–10 of this book. Relationship analysis, as described above, can then be used to identify higher-level misfits that will reveal incompatibilities between the C organization and its parents. From there you plan for needed changes to increase alignment between C and its parents, A and B, thus enhancing the information capacity of C and improving its potential to meet its goals.

Glossary

Complementarities: different (yet compatible) design components, rather than similarities in design components between two parent organizations; often used as a motivation for two organizations forming a multi-organization.

Joint venture: the forming of a new organization by two or more independent organizations; the organization typically remains independent of the parents, except for the resources that they bring together in the joint venture.

Merger: the forming of a new organization by combining two or more independent organizations together.

Multi-organization: the formation of a new organization, C, by multiple parent organizations, A and B; the multi-organizational forms are joint ventures, mergers, and alliances or partnerships.

Strategic alliance: planned collaboration among multiple firms for conducting business activity together for purposes of mutual benefit; typically takes the form of a contract among the collaborating firms; sometimes referred to as a partnership.

Strategic partnership: planned collaboration among multiple firms for conducting business activity together for purposes of mutual benefit; typically takes the form of a contract among the collaborating firms; sometimes referred to as an alliance.

References

Alonso, R., Dessein, W., and Matouschek, N. (2008): "When Does Coordination Require Centralization?", *American Economic Review*, **98**(1), 145–79.

Arrow, K. (1974): *The Limits of Organization*, New York: W. W. Norton.

Ashby, W. R. (1956): *Introduction to Cybernetics*, London: Methuen.

Bartlett, C. A., and Ghoshal, S. (1998): *Managing Across Borders: The Transnational Solution*, 2nd edn, Cambridge, MA: Harvard Business School Press.

Bartol, K. M., and Locke, E. (2000): "Incentives and Motivation," in S. L. Rynes and B. Gerhart (eds.), *Compensation in Organizations: Current Research and Practice*, San Francisco, CA: Jossey-Bass, pp. 104–50.

Basu, A., and Blanning, R. W. (2000): "A Formal Approach to Workflow Analysis," *Information Systems Research*, **11**(1), pp. 17–36.

Boudreau, M.-C., Loch, K. D., Robey, D., and Straub, D. (1998): "Going Global: Using Information Technology to Advance the Competitiveness of the Virtual Transnational Organization," *Academy of Management Executive*, **12**(4), pp. 120–8.

Bourgeois, L. J., III (1980): "Strategy and Environment: A Conceptual Integration," *Academy of Management Review*, **5**, pp. 25–39.

Bourgeois, L. J., and Eisenhardt, K. (1988): "Strategic Decision Processes in High Velocity Environments: Four Cases in the Minicomputer Industry," *Management Science*, **34**, pp. 816–35.

Bower, J. L. (2001): *Merloni Elettrodomestici: Building for a New Century (HBA 9-301-112)*, Cambridge, MA: Trustees of Harvard College.

Burns, T., and Stalker, G. M. (1961): *The Management of Innovation*, London: Tavistock.

Burton, R. M., and Obel, B. (1984): *Designing Efficient Organizations: Modelling and Experimentation*, Amsterdam: North Holland.

(1988): "Opportunism, Incentives, and the M-form Hypothesis: A Laboratory Study," *Journal of Economic Behavior and Organization*, **10**, pp. 99–119.

(2004): *Strategic Organizational Diagnosis and Design: The Dynamics of Fit*, Dordrecht: Kluwer Academic Publishers.

Burton, R. M., Lauridsen, J., and Obel, B. (2002): "Return on Assets Loss from Situational and Contingency Misfits," *Management Science*, **48**(11), pp. 1461–85.

(2004): "The Impact of Organizational Climate and Strategic Fit on Firm Performance," *Human Resource Management*, **43**(1), pp. 67–82.

Burton, R. M., Minton, J. W., and Obel, B. (1991): "Organizational Size And Efficiency: An Information Processing View," *Scandinavian Journal of Management*, **7**(2), pp. 79–93.

Carey, D. C., Ogden, D., and Roland, J. A. (2004): *The Human Side of M & A: Leveraging the Most Important Factor in Deal Making*, Oxford University Press.

Carroll, T. N., Burton, R. M., Levitt, R. E., and Kiviniemi, A. (2005): "Fallacies of Fast Track Heuristics: Implications for Organization Theory and Project Management," submitted to *Management Science.*

Chandler, A. D. (1962): *Strategy and Structure: Chapters in the History of the Industrial Enterprises*, Cambridge, MA: MIT Press.

Choo, C. (1998): *The Knowing Organization*, New York: Oxford University Press.

Cullen, J. B. (2002): *Multinational Management: A Strategic Approach*, New York: Southwestern-Thompson Learning.

Cyert, R. M., and March, J. G. (1963): *A Behavioral Theory of the Firm*, Englewood Cliffs, NJ: Prentice Hall.

Damasio, A., Everitt, B. J., and Bishop, D. (1996): "The Somatic Marker Hypothesis and the Possible Functions of the Prefrontal Cortex," *Philosophical Transactions: Biological Sciences*, 351(1346), pp. 1413–20.

Davidow, W. H., and Malone, M. S. (1992): *The Virtual Corporation*, New York: Edward Burlingame Books/Harper Business.

Denison, D. R. (1996): "What is the Difference between Organizational Culture and Organizational Climate? A Native's Point of View on a Decade of Paradigm Wars," *Academy of Management Review*, 21(3), pp. 619–54.

DeSanctis, G., and Fulk, J. (eds.) (1999): *Shaping Organization Form: Communication, Connection, and Community*, Newbury Park, CA: Sage.

Donaldson, L. (2001): *The Contingency Theory of Organizations*, Thousand Oaks, CA: Sage.

Doty, D., Glick, H. W. H., and Huber, G. P. (1993): "Fit, Equifinality, and Organizational Effectiveness: A Test of Two Configurational Theories," *Academy of Management Journal*, 38(6), pp. 1196–1250.

Duncan, R. B. (1972): "Characteristics of Organizational Environments and Perceived Environmental Uncertainty," *Administrative Science Quarterly*, 17(3), pp. 313–27.

Eisenhardt, K. M., and Brown, S. L. (1998): "Time Pacing: Competing in Markets that Won't Stand Still," *Harvard Business Review*, 76(2), pp. 59–69.

Fenton, E. M., and Pettigrew, A. M. (2000): "Theoretical Perspectives on New Forms of Organizing," in A. M. Pettigrew and E. M. Fenton (eds.), *The Innovating Organization*, London: Sage.

Forgas, J. P., and George, J. M. (2001): "Affective Influences on Judgment and Behavior in Organizations: An Information Processing Perspective," *Organizational Behavior and Human Decision Processes*, 86(1), pp. 2–34.

Galbraith, J. R. (1973): *Designing Complex Organizations*, Reading, MA: Addison-Wesley.

   (1974): "Organization Design: An Information Processing View," *Interfaces*, 4(3), pp. 28–36.

   (2010): "The Multi-Dimensional and Reconfigurable Organization," *Organizational Dynamics*, 39(2), pp. 115–25.

George, G. R., and Zhou, J. (2002): "Understanding When Bad Moods Foster Creativity and Good Ones Don't: The Role of Context and Clarity of Feelings," *Journal of Applied Psychology*, 87, pp. 687–97.

Gibbons, R. (1998): "Incentives in Organizations," *Journal of Economic Perspectives*, 12(4), pp. 115–32.

Gibson, C. B., and Birkinshaw, J. (2004): "The Antecedents, Consequences, and Mediating Role of Organizational Ambidexterity," *Academy of Management Journal*, 47(2), pp. 2009–226.

Gittell, J. H. (2003): *The Southwest Airlines Way*, New York: McGraw-Hill.

Gresov, C. (1989): "Exploring Fit and Misfit with Multiple Contingencies," *Administrative Science Quarterly*, 34(3), pp. 431–54.

Gresov, C., and Drazin, R. (1997): "Equifinality: Functional Equivalence in Organization Design," *Academy of Management Review*, 22(2), pp. 403–28.

Hahn, G. J. (1999): "The Impact of Six Sigma Improvement – A Glimpse into the Future of Statistics," *The American Statistician*, 53(3), pp. 208–16.

Håkonsson, D. D., Obel, B., and Burton, R. (2008a): "Can Organizational Climate be Managed?: Making Emotions Rational," *Journal of Leadership Studies*, 1(4), pp. 62–73.

Håkonsson, D. D., Lauridsen, J., Obel, B., and Burton, R. (2005): "How Misfits between Strategy and Leadership affect Organizational Performance," presented at the AOM Conference, Hawaii (submitted for publication).

Håkonsson, D. D., Obel, B., Burton, R., and Lauridsen, J. (2008b): "How Failure to Align Climate and Leadership Style Affects Performance," *Management Decision*, 46(3), pp. 406–32.

Hambrick, D. C. (2003): "On the Staying Power of Defenders, Analyzers, and Prospectors," *Academy of Management Executive*, 17(4), pp. 115–19.

Hansen, M. T., and Nohria, N. (2004): "How to Build Collaborative Advantage," *MIT Sloan Management Review*, 46(1), pp. 22–30.

Heneman, R. L., Fisher, M. M., and Dixon, K. E. (2001): "Reward and Organizational Systems Alignment: An Expert System," *Compensation and Benefits Review*, 33(6), pp. 18–29.

Hennart, J. F. (1993): "Explaining the Swollen Middle: Why Most Transactions Are a Mix of Market and Hierarchy," *Organization Science*, 4, pp. 529–47.

Heydebrand, W. V. (1989): "New Organizational Forms," *Work and Occupations*, 16(3), pp. 323–57.

Huber, G. (2003): *The Necessary Nature of Future Firms*, Thousand Oaks, CA: Sage Publications.

INSEAD (1994): "The 3M Company: Integrating Europe (A) and (B)," ECCH case collection 494–023–1 and 494–023–2.

Jensen, K. W., Håkonsson, D. D., Burton, R. B., and Obel, B. (2010): "The Effect of Virtuality on The Functioning of Centralized Versus Decentralized Structures – An Information Processing Perspective," *Computational Mathematical Organizational Theory*, 16, pp. 144–70.

Jung, D., Chow, C., and Wu, A. (2003): "The Role of Transformational Leadership In Enhancing Organizational Innovation: Hypothesis and Some Preliminary Findings," *The Leadership Quarterly*, 14, pp. 525–44.

Jung, D., Wu, A., and Chow, C. W. (2008): "Towards Understanding the Direct and Indirect Effects of CEOs' Transformational Leadership on Firm Innovation," *The Leadership Quarterly*, 19(5), pp. 582–94.

Keen, Peter G. W., and McDonald, M. (2000): *The Eprocess Edge*, Berkeley, CA: McGraw-Hill.

Kerr, S. (1975): "On the Folly of Rewarding A while Hoping B," *Academy of Management Journal*, 18(4), pp. 769–83.

Kiel Institute for World Economics (2004): DOME: Database on Mergers in Europe.

Kotter, J. P. (1988): *The Leadership Factor*, New York: Free Press.

Kottler, P. (2000): *Marketing Management: The Millennium Edition*, Upper Saddle River, NJ: Prentice Hall.

Kowtha, N. R. (1997): "Skills, Incentives, and Control: An Integration of Agency and Transaction Cost Approaches," *Group and Organization Management*, 22(1), pp. 53–86.

Lawrence, P. R. (1981): "Organization and Environment Perspective," in A. H. Van de Ven and W. F. Joyce (eds.), *Perspectives on Organization Design and Behavior*, New York: Wiley, pp. 311–27.

Lawrence, P. R., and Lorsch, J. W. (1967): *Organization and Environment*, Boston, MA: Harvard Business Press.

Likert, R. (1967): *The Human Organizations*, New York: McGraw-Hill.

Makadok, R. (2001): "Toward a Synthesis of the Resource-based and Dynamic-capability View of Rent Creation," *Strategic Management Journal*, 22, pp. 387–401.

March, J. G. (1991): "Exploration and Exploitation in Organizational Learning," *Organization Science*, 2, pp. 71–87.

March, J. G., and Simon, H. A. (1958): *Organizations*, New York: John Wiley and Sons.

McCall, M. W. Jr., and Hollenbeck, G. P. (2002): *Developing Global Executives*, Cambridge, MA: Harvard Business School Press.

McGregor, D. (1969): *The Human Side of Enterprise*, New York: McGraw-Hill.

McNabb, D. E., and Sepic, F. T. (1995): "Culture, Climate and Total Quality Management: Measuring Readiness for Change," *Public Productivity and Management Review*, 18(4, Summer), pp. 369–85.

Milakovich, M. E., and Gordon, G. J. (2001): *Public Administration in America*, Thorofare, NJ: Thompson Learning Incorporated.

Miles, R. E., and Snow, C. C. (1978): *Organizational Strategy, Structure, and Process*, New York: McGraw-Hill.

  (1986): "Network Organizations: New Concepts for New Forms," *California Management Review*, 28, pp. 62–75.

Miles, R. E., Snow, C. C., Mathews, J. A., Miles, G., and Coleman, Jr., H. H. (1997): "Organizing in the Knowledge Age: Anticipating the Cellular Form," *Academy of Management Executive*, 11(4), pp. 7–20.

Miller, D. (1992): "Environmental Fit Versus Internal Fit," *Organizational Science*, 3(2), pp. 159–78.

Mintzberg, H. (1983): *Structures in Fives*, Englewood Cliffs, NJ: Prentice Hall.

Mumford, M. D., Scott, G. M., Gaddis, B., and Strange, J. M. (2002): "Leading Creative People: Orchestrating Expertise and Relationships," *The Leadership Quarterly*, 13, pp. 705–50.

Nagar, V. (2002): "Delegation and Incentive Compensation," *The Accounting Review*, 77(2), pp. 379–95.

Naman, J.L., and Slevin, D.P. (1993): "Entrepreneurship and the Concept of Fit: A Model and Empirical Tests," *Strategic Management Journal*, **14**(2), pp. 137–53.

Nissen, M., and Burton, R.M. (2010): "Designing Organizations for Dynamic Fit: System Stability, Maneuverability and Opportunity Loss" (submitted for publication).

Nokia (2003): "Fostering Innovation," ECCH case collection 403–040–1.

Nonaka, I., and Takeuchi, H. (1995): *The Knowledge-Creating Company: How Japanese Companies Create the Dynamics of Innovation*, New York: Oxford University Press.

Obel, B. (1993): "Strategi og Ledelse – Er der en sammenhæng?" in Steen Hildebrandt (ed.), *Strategi og Ledelse, Veje og Visioner mod år 2000*, Herning: Systime, pp. 396–408.

Ocasio, W. (1997): "Towards an Attention-Based View of the Firm," *Strategic Management Journal*, **18**, pp.187–206.

Ouchi, W.G. (1980): "Markets, Bureaucracies, and Clans," *Administrative Science Quarterly*, **25**, pp. 129–41.

PHP Institute (1994): *Matsushita Konosuke: His Life and His Legacy*, Tokyo: PHP Institute.

Polanyi, M. (1966): *The Tacit Dimension*, London: Routledge & Kegan Paul.

Porter, M.E. (1985): *Competitive Advantage: Creating and Sustaining Superior Performance*, New York: The Free Press.

Powley, E.H., Fry, R.E., Barrett, F.J., and Bright, D.S. (2004): "Dialogic Democracy Meets Command and Control: Transformation through the Appreciative Inquiry Summit," *Academy of Management Executive*, **18**(3), pp. 67–81.

Quinn, R.E., and Kimberly, J.R. (1984): "Paradox, Planning, and Perseverance: Guidelines for Managerial Practice," in J.R. Kimberly and R.E. Quinn (eds.), *Managing Organizational Transitions*, New York: Dow-Jones-Irwin, pp. 295–314.

Raisch, S., and Birkinshaw, J. (2008): "Organizational Ambidexterity: Antecedents, Outcomes, and Moderators," *Journal of Management*, **34**, pp. 375–409.

Richard, M. (2001): "Toward a Synthesis of the Resource-based and Dynamic-capability Views of Rent Creation," *Strategic Management Journal*, **22**(5), pp. 387–401.

Rivkin, J., and Fleming, L. (2004): "Complexity, Networks, and Knowledge Flow," *Research Policy*, **33**(10), pp. 1615–34.

Robbins, S.P. (1990): *Organization Theory: Structure, Design and Applications*, Englewood Cliffs, NJ: Prentice-Hall.

Roberts, J. (2004): *The Modern Firm: Organizational Design for Performance and Growth*, New York: Oxford University Press.

Robinson, D.T. (2008): "Strategic Alliances and the Boundaries of the Firm," *The Review of Financial Studies*, **21**(2), pp. 649–81.

Rynes, S.L., and Gerhart, B. (2000): *Compensation in Organizations: Current Research and Practice*, San Francisco, CA: Jossey-Bass.

Sastry, M.A. (1997): "Problems and Paradoxes in a Model of Punctuated Organizational Change," *Administrative Science Quarterly*, **42**, pp. 237–75.

Scott, W.R. (1998): *Organizations, Rational, Natural and Open Systems*, Englewood Cliffs, NJ: Prentice-Hall.

Sharma, P., and Manikutty, S. (2005): "Strategic Divestments in Family Firms: Role of Family Structure and Community Culture," *Entrepreneurship Theory and Practice*, 24(3), pp. 293–311.

Siggelkow, N., and Levinthal, D. A. (2003): "Centralized, Decentralized, and Reintegrated Organizational Approaches," *Organization Science* 14(6), pp. 650–69.

Siggelkow, N., and Rivkin, J. (2005): "Speed and Search: Designing Organizations for Turbulence and Complexity," *Organization Science*, 16(2), pp. 101–22.

Sinha, K. K., and Van de Ven, A. (2005): "Design of Work Within and Between Organizations," *Organization Science*, 16(4), pp. 389–408.

Smith, A. (1904): *An Inquiry into the Nature and Causes of the Wealth of Nations*, Oxford University Press.

Sorenson, O., Rivkin, J., and Fleming, L. (2004): "Complexity, Networks, and Knowledge Flow," *Research Policy*, 33(10), pp. 1615–34.

Stinchcome, A. L. (1965): "Social Structure and Organizations," in James D. March (ed.), *Handbook of Organizations*, Chicago, IL: Rand McNally, pp. 142–93.

Tagiuri, R., and Litwin, G. H. (1968): *Organizational Climate*, Cambridge, MA: Harvard University Press.

Thompson, J. D. (1967): *Organizations in Action*, Oxford University Press.

Tushman, M. L., and Romanelli, E. (1985): "Organizational Evolution: A Metamorphosis Model of Convergence and Reorientation," in L. L. Cunnings and B. M. Stacer (eds.), *Research in Organizational Behavior*, San Francisco, CA: SAI Press, pp. 171–222.

Velstring, T., Rouse, T., and Rovit, S. (2004): "Integrate Where It Matters," *MIT Sloan Management Review*, 46(1), pp. 15–18.

Venkatraman, N. (1989): "The Concept of Fit in Strategy Research: Towards a Verbal and Statistical Correspondence," *Academy of Management Review*, 14(3), pp. 423–44.

Williamson, O. E. (1975): *Markets and Hierarchies: Analysis and Antitrust Implications*, New York: Free Press.

Woodward, J. (1965): *Industrial Organization, Theory and Practice*, Oxford University Press.

Zammuto, R. F., and Krakower, J. Y. (1991): "Quantitative and Qualitative Studies in Organizational Culture," *Research in Organizational Change and Development*, 5, pp. 83–114.

Zuboff, S. (1988): *In the Age of the Smart Machine: The Future of Work and Power*, Oxford University Press.

Index